HONDA
WORKSHOP MANUAL
1974 - 1977
TWIN CYLINDER
5 & 6 SPEED 250 & 360cc
MODELS
CB250 - CJ250T
CB360 - CL360
CB360T - CJ360T

**A Floyd Clymer Publication
This edition published in 2023 by
www.VelocePress.com**

All rights reserved. This work may not be reproduced or transmitted in any form without the express written consent of the publisher.

INTRODUCTION

Welcome to the world of digital publishing ~ the book you now hold in your hand was printed using the latest state of the art digital technology. The advent of print-on-demand has forever changed the publishing process, never has information been so accessible and it is our hope that this book serves your informational needs for years to come. If this is your first exposure to digital publishing, we hope that you are pleased with the results. Many more titles of interest to the classic automobile and motorcycle enthusiast, collector and restorer are available via our website at www.VelocePress.com. We hope that you find this title as interesting as we do.

NOTE FROM THE PUBLISHER

The information presented is true and complete to the best of our knowledge. All recommendations are made without any guarantees on the part of the author or the publisher, who also disclaim all liability incurred with the use of this information.

TRADEMARKS

We recognize that some words, model names and designations, for example, mentioned herein are the property of the trademark holder. We use them for identification purposes only. This is not an official publication.

INFORMATION ON THE USE OF THIS PUBLICATION

This manual is an invaluable resource for those interested in performing their own maintenance. However, in today's information age we are constantly subject to changes in common practice, new technology, availability of improved materials and increased awareness of chemical toxicity. As such, it is advised that the user consult with an experienced professional prior to undertaking any procedure described herein. While every care has been taken to ensure correctness of information, it is obviously not possible to guarantee complete freedom from errors or omissions or to accept liability arising from such errors or omissions. Therefore, any individual that uses the information contained within, or elects to perform or participate in do-it-yourself repairs or modifications acknowledges that there is a risk factor involved and that the publisher or its associates cannot be held responsible for personal injury or property damage resulting from the use of the information or the outcome of such procedures.

WARNING!

One final word of advice, this publication is intended to be used as a reference guide, and when in doubt the reader should consult with a qualified technician.

CONTENTS

I. GENERAL SERVICE PRECAUTIONS 1
II. CONSTRUCTION
    1. Cam shaft and valve mechanism 2
    2. Cam chain tensioner mechanism 3
    3. Lubricating system 4
    4. Power transmitting system 5
    5. Carburetor 8
    6. Frame 11
    7. Electrical system 16
III. INSPECTION AND ADJUSTMENT
    1. Tappets 17
    2. Breaker point gap and ignition timing 18
    3. Carburetor 20
    4. Throttle cable 21
    5. Clutch 22
    6. Cam chain 23
    7. Engine oil 23
    8. Oil filter screen and rotor 24
    9. Front brake 25
    10. Rear brake 28
    11. Drive chain 28
    12. Front fork 29
    13. Rear shock absorber 29
    14. Air cleaner 30
    15. Compression pressure 30
IV. ENGINE
    1. On-frame servicing 31
    2. Engine removal and installation 31
    3. Cylinder head, camshaft, cylinder and pistons . 37
    4. A.C. generator and starting motor 45
    5. Right crankcase cover and clutch 47
    6. Oil pump and oil filter rotor 50
    7. Kick starter and lower crankcase 53
    8. Gearshift mechanism 57
    9. Crankshaft and upper crankcase 61
    10. Carburetor 63
V. FRAME
    1. Front wheel and front brake 68
    2. Front disc brake 73
    3. Rear wheel and rear brake 78
    4. Steering handlebar 81
    5. Front suspension 85
    6. Steering stem 87
    7. Rear shock absorbers and rear fork 90
    8. Frame body and other related parts 93
VI. ELECTRICAL SYSTEM
    1. Charging system 97
    2. Ignition system 100
    3. Starting system 103
    4. Other electrical parts 105
VII. SERVICE DATA
    1. Special tools 108
    2. Maintenance schedule 110
    3. Tightening torque standard 111
    4. Maintenance standard 112
    5. Trouble shooting 114
    6. Specifications 118
    7. Wiring diagram 120
VIII. CB360T, CL360K1 SUPPLEMENT 127
IX. CB360T, CL360K1 SUPPLEMENT 131
    (LATE MODEL)
X. CJ250T/CJ360T SUPPLEMENT 137

I. GENERAL SERVICE PRECAUTIONS

1. Always replace gaskets, O-rings, cotter pins, etc with new ones when reassembling.
2. When tightening bolts, nuts or screws, begin on larger-diameter or inner one first and tighten them to specified torque in a criss-cross pattern.
3. Use genuine Honda or Honda-recommended parts and lubricants when servicing.
4. Be sure to use a special tool or tools where so specified.
5. A joint work of more than two persons must be carried out with mutual safety attention paid.
6. Wash clean engine parts upon disassembly. Coat their sliding surfaces with high-quality lubricant when reassembling.
7. Coat or pack grease where so specified.
8. After reassembling, check to be sure each part is tightened properly. Also check for proper operation.
9. Be sure to retain fuel and oil pipes with clips.

Electrical System

1. When tracing electrical system problems, refer to the wiring diagram at the end of this manual.
2. Check cables and wires for disconnection, open circuit, binding or breakage of coverings, and grommets and covers for removal or breakage. Repair or replace them if necessary.
3. Check if fuse failures are due to blow-out or to mechanical open circuit. If a fuse is blown, locate the cause before installing a new fuse. Always use a specifically rated fuse.
4. Route the battery breather tube as shown on the label.

NOTE:
It is advisable to check the electrical parts at a temperature of about 20°C/68°F (room temperature).

II. CONSTRUCTION

1. CAMSHAFT AND VALVE MECHANISM

Cylinder head

The cylinder head is so designed that the rocker arm shafts and rocker arms are incorporated into the cylinder head cover.
It can be removed or installed with the engine mounted on the frame to enable the cylinder and pistons to be replaced easily.

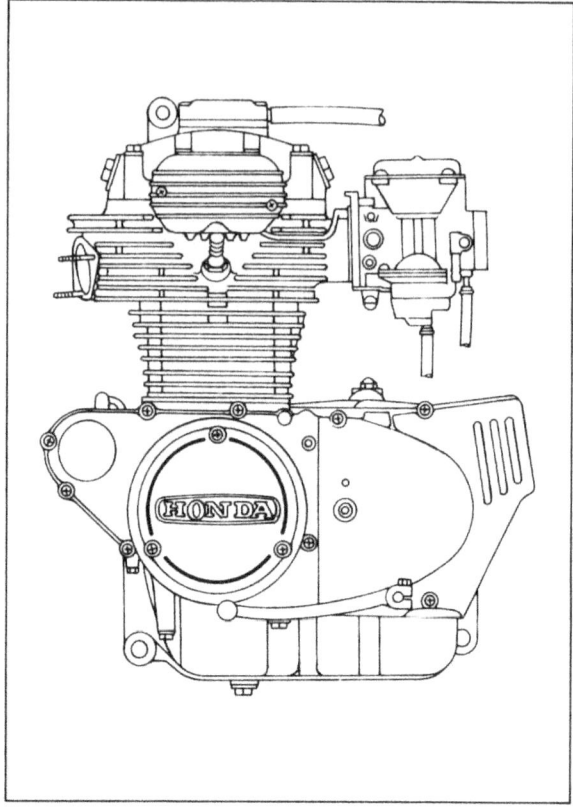

Fig. 2-1

Valve guides

Each valve guide is securely supported by the spring seats as shown at right. It is also provided with the stem seals to prevent oil from leaking into the combustion chamber.
When disassembling the valve guide, take care not to compress the valve compressor (Tool No. 07957-3290000) more than necessary; otherwise the stem seals may be damaged.

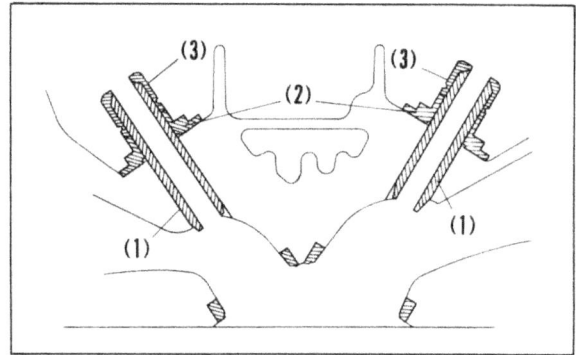

Fig. 2-2 (1) Valve guide
(2) Spring seat
(3) Stem seal

Cylinder

The cylinder is an aluminum die casting which is light-weight and has great cooling efficiency. Two special cast iron sleeves are pressed into the cylinder.
Eight stud bolt holes are provided in the cylinder and the two holes at the rear outside act as oil passages to the cylinder head. In the two holes O-rings are inserted to prevent oil leakage.

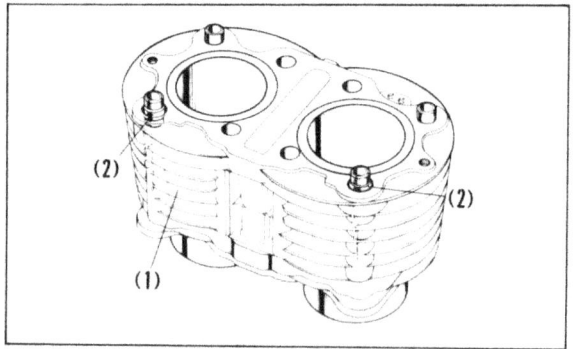

Fig. 2-3 (1) Cylinder
(2) Cylinder stud bolt gasket

II. CONSTRUCTION

Pistons

The pistons are made of aluminum alloy. They are three-stage tapered as shown to provide for unequal expansion that occurs at operating temperature.

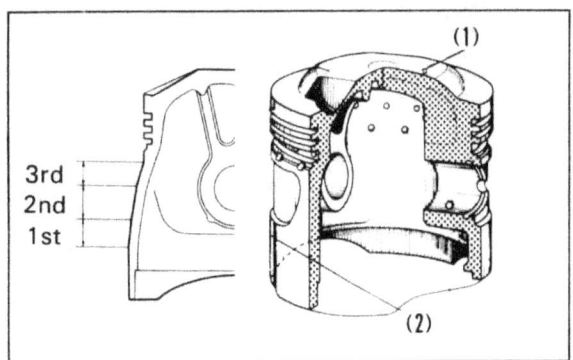

Fig. 2-4 Sectional view of piston
(1) Piston head
(2) Piston skirt

Piston pins

Each piston pin is full floating in both the connecting rod and piston with snap rings in both piston bosses. It is **1 mm** offset **(0.039 in.)** to the intake side with respect to the center of the piston. The reason for this is that since the pressure on the piston on the explosion stroke rises to the maximum after the top dead center position, the side thrust on the piston is moved before the top dead center position to avoid rapid movement of the side thrust on the explosion stroke, preventing the piston from slapping the cylinder sleeve. The head of each piston is marked to make it easier to install it correctly.

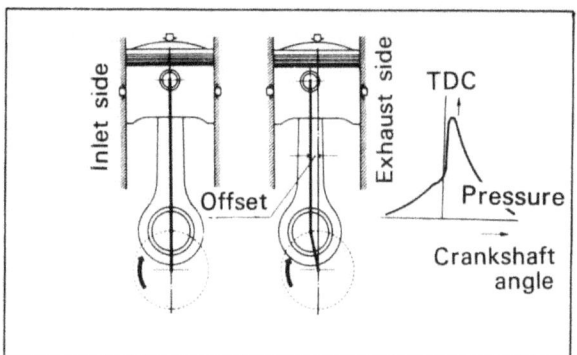

Fig. 2-5 Piston pin offset

2. CAM CHAIN TENSIONER MECHANISM

1. The cam chain tensioner is made of spring steel on which heat-resistant rubber is lined by paking and then heatresistant teflon having less frictional resistance is coated, minimizing chain noise and improving durability.
2. The chain tension can be easily adjusted by loosening the adjusting bolt and then retightening it.

Cam chain slipper

1. The cam chain slipper installed to the cylinder block prevents chain vibrations often developed due to temporalily disturbed engine speed during deceleration.
2. The cam chain slipper is so constructed that the synthetic rubber is attached to the steel plate and it has great durability.

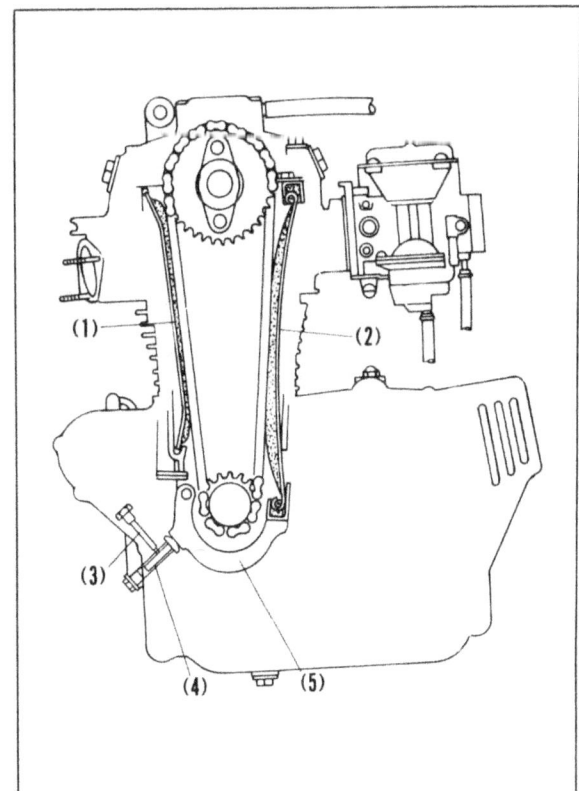

Fig. 2-6 (1) Cam chain slipper
(2) Cam chain tensioner
(3) Adjusting bolt
(4) Tensioner push bar
(5) Tensioner arm

3. LUBRICATING SYSTEM

The models CB250, CB360 and CL360 are continuously pressure-lubricated with a trochoid oil pump.

Lubricating oil is fed to the engine parts through the centrifugal oil filter coupled directly to the crankshaft and the oil filter screen located at the suction port of the oil pump.

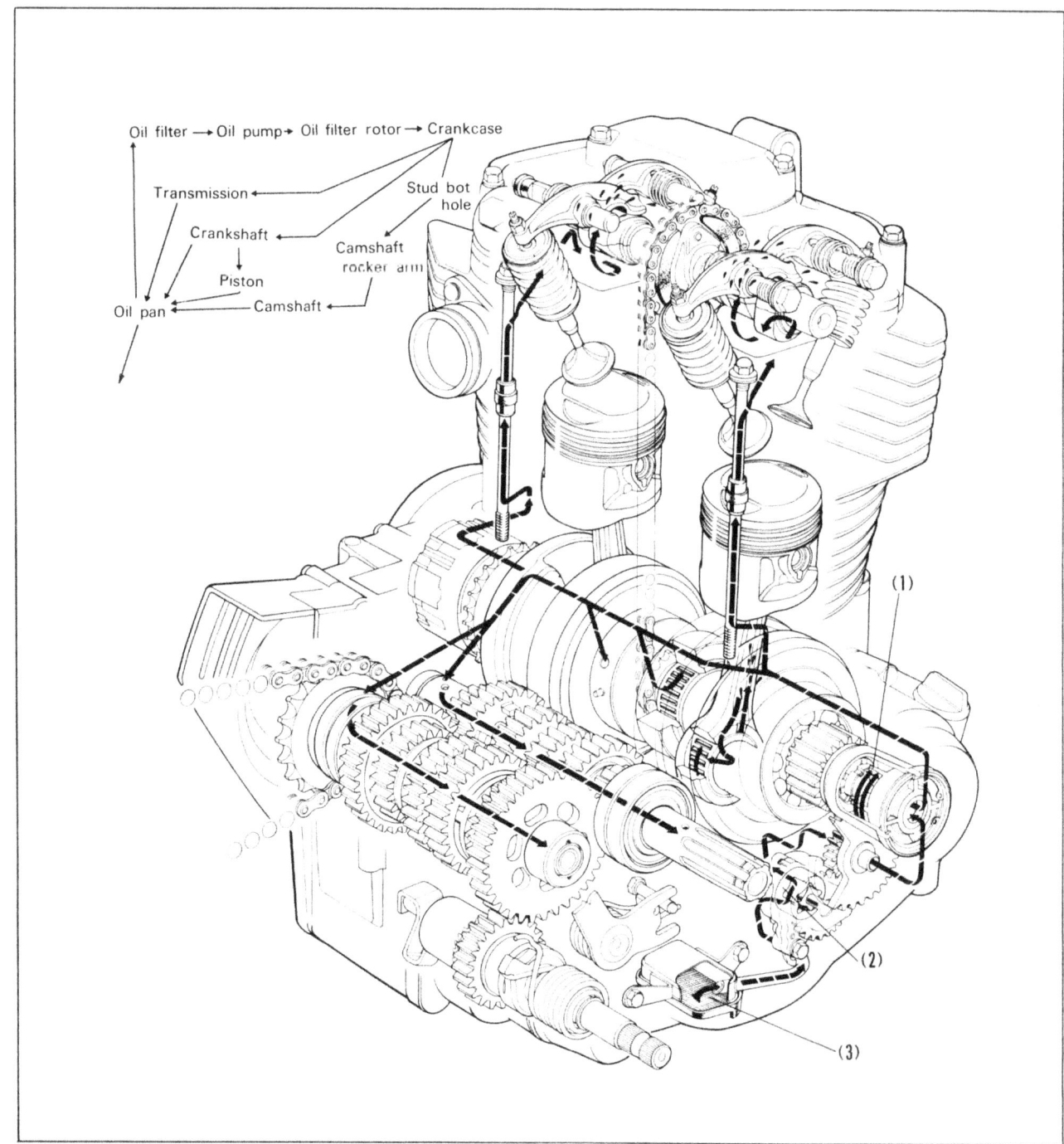

Fig. 2-7 Lubricating oil circuit

(1) Oil filter rotor (2) Trochoid oil pump (3) Oil filter screen

II. CONSTRUCTION

Trochoid oil pump

The trochoid oil pump is driven by the crankshaft through the pump idle gear and drive gear.

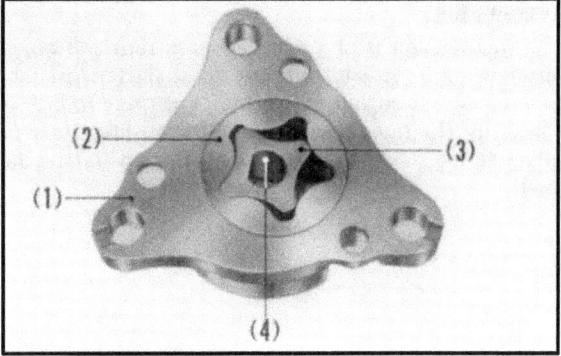

Fig. 2-8 (1) Oil pump body
(2) Outer rotor
(3) Inner rotor
(4) Drive gear

Centrifugal oil filter

As the oil from the pump enters the filter rotor through the guide metal and is picked up by the spinning vanes of the filter cap, foreign materials such as metallic dust and carbon particles are separated from the oil by centrifugal force and are attached to the inner wall of the rotor. The oil cleaned in this manner is fed to the engine parts through the outlet port in the center section of the filter cap.

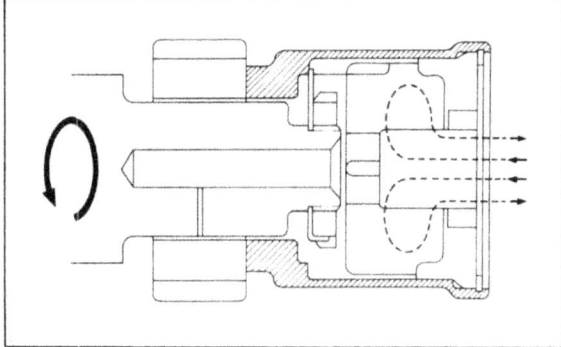

Fig. 2-9 Oil flow in oil filter

4. POWER TRANSMITTING SYSTEM

Clutch

The clutch is provided to transmit engine power to the transmission mainshaft or disconnect it from the shaft through friction between the clutch friction discs (3) and clutch plates (4).

When the clutch is engaged, the friction discs and plates are "sandwiched" between the clutch pressure plate (7) and clutch center (5) by means of the clutch spring (6), thereby causing the clutch outer (2) and clutch center to be pressed together. Under this condition, engine power is transmitted from the crankshaft to the main shaft through the primary drive gear, clutch outer, friction discs, plates and clutch center.

As the clutch lever is squeezed, the clutch lifter cam (11) connected to the clutch cable is rotated and then is pushed out by means of the ♯10 steel ball (12) located between the lifter cam and clutch adjusting cam. Then the force is transmitted to the steel ball (10), lifter rod, lifter joint piece and pressure plate to cause the clutch springs to be compressed. Now the friction discs are separated from the plates, resulting in disengagement.

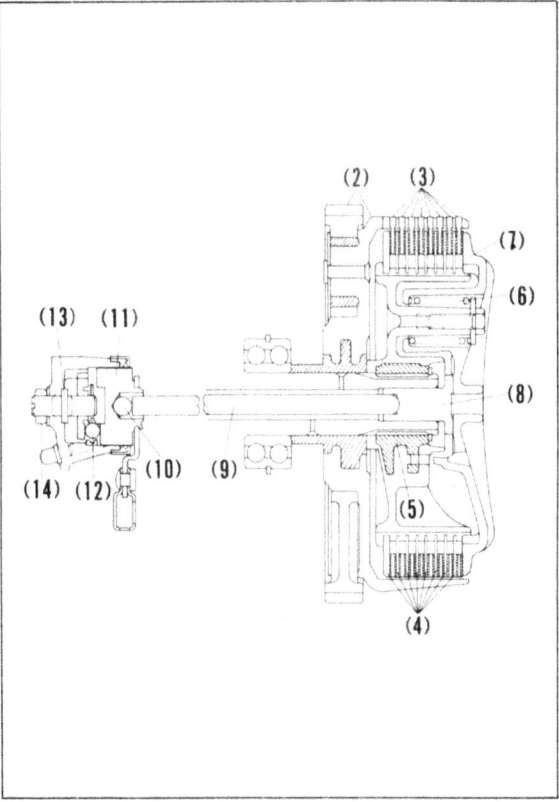

Fig. 2-10

Transmission

The transmission is of a constant-mesh type and provides a selection of six speeds, fulfilling the characteristics inherent to a four-stroke engine ranging from low speed to high speed. Especially the transmission plays its most important role in riding at the overtop (sixth) speed. Return shifting type is used.

The engine power, transmitted from the crankshaft to the mainshaft through the clutch, is changed in speed and torque by gearing. It is then transmitted from the drive sprocket to the rear wheel through the drive chain.

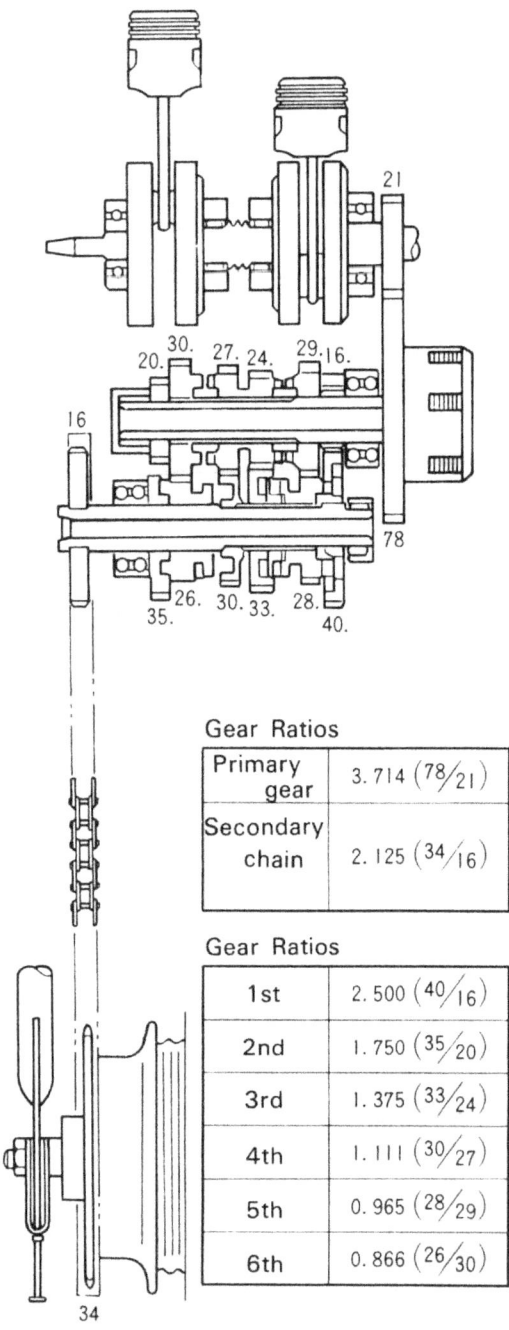

Gear Ratios

Primary gear	3.714 (78/21)
Secondary chain	2.125 (34/16)

Gear Ratios

1st	2.500 (40/16)
2nd	1.750 (35/20)
3rd	1.375 (33/24)
4th	1.111 (30/27)
5th	0.965 (28/29)
6th	0.866 (26/30)

Fig. 2−11

II. CONSTRUCTION

Gearshift mechanism

The gearshift mechanism is a linkage between the gear change pedal and the shift forks and includes a shift arm, a shift drum, a neutral stop, a drum stop, etc.

When the pedal is depressed for shifting, the shift spindle rotates, causing the arm to push the drum pins to rotate the drum. As the drum is so rotated, the fork is moved by the cam action of a groove cut in the drum to shift a gear. After shifting, the arm is returned to its original position by means of the return spring. The drum stop is provided to prevent unintentional gear engagement, shifting the gears smoothly. The drum is pressed by the #10 steel ball to make it possible to shift into the neutral position properly.

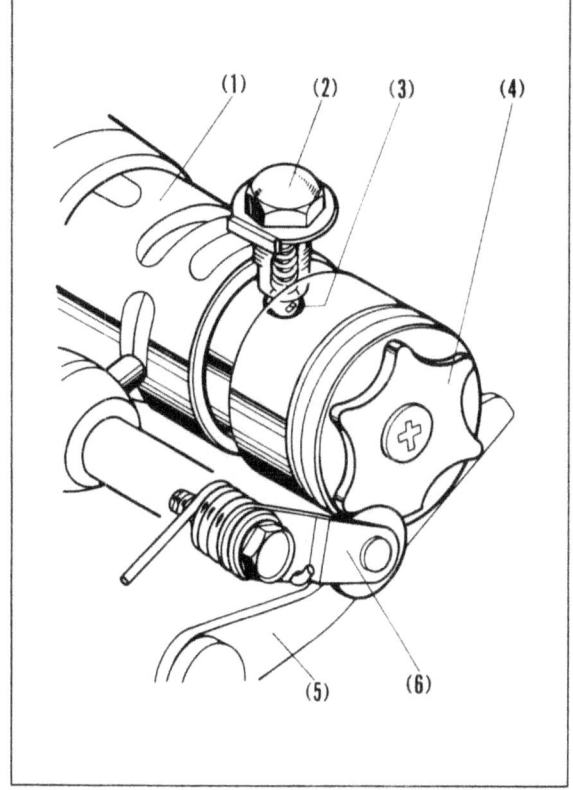

Fig. 2–12 (1) Gearshift drum (4) Drum stop cam plate
(2) Neutral stop (5) Gearshift spindle arm
(3) #10 steel ball (6) Shift drum stop

Crankshaft

The crankshaft serves to change the reciprocating motion of the piston into rotary motion in connection with the connecting rod. It also serves as a flywheel limiting the torque fluctuation. The crankshaft is supported at four places by antifriction bearings—two needle roller bearings on the inside and two ball bearings on the outside, increasing the load capacity and improving the strength and durability at high speeds.

Fig. 2–13 Crankshaft

The crankshaft bearings are lubricated by oil from the oil pump. The oil enters from the upper crankcase, passes through the oil holes in the center bearing outer rings and lubricates the bearings. Then the oil collects into the notches in the sides of the crank weights and enters the crankpins to lubricate the big ends of the connecting rods.

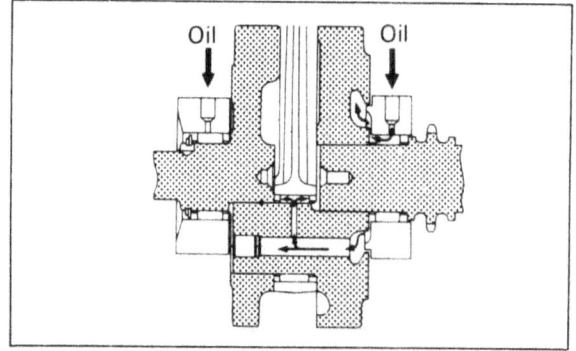

Fig. 2–14 Lubrication to crankshaft

5. CARBURETORS

Two sets of carburetors, one for each cylinder, are equipped. They are of a single-barrel, CV (Constant Vacuum type, the venturi area is automatically changed by the negative pressure created by air to be drawn into the cylinder) type. Following are the remarkable features:

(1) Because of a variable-venture type, smooth power transition between low-speed and high-speed operations is provided.
(2) The construction is simple.
(3) Acceleration is good and fuel consumption is less.

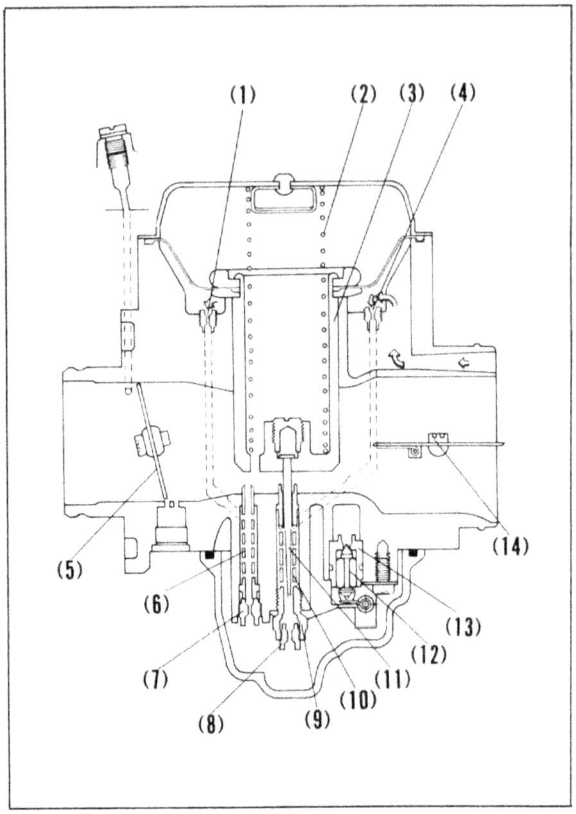

Fig. 2-15
(1) Primary air jet
(2) Vacuum piston spring
(3) Vacuum piston
(4) Secondary air jet
(5) Throttle valve
(6) Main nozzle
(7) Primary main jet
(8) Secondary main jet
(9) Needle jet holder
(10) Needle jet
(11) Jet needle
(12) Float valve
(13) Valve seat
(14) Choke valve

1. Starting circuit

When the engine is started while it is cold, a richer fuel-air mixture is required.

When the choke lever is raised, the choke valve is closed to cause the amount of incoming air to be reduced, resulting in an increased negative pressure within the main bore. Now fuel is fed to the bore from the low-speed and main circuits. The choke valve is controlled by the relief valve depending on vacuum created by air to be drawn into the main bore.

2. Low-speed circuit

The low-speed circuit is provided to supply the proper amount of mixture to the engine at idle and low speeds.

Fuel passes through the primary main jet and slow jet and is mixed with the air bled by the slow air jet here. Then the mixture is squirted from the bypass and pilot outlet. The mixture to be squirted from the pilot outlet is regulated by the pilot screw.

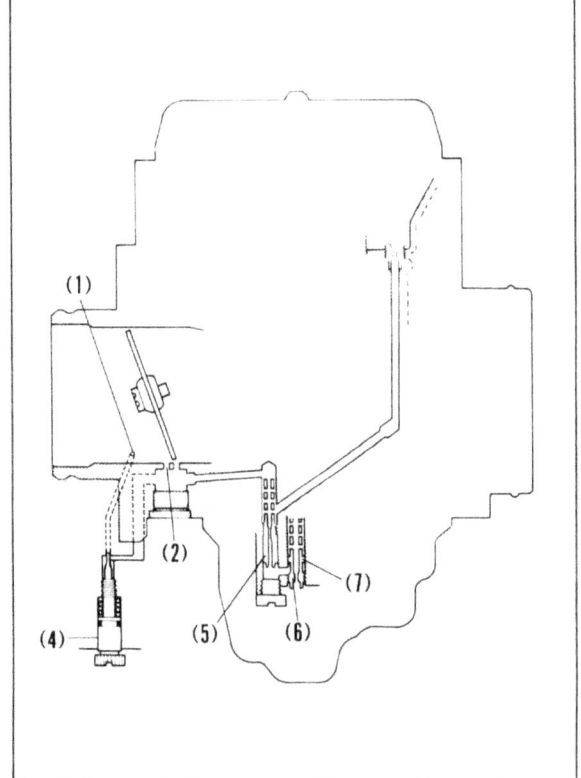

Fig. 2-16
(1) Pilot outlet
(2) Bypass
(3) Slow air jet
(4) Pilot screw
(5) Slow jet
(6) Primary main jet
(7) Main nozzle

3. Main circuits

Primary circuit

The primary main circuit is provided chiefly for the low speed engine operation. Fuel flows into the main nozzle through the primary main jet and is mixed with the air bled by the primary air jet in the main nozzle. Then the mixture is squirted from the tip of the main nozzle.

Secondary circuit

The secondary main circuit is provided chiefly for the normal and high speed engine operations.
Fuel flows into the needle jet through the secondary main jet and is mixed with the air bled by the secondary air jet in the needle jet. Then the mixture passes between the jet needle and needle jet and is spurted from the tip of the needle jet.

Operation of vacuum piston

The vacuum piston is operated by the vacuum within the venturi. When the negative pressure is low, the piston is pushed down by the spring pressure. As the vacuum rises, the piston overcomes the spring pressure and moves up. The jet needle built in the piston is used to supply a charge of optimum fuel-air mixture to the engine.

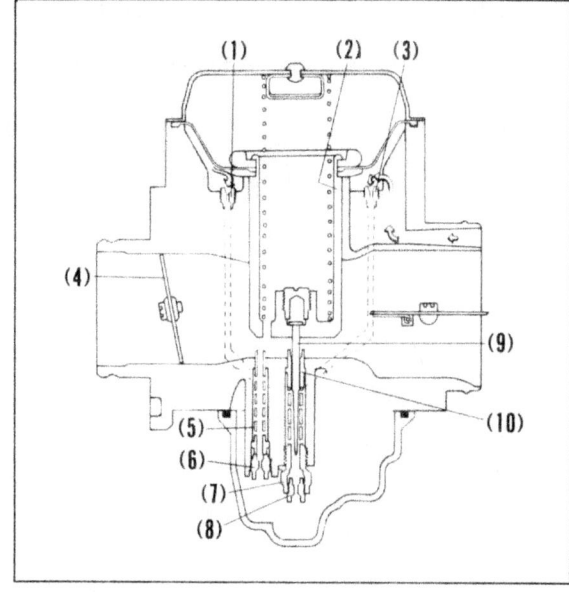

Fig. 2-17 (1) Primary air jet   (6) Primary main jet
(2) Vacuum piston   (7) Needle jet holder
(3) Secondary air jet (8) Secondary main jet
(4) Throttle valve   (9) Jet needle
(5) Main nozzle   (10) Needle jet

4. Float circuit

Fuel flows into the float chamber from the fuel tank through the pipe adapter and the clearance between the float valve and seat. When the fuel level exceeds the specified height, the float moves up on the fuel to cause the float valve to be closed, shutting off the supply of fuel. As the level drops below the specified height, the float valve is opened to permit fuel to flow into the float chamber. By repeating this process, the level of the fuel in the float chamber is always maintained at the same level.

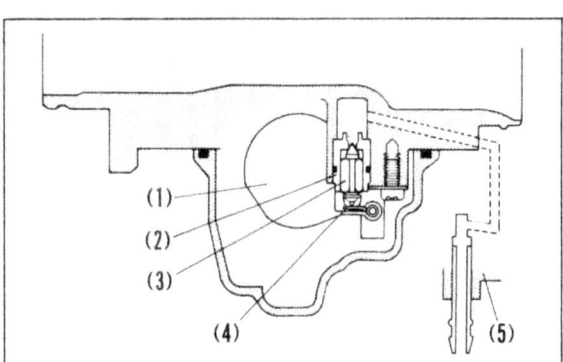

Fig. 2-18 (1) Float   (5) Pipe adapter
(2) Valve seat
(3) Float valve
(4) Special clip

The float valve is provided with a spring at the area where the valve comes in contact with the arm. The spring prevents the float valve from vibrating when the float moves abnormally due to riding and road conditions, maintaining the fuel level constant. The float valve is also provided with a special clip at the tip, which is hooked over the arm, to cause the float valve to be operated together with the float.

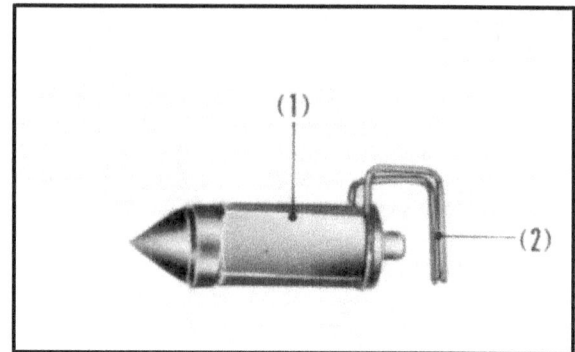

Fig. 2-19 (1) Float valve
(2) Special clip

5. Linkage

The opening and closing of the throttle valves are controlled by the two cables, one for opening the valves and the other for closing them.

The linkage mechanism, which operates the opening and closing of the two carburetor throttles at the same time, which are respectively coupled to the link arm, by means of the adjusting holder.

The throttle stop screw is of a flexible type and the right and left carburetors can be adjusted at the same time.

Each pilot screw is provided with the idle limiter to obtain the constant CO content (%) in exhaust gases at engine idle speed.

Idle limiters

The CO content in exhaust gases varies excessively with the adjustment by the pilot screw. This is why each pilot screw is equipped with the idle limiter to limit the adjustment range.

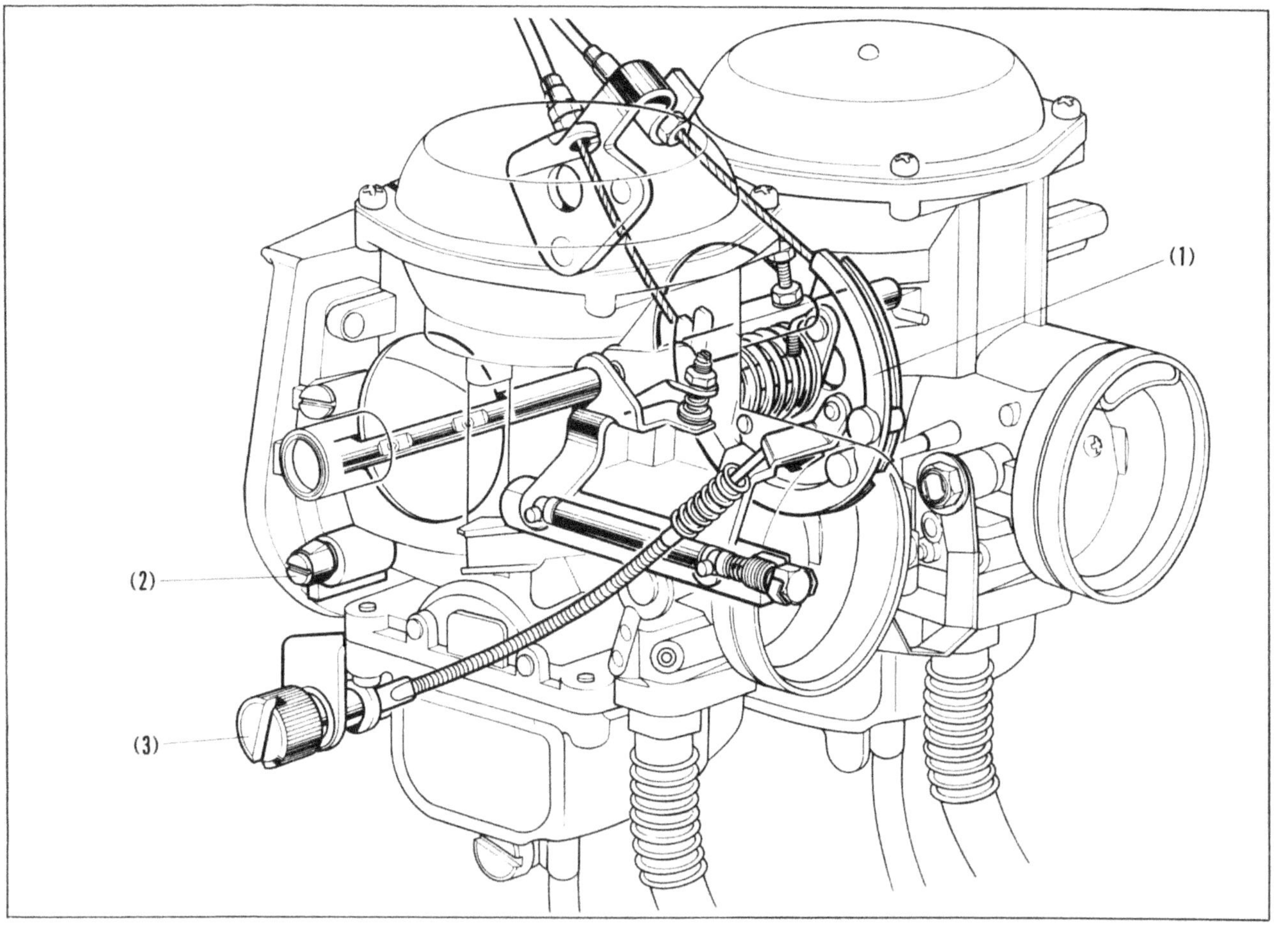

Fig. 2-20 (1) Throttle lever (2) Idle limiter (3) Throttle stop screw

II. CONSTRUCTION

6. FRAME

Front disc brake

The front disc brake consists mainly of a brake lever on the right side of the handlebar, a master cylinder, calipers installed to the left front fork and a brake disc installed to the wheel hub, increasing safety in the operation of the motorcycle. The brake disc is provided with the cover not to allow mud and dust to come in contact with the disc, resulting in a longer life of the pads.

Operation

1. As the brake lever (1) is squeezed, the cam (2) at the bottom of the lever moves the piston (3) within the master cylinder.
2. The piston so moved causes the primary cup (4) to cover up the oil passage to force the brake fluid in the chamber A.
3. The brake fluid so forced throughout the chamber A passes through the brake hose (6) to cause the stop switch (8) to operate at the joint (7). Then the brake fluid passes through the brake hose (9) and enters the chamber B of the caliper A (12).
4. The brake fluid moves the piston (10) within the chamber B to force the pad A against the disc.
5. Since the calipers A and B are "free-joined" with the holder, the reaction of the pad A is exerted on the pad B (13) through the calipers A and B to cause the disc to be "sandwiched" between the pads A and B.

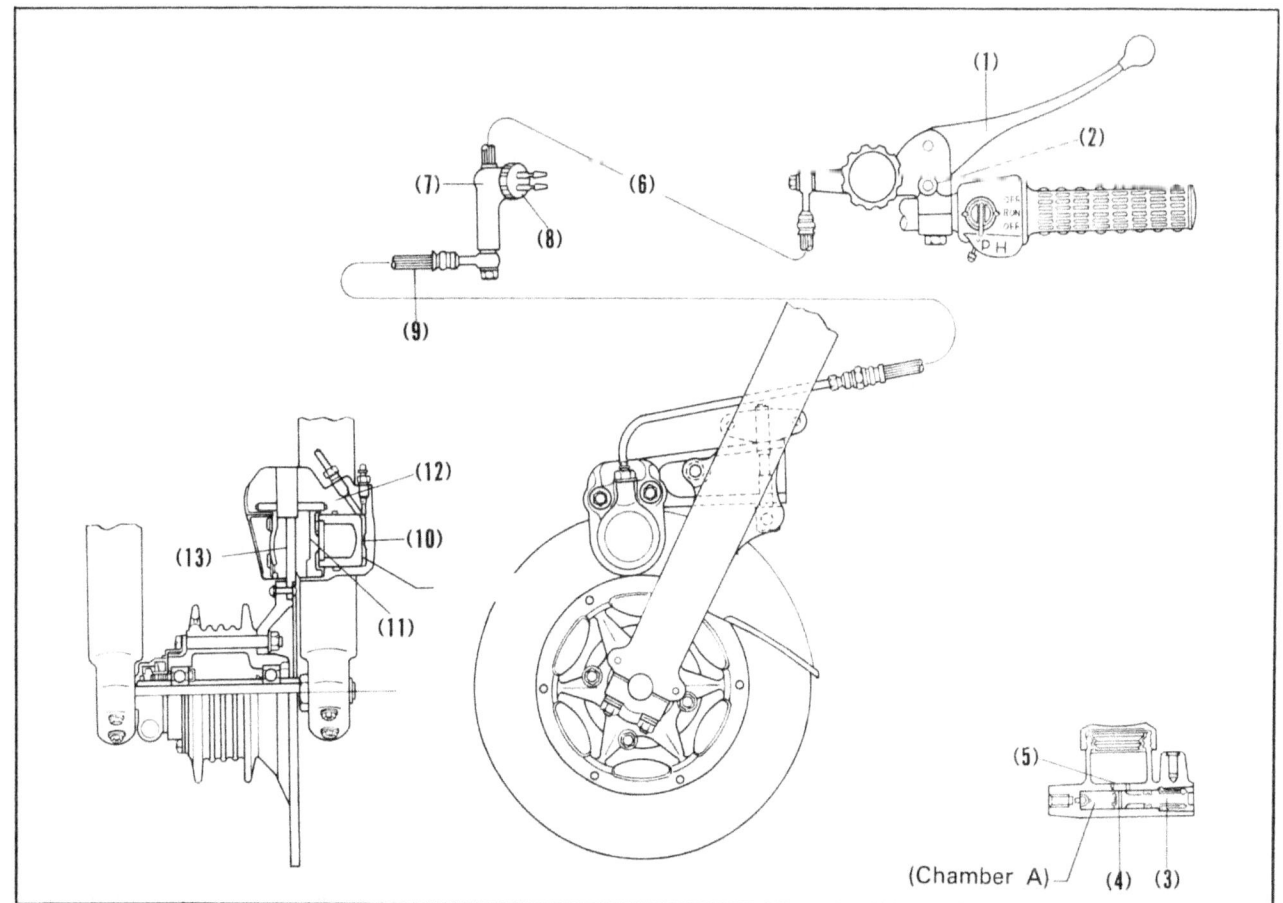

Fig. 2-21

Rear brake

The rear brake is of a drum type (**drum dia.: 160 mm or 6.30 in.**) and uses the leading and trailing type shoes. The brake linings are specifically molded and, therefore, the coefficient of friction hardly varies with high temperature and pressure.
The rear brake is equipped with the brake indicator to make it possible find wear of the brake shoes and drum earlier.

Fig. 2-22

Brake indicator

The brake panel is provided with the index mark, and the brake arm is installed on the brake cam shaft with the brake indicator plate in between.
If the index marks on the panel and on the indicator are not aligned when the brake pedal is depressed, it indicates that the brake shoes and drum are in good condition. As the brake shoes wear, the brake cam moves as shown and, therefore, the index marks reach alignment. Check the brake shoes and drum for wear and replace if the service limit is exceeded.

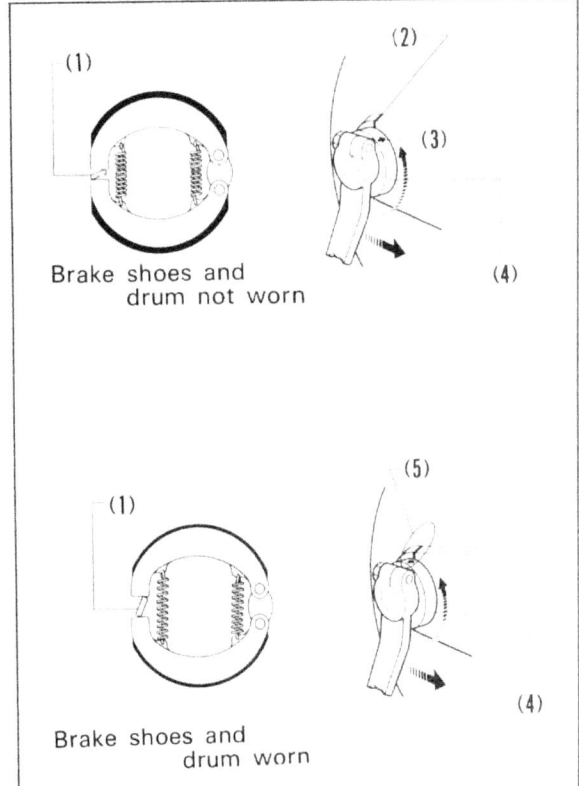

Fig. 2-23 (1) Brake cam
(2) Index mark
(3) Arrow mark
(4) Brake indicator plate
(5) Wear limits

II. CONSTRUCTION

Front shock absorber assemblies

The front forks are of a hydraulically-damped telescopic type using a free valve. Each front fork consists mainly of a fork pipe, a fork bottom case and a shock absorber spring. The shock absorber having a long stroke absorbs shocks very well. The fork bottom cases are made of aluminum-alloy which is light in weight and has high rigidity.

Travel of front shock absorber:
Compression side: **90 mm (3.54 in.)**
Extension side: **24.5 mm (0.96 in.)**

Operation

(On compression stroke)

Shocks from a road are transmitted to the fork bottom case through the front wheel and are absorbed by the rebound spring at the upper end of the bottom pipe in one piece with the case. At this time the oil in the chamber B lifts the free valve off its seat and flows into the chamber A smoothly. At the same time the oil in the chamber B also flows by the amount of oil entered the fork pipe into the chamber C through the orifice in the lower part of the spring under seat.

(On extension stroke)

The spring, now compressed, exerts a reaction to extend the fork bottom case, together with the unspriung weight of the front axle. At this time the oil in the chamber A is trapped because the free valve is closed and then flows into the chamber C through the orifice in the wall between the spring under seat and bottom pipe. By the resisting force of this oil, the damping action is provided.

(1) Front shock absorber spring
(2) Front fork pipe
(3) Front fork dust seal
(4) Oil seal
(5) Front fork bottom case
(6) Piston ring
(7) Rebound stop spring
(8) Free valve
(9) Bottom pipe
(10) Oil lock piece

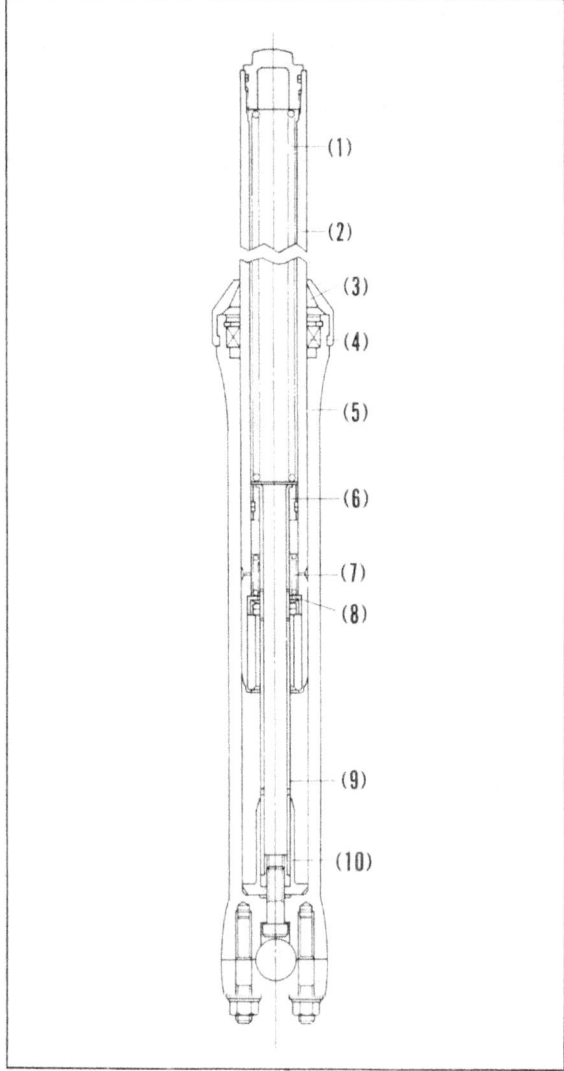

Fig. 2-24

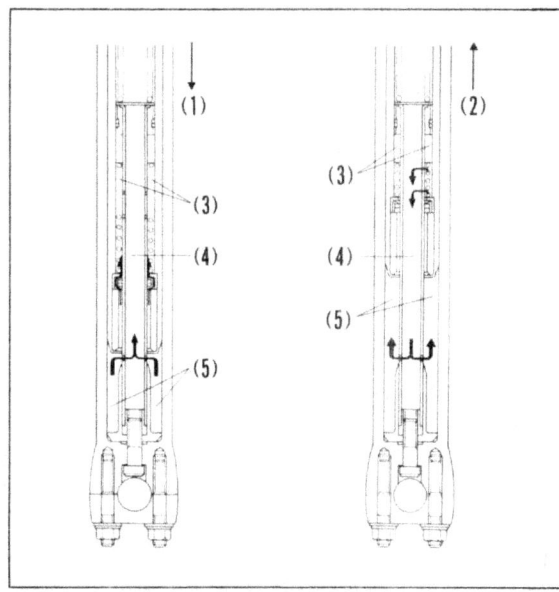

Fig. 2-25 (1) Compression   (4) Chamber "C"
          (2) Extension   (5) Chamber "B"
          (3) Chamber "A"

Rear shock absorber assemblies

The rear shock absorber assemblies feature the telescopic type oil dampers with bottom valve to give an optimum damping performance under all bumping and rebounding conditions. The damping performance on the extension side is well matched with that on the compression side, providing maximum damping.

Stroke of rear shock absorber: **77.6 mm (3.06 in.)**

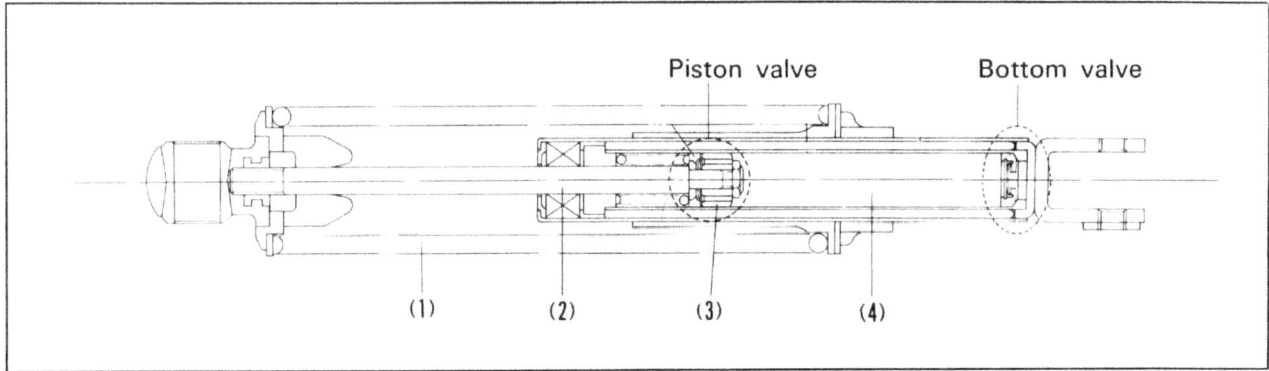

Fig. 2-26 (1) Rear shock absorber spring
(2) Damper rod
(3) Damper piston
(4) Damper cylinder

Operation

Each oil damper is equipped with the piston valves A and B and bottom valve. On the extension side, the damping action is provided by means of the piston valves. While, on the compression side, the damping action is provided by means of the bottom valve.

On extension side:
The oil in the chamber [a] flows into the chamber [b] through the orifice (I) in the valve A (sheet metal). By the resisting force of this oil, the damping action is provided. The valve A is overlapped with the valve B (leaf spring) which covers the half of the orifice. The damping action is regulated by the deflection of the valve B. Under such a condition, the bottom valve is opened and the oil in the chamber [c] flows into the chamber [b] smoothly to prevent air bubbles from being produced.

On compression side:
The oil in the chamber [b] flows by amount of oil equivalent to the volume of damper rod into the chamber [c] through the orifice in the bottom valve. By the resisting force of this oil, the damping action is provided. At this time the piston valves are opened and the oil flows from the chamber [b] into the chamber [a] smoothly.

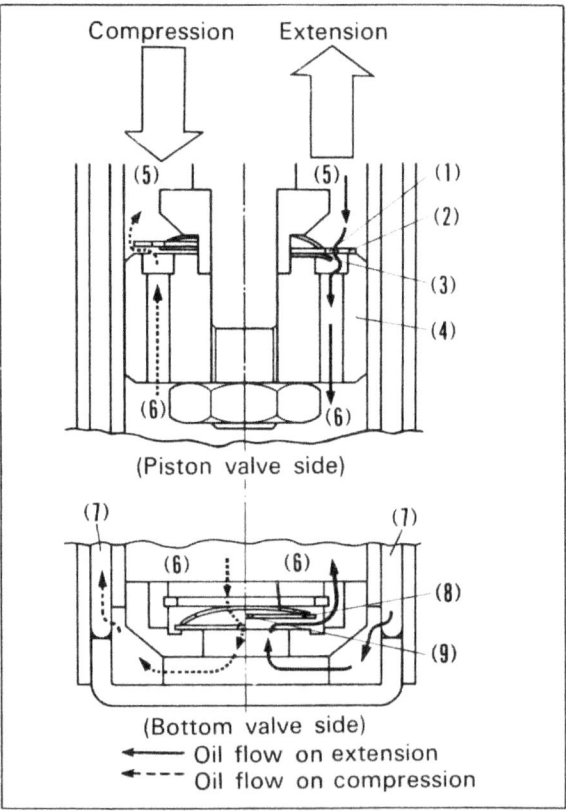

Fig. 2-27 (1) Orifice (I)   (4) Piston   (7) Chamber "c"
(2) Valve "A"   (5) Chamber "a"   (8) Bottom valve
(3) Valve "B"   (6) Chamber "b"   (9) Orifice (II)

Air cleaners

Air that is taken into the carburetor (cylinder) and mixed with fuel must be as free from dust as possible. If this is not done, the dust acts as an abrasive and under extreme conditions, the resulting wear will reach such proportions that it soon becomes necessary to recondition the engine. To reduce the amount of dust entering the carburetor, two air cleaners, one for each carburetor, are installed at the air entrance so all air is screened and filtered. In addition to filtering the air, the air cleaner is also designed to act as a silencer to reduce air suction noise.

Each air cleaner uses a replaceable, bellows type paper element. Both air cleaners are connected with each other by a central air passage to assure constant supply of clean air to the engine even if any one of the elements is clogged, resulting in a high efficiency. A clogged element reduces the amount of air to be taken into the carburetor, resulting in excessive fuel consumption and poor acceleration. The elements should, therefore, be cleaned periodically.

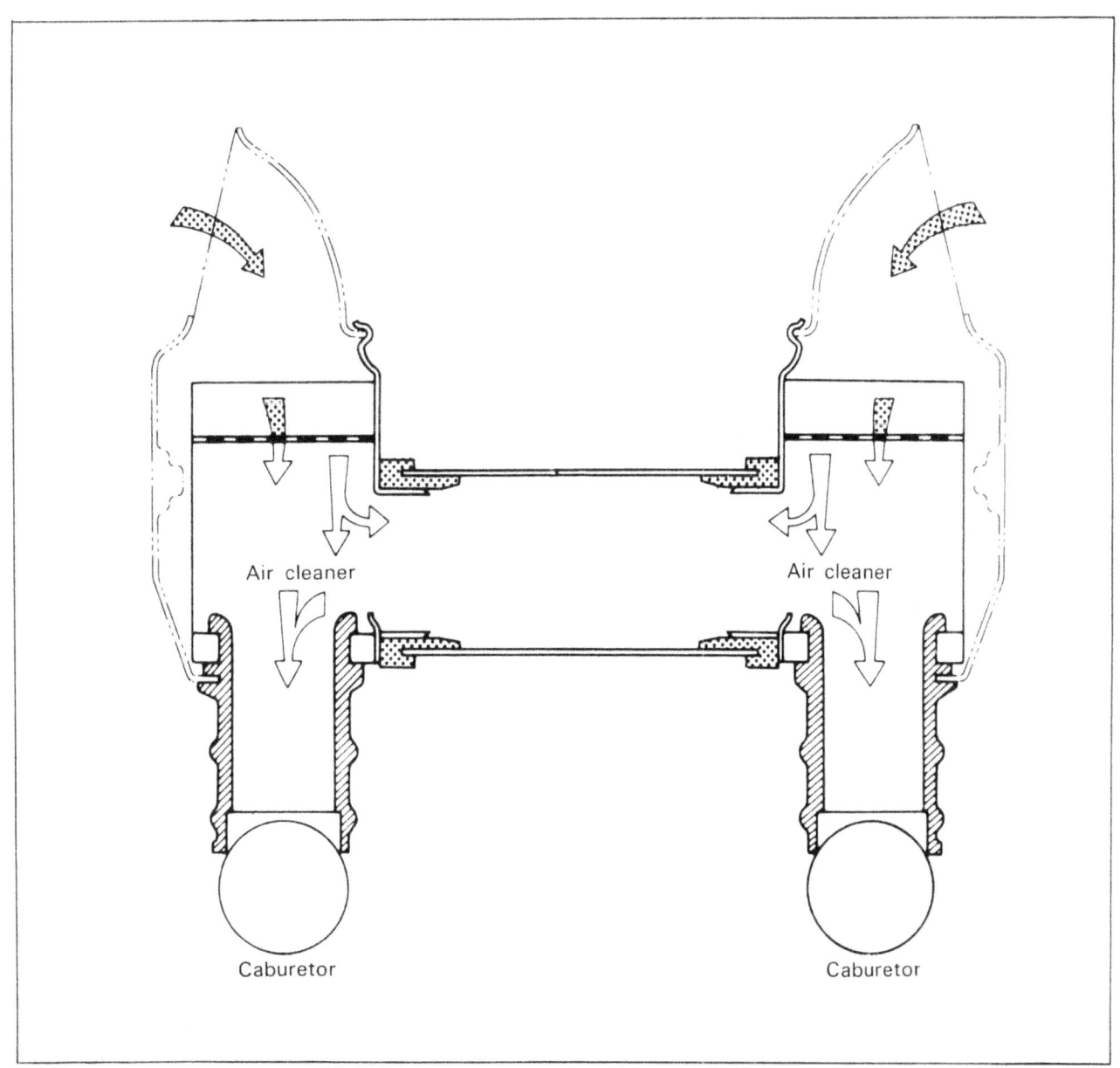

Fig. 2-28 Air cleaners communicated by central air passage

7. ELECTRICAL SYSTEM

Fuses

Three fuses are placed in the fuse box and they are easily checked by opening the seat. The main fuse is 15A fuse and the sub-fuses are 7A fuses, one for the headlight and the other for the position lamp, taillight and meter lamp, to make it easier to find circuit failure. Even if the 7A fuses are burnt down, as long as the 15A fuse is normal, the horn, turn signals, ignition switch and stop switches are operated properly. However, it is recommended that the cause be located before the damaged fuses is replaced.

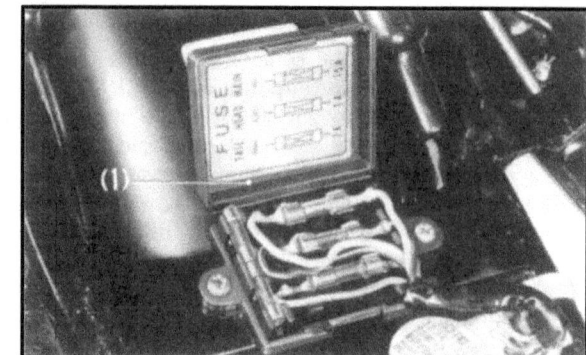

Fig. 2-29 (1) Fuse box

MEMO

III. INSPECTION AND ADJUSTMENT

This section covers the inspection and adjustment of important ones of the items involved in the MAINTENANCE SCHEDULE on page 110. For other items, see the paragraph for "Inspection" of each group.

1. TAPPETS

The tappet clearance must be adjusted when the engine is cold. For ease of service, open the seat and pull the rear fuel tank rubber mounting away from the rear tank mount. Raise the back of the fuel tank slightly.

1. Remove the tappet adjusting hole caps.
2. Remove the generator cover.
3. While slowly rotating the generator rotor counterclockwise watch the left (L) cylinder inlet valve tappet. When this tappet goes down all the way and then starts to lift, then watch for alignment of the index mark and "LT" mark. In this position, the piston in left cylinder will be at T.D.C. (top dead center) of the compression stroke, and the inlet and exhaust valves in that cylinder should be fully closed.

4. Check the clearance of both valves by inserting the feeler gauge between the tappet adjusting screw and the valve stem. If clearance is correct there will be slight drag or resistance as the gauge is inserted. If clearance is too close or loose, adjustment is necessary.
   The standard tappet clearance is
   In. 0.05 mm (0.002 in.)
   Ex. 0.08 mm (0.003 in.)

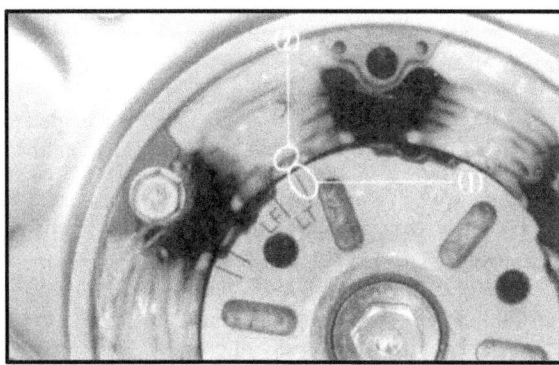

Fig. 3-1 Place piston at T.D.C. position on compression stroke
(1) "LT" mark (2) Index mark on stator

5. Adjustment is made by loosening the adjusting screw lock nut and turning the adjusting screw until there is slight drag on the feeler gauge. Hold the tappet adjusting screw in this position and tighten the lock nut.
   Recheck the clearance with the gauge.

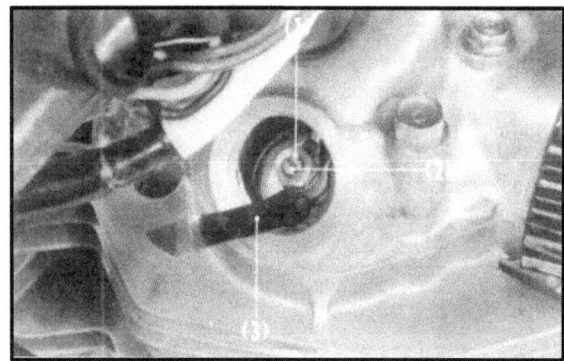

Fig. 3-2 (1) Lock nut
         (2) Adjusting screw
         (3) Feeler gauge

6. Turn the generator rotor 180° counterclockwise to position the right piston at top dead center. In this position the "T" mark will be aligned with the index mark.
7. Check right cylinder valve tappet clearance. The adjustment procedure is the same as described in step 5.
8. Reinstall the fuel tank.

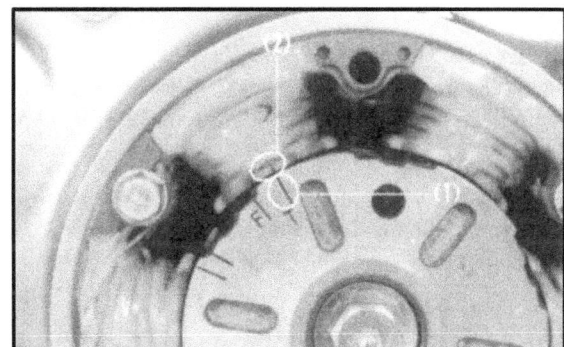

Fig. 3-3 (1) "T" mark
         (2) Index mark on stator

2. CONTACT BREAKER POINT GAP AND IGNITION TIMING

Contact Breaker Point Gap Adjustment

1. Remove the contact breaker point cover and generator cover.
2. Clean and inspect the contact breaker points. Replace if worn or badly pitted. Light pitting may be removed with an ignition point file.
3. Turn the generator rotor counterclockwise until one set of contact breaker points opens to maximum clearance.

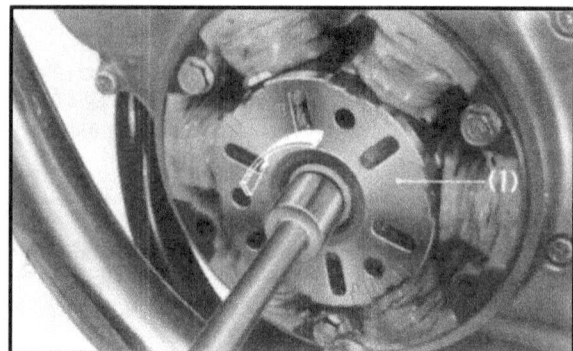

Fig. 3-4 (1) Generator rotor

4. Check contact breaker point gap with a feeler gauge. The correct gap is **0.3-0.4 mm (0.012-0.016 in.)**. If the gap is not within these limits, loosen the breaker plate locking screws and move the breaker plate to obtain the correct gap.
   Tighten the locking screws and recheck the gap.
5. Turn the generator rotor counterclockwise until the other set of contact breaker points opens to maximum clearance. Check gap and adjust if necessary.
6. Lubricate the breaker point cam with a thin film of grease.

NOTE:
Contact breaker point gap adjustment will affect ignition timing. Ignition timing must be checked after contact breaker point gap adjustment.

Fig. 3-5 (1) Point cam (5) Contact breaker plate locking
        (2) L/H contact breaker point   screw
        (3) R/H contact breaker point
        (4) Contact breaker plates

Ignition Timing

Check ignition timing upon completion of the contact breaker point gap adjustment.

1. Turn the generator rotor counterclockwise until the "LF" timing mark on the rotor aligns with the index mark on the generator stator.
   If left cylinder ignition timing is correct, the left breaker points will just begin to open as these marks align.

Start of advance (at crankshaft)	1,800 rpm
Full advance (at crankshaft)	3,400 rpm
Advance angle	0-12.5

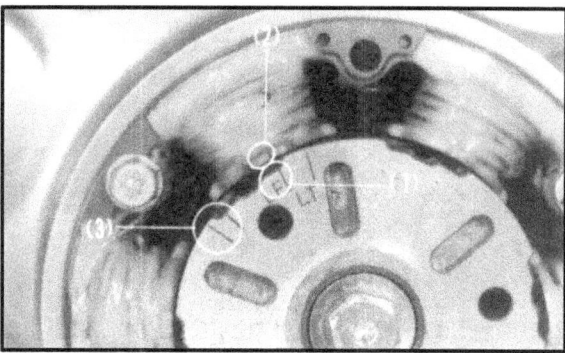

Fig. 3-6 (1) "LF" mark
        (2) Index mark on stator
        (3) Index marks at full advance

NOTE:
Static ignition timing may be checked with a 12V-3W continuity light. When connected as illustrated in Fig. 3-7, with the main switch in the ON position, the light will come on as the breaker points open.
Static timing is relatively accurate, but for best results a stroboscopic timing light should be used to check ignition timing in both retarded and full advanced positions.

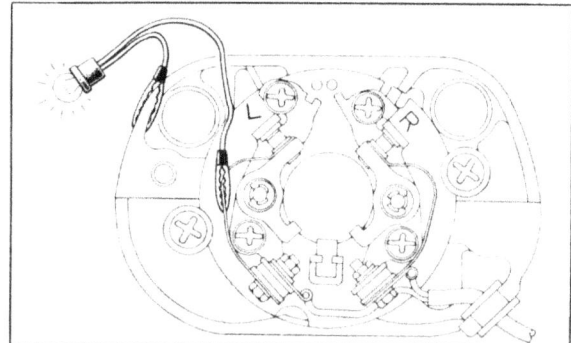

Fig. 3-7

III. INSPECTION AND ADJUSTMENT

2. If left cylinder ignition timing is incorrect, loosen the base plate locking screws and rotate the base plate to obtain correct timing. Rotate the base plate clockwise to advance timing, or counterclockwise to retard timing. Tighten the base plate locking screws and recheck left breaker point gap.
3. Turn the generator rotor counterclockwise until the "F" timing mark on the rotor aligns with the index mark on the generator stator. If right cylinder ignition timing is correct, the right breaker points will just begin to open as these marks align.
4. If right cylinder timing is incorrect, loosen the right breaker plate locking screws and increase or decrease point gap to obtain correct timing. Do not loosen the base plate locking screws. Increasing the point gap advances ignition timing. Decreasing the point gap retards ignition timing.

NOTE:
Ignition point gap must remain within limits of 0.3-0.4 mm (0.012-0.016 in.) after ignition timing has been set. If correct timing results in a point gap which is outside these limits, increase or decrease both point gaps equally to bring gaps within limits, then retime by rotating base plate.

e.g. If left point gap is set at 0.35 mm (0.014 in.) and right point gap produces correct timing at 0.42 mm (0.017 in.), and rotate base plate to time ignition.

If both point gaps cannot be adjusted within limits, replace point assemblies.

Fig. 3-8 (1) Base plate locking screws
(2) Base plate
(3) L/H contact breaker plate locking screws
(4) R/H contact breaker plate locking screws

Fig. 3-9 (1) "F" mark
(2) Index mark on stator
(3) Index mark at full advance

MEMO

3. CARBURETOR

Carburetor adjustment should only be made when the engine is at operating temperature.

Checking idle speed

1. Set the idle speed to 1,200 rpm with the throttle stop screw.
   Turning the screw clockwise will increase engine speed.

Fig. 3–10 (1) Throttle stop screw

2. Starting with either the right or left carburetor, turn each pilot screw to find the point of highest rpm; the same should be done with the opposite carburetor. Turning the pilot screw in produces a lean fuel air mixture, turning the screw out produces a rich mixture.
3. Readjust the throttle stop screw if it is necessary to rest the idle speed.
   After performing the adjustment above if the proper idling speed cannot be obtained or if the exhaust back pressures from the cylinders are not uniform, the carburetors require individual adjustment and synchronization.

Fig. 3–11 (1) Pilot screw

Checking synchronization

1. Remove the fuel tank and connect it to the right and left carburetors by the longer fuel tubes provided for this purpose. Hold the fuel tank higher than the carburetors.
2. Remove the plugs from the right and left carburetors and attach vacuum gauges. (Tool No. 07504–3000100).

Fig. 3–12 (1) Plug

3. Start the engine and check if the pointers of the two vacuum gauges remain between **16** and **24 cmHg**. If necessary, loosen the lock nut and turn the adjusting screw. The difference in the negative pressure between the two carburetors should be within **2.0 cmHg**.

   NOTE:
   If each pointer fluctuate excessively, adjust it with the vacuum gauge adjuster.

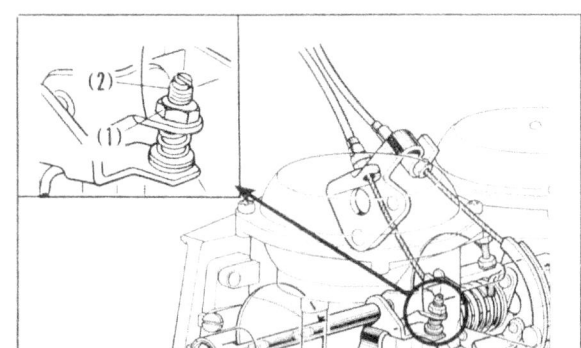

Fig. 3–13 (1) Lock nut
(2) Adjusting screw

III. INSPECTION AND ADJUSTMENT

4. Upon noting that the pointers of two vacuum gauges remain between **16** and **24 cmHg**, snap the engine two or three times.
   If the pointers come outside the specification, repeat the step 3 above.
   * If the pointers are below 15 cmHg, check the following items.
     (1) Ignition timing (see page 18)
     (2) Tappet clearance (see page 17)
     (3) Spark plug gap (see page 102)
     (4) Compression pressure (see page 30)

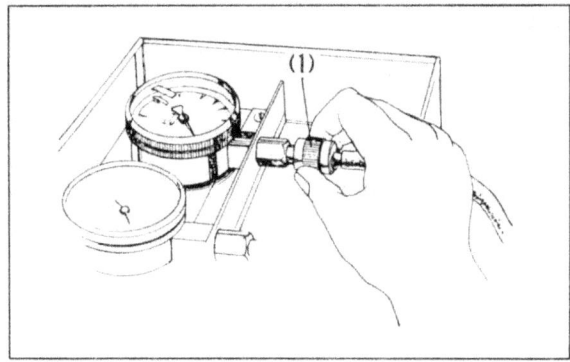

Fig. 3–14 (1) Vacuum gauge adjuster

5. Upon noting that the vacuum of the two carburetors reach the specified value, turn the throttle stop screw to obtain the standard idle speed.
6. Adjust each carburetor with the pilot screw.
7. Turn the throttle stop screw to again adjust the idle speed to **1,200 rpm**

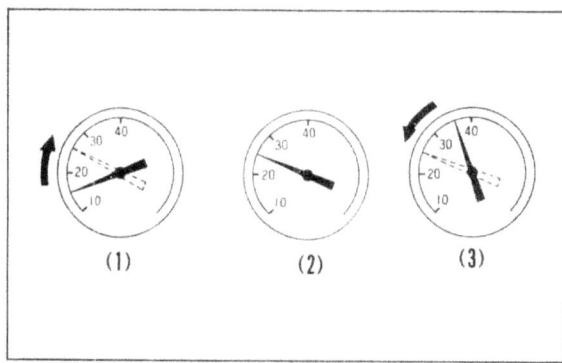

Fig. 3–15 (1) High speed (throttle too open)
        (2) Standard
        (3) Low speed (throttle too closed)

4. THROTTLE CABLE

Two control cables connect the throttle grip to a linkage on the carburetor operating bar. One cable opens the throttle valves, while the other cable ensures positive closure.

Standard throttle grip play is approximately 10-15° of grip rotation. This play can be adjusted at the grip play adjuster and also with the cable adjuster at the lower end of the opening cable at the throttle crank. To adjust, loosen the lock nut and turn the adjuster. Tighten the lock nut upon completion of adjustment and check for smooth operation of throttle grip through the engine range from full open to full close with the handlebar set to the extreme right and left steering positions.

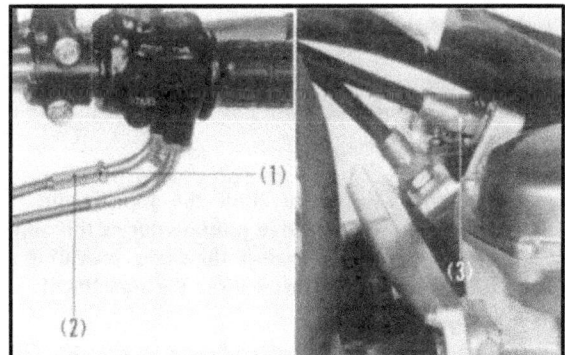

Fig. 3–16 (1) Lock nut
        (2) Grip play adjuster
        (3) Cable adjuster

5. CLUTCH

The normal clutch lever free play is **10-20 mm (0.4-0.8 in.)** at the lever tip.
To adjust the clutch, perform the following steps.
1. Loosen the lock nut and turn the clutch cable upper adjuster located at the clutch lever, all the way into the clutch lever bracket.

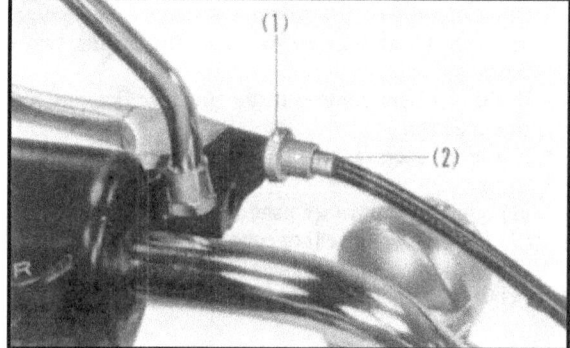

Fig. 3–17 (1) Lock nut
(2) Clutch cable upper adjuster

2. Turn the clutch cable lower adjuster located at the clutch housing, in direction (A) all the way down to loosen the clutch cable.

Fig. 3–18 (1) Clutch cable lower adjuster
(2) Lock nut

3. Loosen the clutch adjuster lock nut until nut is flush with screw adjuster, turn the clutch adjuster in direction (B) until a slight resistance is felt.
   From this position, turn the adjuster in direction (A) ¼ turn.
   CAUTION:
   During this adjustment, allow the adjuster nut to rotate freely. If the nut is held in position during this adjustment, the nut may tighten against the cover, providing with the resistance which may throw away the adjustment.

   Tighten the lock nut.
4. Turn the clutch cable lower adjuster in direction (B) so that there is **10-20 mm (0.4-0.8 in.)** of the play at the clutch lever, then tighten the lock nut.
   Perform any subsequent minor adjustment with the clutch cable upper adjuster.
5. After the adjustment has been made, ensure that the clutch is not slipping and that the clutch is properly disengaging. After the engine starts, pull in the clutch lever and shift into gear, and ensure that the engine does not stall, nor the motorcycle start to creep. Gradually release the clutch lever and open the throttle. The motorcycle should start smoothly and accelerate gradually.

Fig. 3–19 (1) Clutch adjuster lock nut
(2) Clutch adjuster

III. INSPECTION AND ADJUSTMENT

6. CAM CHAIN

A loose cam chain will cause the valve timing to change, resulting in poor performance. It will also cause excessive engine noise.

1. Adjustment must be made when the four valves are closed completely and the tappets are free. This position occurs at 90° A.T.D.C. on the compression stroke of the left side cylinder. Rotate the generator rotor counterclockwise until index mark on the stator is 90° A.T.D.C. (after 90° "LT" mark). If the valves are still lifted, rotate the rotor 360° and repeat realignment above.
2. Loosen the tensioner lock nut and the tensioner bolt. When these are loosened, the cam chain tensioner will automatically position itself to provide the correct cam chain tension.
3. Retighten the tensioner bolt and lock nut.

Fig. 3–20 (1) Lock nut
(2) Tensioner bolt

7. ENGINE OIL

Checking oil level and refilling

1. Remove the oil filler cap and check the oil level using the oil level gauge with the motorcycle in the up-right position.
2. The oil level should be between the upper and lower level marks. Do not screw the level gauge in.
3. If necessary, refill the crankcase with the recommended oil through the oil filler hole.
4. Again check the oil level.
* Excessive oil may cause abnormal noise and inoperative clutch.

Fig. 3–21 (1) Oil level gauge
(2) Upper level mark
(3) Lower level mark

Oil Recommendation

Use only high detergent, premium quality engine oil.
The regular use of special oil additives is unnecessary and will only increase operating expenses.

NOTE:
Non-detergent and low quality oils are specifically not recommended.

Viscosity

Viscosity selection should be based on the average atmospheric temperature in riding area. Change to the proper viscosity oil whenever the changes in average atmospheric temperature require it.

Recommended oil viscosity:

General, all temperatures
SAE 10W-30 or SAE 10W-40

Alternate:

Above 59°F (15°C)	SAE 30
32° (0°) to 59°F (15°C)	SAE 20 or 20W
Below 32°F (0°C)	SAE 10W

Changing Oil

1. Remove the oil filler cap from the right crankcase cover.
2. Remove the oil drain plug with a 17 mm wrench.
3. After the oil stops draining from the crankcase, operate the kick starter several times to drain any oil which may be left in the recesses of the engine.
4. When the oil has been completely drained, reinstall the drain plug making sure that the O-ring used on the drain plug is in good condition.
5. Fill the crankcase through the oil filler opening with recommended grade oil. Check the oil level with the filler cap dipstick, however, when making this check, do not screw in the cap. Oil level should be between the upper and lower level marks on the dipstick. When checking the oil make certain that the motorcycle is in upright and level position.

Fig. 3–22 (1) Drain plug

Unit: liter (U.S. qt.)

Amount of oil to be filled	When changing oil	1.5 (1.6), approx.
	When separating crankcase	2.0 (2.1), approx.

8. OIL FILTER SCREEN AND ROTOR

A dual system of metal screening and centrifugal oil filtering is utilized to provide engine components with highly purified oil to minimize wear and improve engine cooling. The oil filters are serviced in the following manner.

1. Drain the engine oil.
2. Remove the foot rest, the muffler and the kick starter pedal.
3. Loosen the right crankcase cover mounting screws and remove the crankcase cover and cover gasket.
4. Remove the snap ring and disassemble the oil filter cap from the oil filter rotor.

Fig. 3–23 (1) Oil filter cap
(2) Snap ring
(3) Oil filter rotor

5. Clean any sludge from the center of the oil filter rotor.

Fig. 3–24 (1) Oil filter rotor

III. INSPECTION AND ADJUSTMENT

6. Remove the screen filter for cleaning. Wash the screen filter in clean solvent and then install.
7. Reassemble all parts removed in the proper order. If the crankcase cover gasket is damaged, replace it with a new gasket.

Fig. 3–25 (1) Screen filter
(2) Screen filter attaching bolts

NOTE:
* When assembling the oil filter cap and the oil filter rotor ensure that either of the cap ribs is aligned with the rotor index marks.

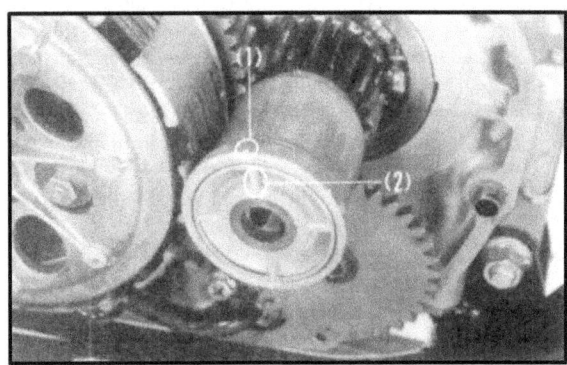

Fig. 3–26 (1) Index mark
(2) Rib

9. FRONT BRAKE

(Disc Type)

Replenishing brake fluid

Remove the reservoir cap, washer and diaphragm, and whenever the level is lower than the level mark engraved inside the reservoir, fill the reservoir with **DOT 3 BRAKE FLUID** up to the level mark. Reinstall the diaphragm and washer, and tighten the reservoir cap securely.

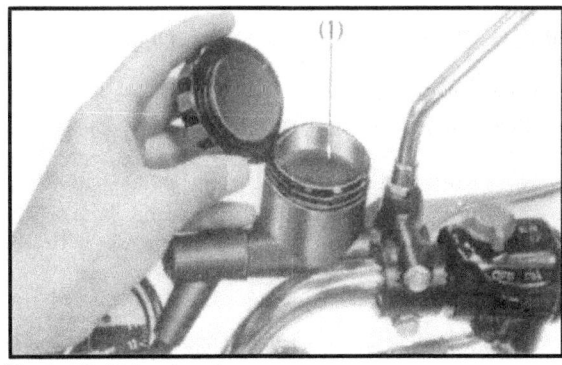

Fig. 3–27 (1) Level mark

Adjusting brake caliper

Whenever the brake pads are replaced, the brake caliper must be adjusted. This adjustment is made in the following manner, so that there is a small clearance between the fixed friction pad and the brake disc.
1. Raise the front wheel off the ground using a suitable prop.
2. Loosen the caliper stopper bolt lock nut.
3. Using a suitable screw driver, turn the stopper bolt in direction (A) until the friction pad contacts the brake disc. When the wheel is rotated, slight drag should be noticed.
4. While rotating the front wheel, turn the stopper bolt in direction (B) until the front wheel rotates freely.
5. Turn the stopper bolt ½ turn in direction (B) further and tighten the lock nut.

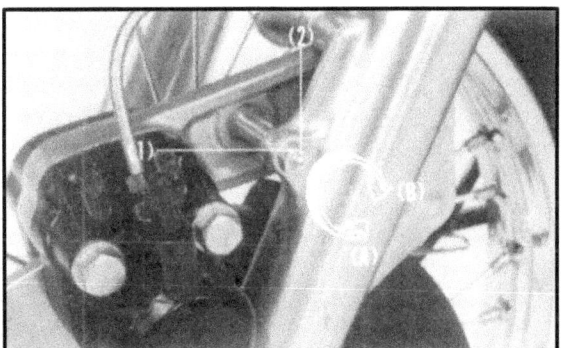

Fig. 3–28 (1) Stopper bolt lock nut
(2) Stopper bolt

III. INSPECTION AND ADJUSTMENT

Bleeding the brake system

The brakes must be bled with great care subsequent to work performed on the brake system, when the lever becomes soft or spongy, or when lever travel is excessive. The procedure is best performed by two mechanics.

1. Remove the dust cap from the bleeder valve and attach bleeder hose.
2. Place the free end of the bleeder hose into a glass container which has some hydraulic brake fluid in it so that the end of the hose can be submerged.
3. Fill the reservoir using only the recommended brake fluid. Screw the cap partially on the reservoir to prevent entry of dust.
4. As shown at right (Fig. 3–30B), attach a rubber of about 15 mm thick to the end of the handle grip to decrease the stroke as measured at the tip of the handle lever.
5. Pump the brake lever several times until pressure can be felt, holding the lever tight, open the bleeder valve by about one-half turn and squeeze the lever all the way down.
   Do not release the lever until the bleeder valve has been closed again. Repeat this procedure until bubbles cease to appear in the fluid at the end of the hose.
6. Remove the bleeder hose, tighten the bleeder valve and install the bleeder valve dust cap.
7. Do not allow the fluid reservoir to become empty during the bleeding operation as this will allow air to enter the system again. Replenish the fluid as often as necessary while bleeding.
8. Check for proper effect of bleeding and absence of leaks in the front brake lines while holding pressure against the brake lever. Replenish fluid in the reservoir when bleeding is completed. Reinstall the diaphragm, washer and reservoir cap and tighten.

When the hydrulic brake system has been drained, it should be first filled as outlined below.

1. Fill the fluid reservoir.
2. Open the bleeder valve by one-half turn, squeeze the brake lever, close the valve and release the brake lever. This procedure must be repeated in this sequence until hydraulic fluid begins to flow through the bleeder hose. Having filled the hydraulic system with fluid, proceed with the actual bleeding operation.

NOTES:
* Brake fluid which has been pumped out of the system must not be used again.
* Care must be taken, as brake fluid will damage the paint finish and instrument lenses.

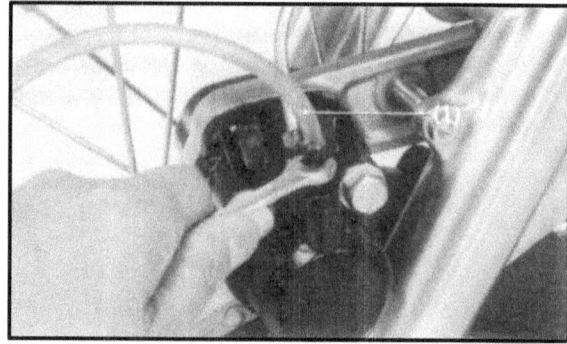

Fig. 3–29 (1) Bleeder hose

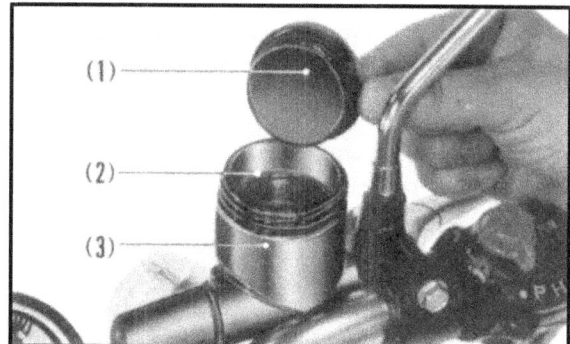

Fig. 3–30A (1) Diaphragm
(2) Level mark
(3) Reservoir

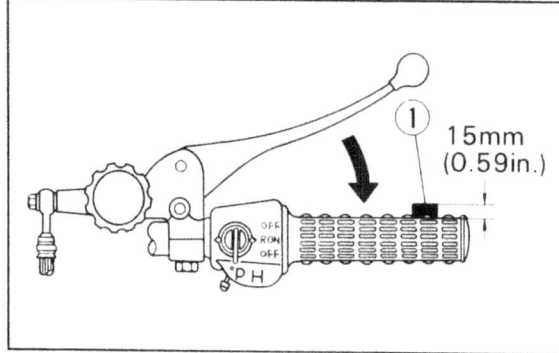

Fig. 3–30B (1) Rubber

III. INSPECTION AND ADJUSTMENT

(Drum Type)

1. Raise the front wheel off the ground by placing a support block under the engine, spin the front wheel by hand and measure the travel the front brake lever must be moved before the brake starts to take hold. The lever free play should be **20–30 mm (0.8–1.2 in)** at the end of the brake lever.

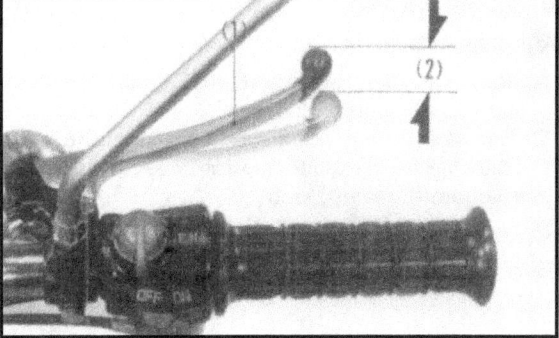

Fig. 3–31 (1) Front brake lever
(2) Lever free play

2. Normally the adjustment can be made at the front brake arm on the front brake panel.
First loosen the lock nut and then turn the front brake adjusting nut. Turning the nut in the clockwise direction (A) will decrease the brake lever play and turning in the counterclockwise direction (B) will increase the play.

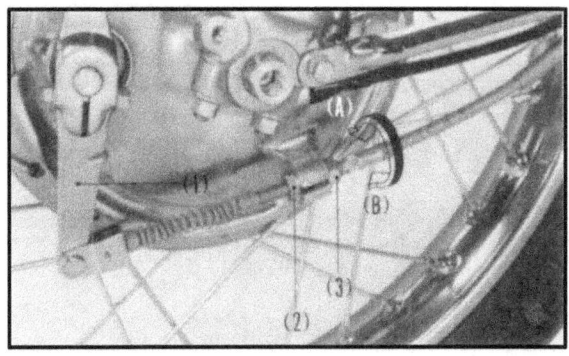

Fig. 3–32 (1) Front brake arm
(2) Lock nut
(3) Adjusting nut

3. Minor adjustment can also be made with front brake cable adjuster on the front brake lever by turning in the same direction as above.

Fig. 3–33 (1) Front brake cable adjuster
(2) Lock nut

Brake wear indicator

The wear indicator is provided in the front brake.
When the brake is applied, a red arrow, adjacent to the brake arm, moves toward a red reference mark on the brake panel. The distance between the arrow and the reference mark, on full application of the brake, indicates brake lining thickness.
If the arrow aligns with the reference mark on full application of the brake, the brake shoes should be removed and inspected for wear. Replace the brake shoes, if the thickness of the lining is **2.0 mm (0.08 in)** or less.

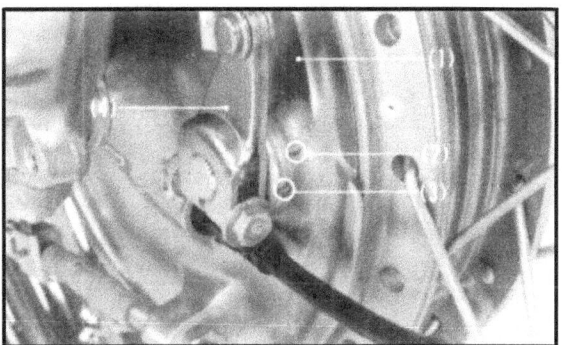

Fig. 3–34 (1) Front brake panel
(2) Reference mark
(3) Arrow mark
(4) Front brake arm

10. REAR BRAKE

Adjusting pedal height

1. Raise the rear wheel off the ground by placing the motorcycle on its center stand.
2. The stopper bolt is provided to allow adjustment of the pedal height. To adjust the rear brake, loosen the lock nut, and turn the stopper bolt.

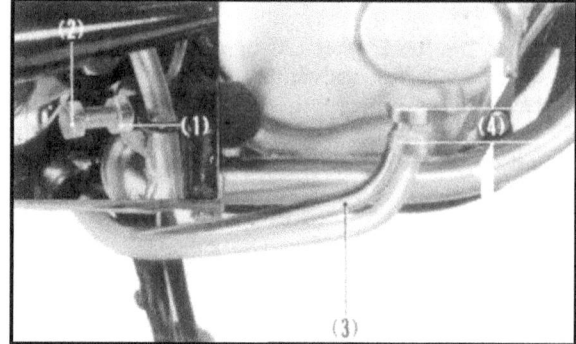

Fig. 3-35 (1) Lock nut
(2) Pedal stopper bolt
(3) Rear brake pedal
(4) Free play

Adjusting rear brake pedal free play

The rear brake pedal free play should be **20-30 mm (0.8-1.2 in)** as measured at the tip of the pedal.

1. To adjust, turn the rear brake adjusting nut. Turn clockwise for less free travel, counterclockwise for greater free travel.

NOTE:
After adjusting, check the lighting time of the rear brake stop lamp. (See page 105.)

Fig. 3-36 (1) Rear brake adjusting nut

Brake wear indicator

The wear indicator is provided in the rear brake.
When the brake is applied, a red arrow, adjacent to the brake arm, moves toward a red reference mark on the brake panel. The distance between the arrow and the reference mark, on full application of the brake, indicates brake lining thickness.
If the arrow aligns with the reference mark on full application of the brake, the brake shoes should be removed and inspected for wear. Replace the brake shoes, if the thickness of the lining is **2.0 mm (0.08 in)** or less.

Fig. 3-37 (1) Rear brake panel
(2) Reference mark
(3) Arrow mark
(4) Rear brake arm

11. DRIVE CHAIN

Checking drive chain tension

1. Place the motorcycle on its center stand to raise the rear wheel off the ground. Shift the transmission into neutral.
2. Check vertical movement of the lower length of the drive chain at a point midway between the sprockets. Move the chain up and down with your fingers and observe the amount of slack. Drive chain tension should be adjusted to allow approximately **20 mm (¾")** vertical movement at this point.

Fig. 3-38 (1) Drive chain

III. INSPECTION AND ADJUSTMENT

3. Remove the rear axle nut cotter pin and loosen the rear axle nut.
4. Loosen the lock nut and turn the adjusting bolts on both the right and left chain adjusters to increase or decrease chain tension.
   Align the chain adjuster index marks to corresponding scale graduations on both sides of the rear fork.
5. Tighten the rear axle nut and secure the nut with a new cotter pin.
   Tighten the lock nuts.
6. Recheck drive chain tension.
7. Rear brake pedal free travel is affected when repositioning the rear wheel to adjust drive chain tension. Check rear brake pedal free travel and adjust as necessary.

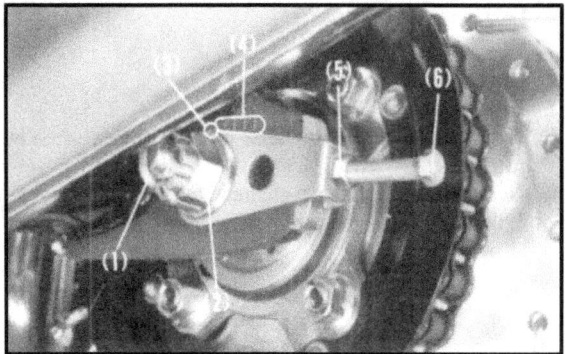

Fig. 3-39 (1) Cotter pin   (5) Lock nut
(2) Rear axle nut   (6) Adjusting bolt
(3) Index mark
(4) Corresponding scale

12. FRONT FORK

Changing fork oil

1. Unscrew the front fork drain plug at the bottom of fork leg. Drain the oil by pumping the fork while plug is out. Replace the plug securely after draining.
2. Set the motorcycle on the center stand.
3. Place a jack under the crankcase to control lowering of the front end.
4. Remove the handlebar by removing the four handlebar bolts.
5. Unscrew the fork filler plugs until free.
6. Lower the jack under the engine to extend the fork springs with the attached filler plugs.
7. Move the fork springs to one side and pour **135–140cc (4.6–4.7 ozs.)** of premium quality **ATF** (automatic transmission fluid) into each fork leg.
8. Raise the jack under the engine to allow the fork springs and filler plugs to return into the fork legs.
9. Securely tighten the fork filler plugs.
10. Reinstall handlebar, tightening the two front bolts first, then securely tightening the two rear bolts.
11. Remove the jack from under the engine.

Fig. 3-40 (1) Front fork drain plug

Fig. 3-41 (1) Fork filler plugs

13. REAR SHOCK ABSORBER

Each rear shock absorber has five adjustment positions for different types of road or riding conditions.
Position I is for light loads and smooth road conditions. Positions II to V progressively increase spring tension for stiffer rear suspension, and are used when the motorcycle is heavily laden or operated on rough roads.

Fig. 3-42 (1) Rear shock absorber
(2) Pin spanner

III. INSPECTION AND ADJUSTMENT

14. AIR CLEANER

1. Open the seat.
2. Remove the air cleaner cover.
3. Remove the air cleaner case by unscrewing the case fixing nut.
4. Remove the air cleaner element by unscrewing the element fixing bolt and connecting tube fixing screw.

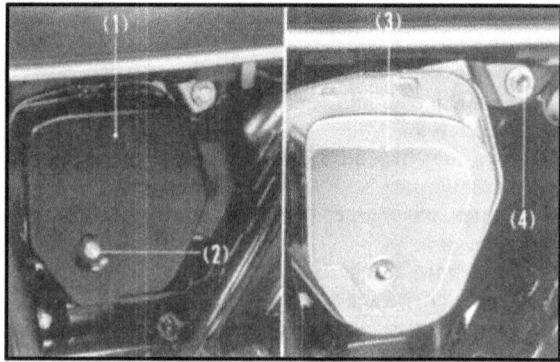

Fig. 3–43 (1) Air cleaner case
(2) Case fixing nut
(3) Element fixing bolt
(4) Fixing screw

5. Clean the air cleaner element by tapping it lightly to loosen dust. The remaining dust can be brushed from the outer element surface or blown away by applying compressed air from the inside of the element.

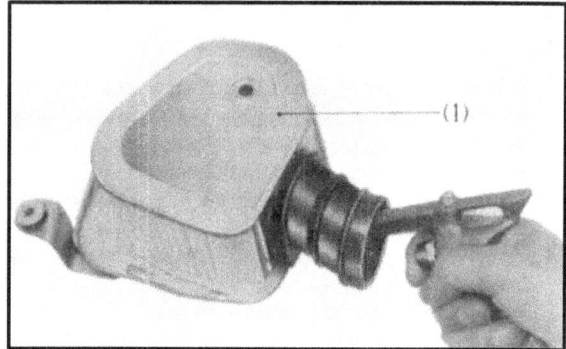

Fig. 3–44 (1) Air cleaner element

15. CYLINDER COMPRESSION PRESSURE

1. Remove the spark plug.
2. Put a compression gauge attachment into the plug hole and hold the gauge securely to prevent leaks of compressed gases.
3. Fully open the throttle and choke valves and continuously operate the kick starter vigorously and quickly.

   The specified compression pressure is 12kg/sq.cm (171 lb/sq.in.)
   If the actual compression pressure is above 12kg/sq.cm, it indicates that carbon is accumulated in the combustion chambers or on the piston heads. Disassemble the cylinder head and cylinder and decarbonize. If the actual pressure is below 10.5kg/sq.cm (149 lb/sq.in.), compressed gases leak from the valves, piston rings, cylinder head or cylinder gasket. Readjust the tappet clearance or disassemble the cylinder head, cylinder and pistons to check the piston rings and gaskets for condition.

Fig. 3–45 (1) Compression gauge attachment
(2) Compression gauge

IV. ENGINE

1. ON-FRAME SERVICING (Engine Disassembly)

No.	Item	Ref. page
1	Cylinder head, cylinder and pistons	37
2	Left crankcase cover, A.C. generator and starting motor	45
3	Right crankcase cover and clutch	47

No.	Item	Ref. page
4	Oil pump and oil filter	50
5	Gearshift spindle	57
6	Carburetor	63

2. ENGINE REMOVAL AND INSTALLATION

Removal

Dismount the engine for disassembly after the engine oil has been drained out.

(1) Open the seat and remove the battery.
* Remove the battery cable first.

(1) Battery   (3) Positive terminal
(2) Negative terminal

(2) Disconnect the starting motor cable at the starter magnetic switch.

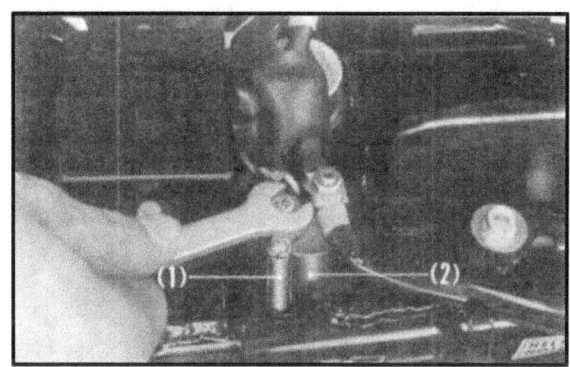

(1) Starting motor cable   (2) Starter magnetic switch

(3) Remove the fuel tank
* With the fuel valve in "OFF" position, remove the tank taking care not to break the fuel tubes.

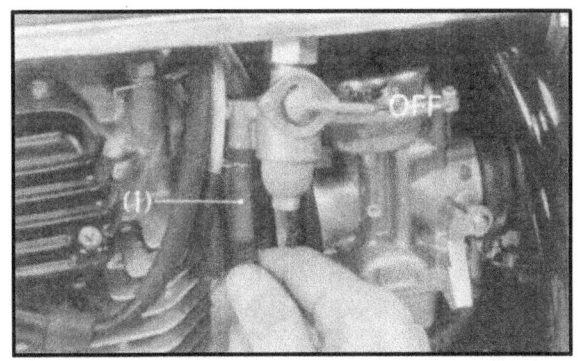

(1) Fuel tube

(4) Remove the right and left mufflers
* Remove the two nuts (2) and bolt (3) and remove the left muffler.
Repeat the above for the right muffler.

(1) Left muffler   (Indicates CB type)

IV. ENGINE

(5) Remove the change pedal and left crankcase rear cover.

(1) Change pedal (2) Left crankcase rear cover

(6) Remove the drive chain with the drive sprocket.
 * Remove the drive sprocket fixing bolts.

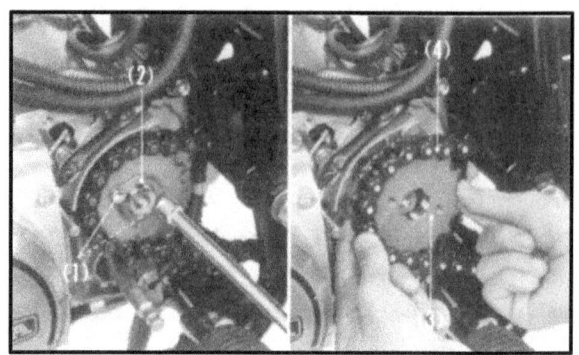

(1) Drive sprocket fixing bolts (3) Drive sprocket
(2) Fixing plate (4) Drive chain (endless)

(7) Drain the carburetor and loosen the connecting tube band.
 * Remove the drain screw and drain gasoline.

(1) Drain screw (3) Carburetor insulator band
(2) Connecting tube band

(8) Remove the carburetor.
 * Disconnect the carburetor at the insulator side and push it toward the air cleaner.
 Then remove the carburetor toward left by lowering it.

(9) Remove the A.C. generator connector.
 * Pull out the starting motor cable.

(1) A.C. generator connector (2) Starting motor cable

(10) Remove the brake pedal.
 * Remove the bolt and brake pedal pivot shaft and remove the pedal.

(1) Brake pedal pivot shaft (2) Brake pedal

IV. ENGINE 33

(11) Disconnect the tachometer cable and primary lead. Remove the spark plug caps.

(1) Primary lead

(12) Remove the UBS nuts (2) and nut (3) and remove the engine upper hanger.

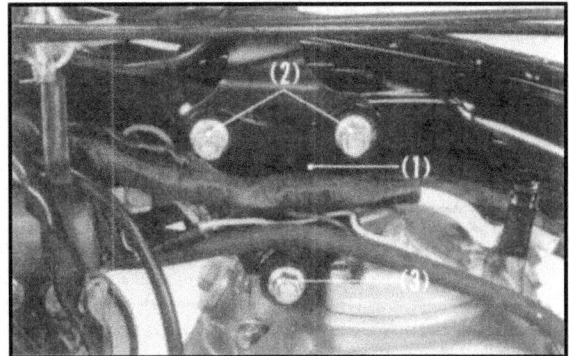

(1) Engine upper hanger

(13) Remove the UBS nuts (2), (3) and (4).
* Remove the nut (2) and remove the foot peg.
* Remove the nut (4) and pull out the bolt.

(1) Left foot peg

(14) Remove the bolt (3), pull out the bolt (4) and remove the engine hanger plate.
Remove the bolt (5) with nut and right foot peg together.

(1) Right foot peg (2) Engine hanger plate

(15) Remove the bolts (2) and (3).

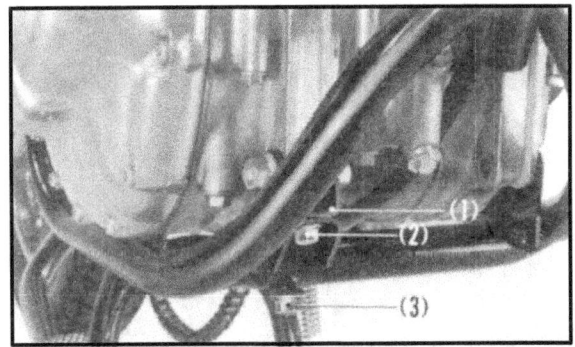

(1) Engine bottom hanger

(16) Lower the engine toward right as shown.
* Be careful of your feet. It is advisable to lower the engine by two persons.

IV. ENGINE

Installation

To install the engine, reverse the removal procedures.
1. Install the engine on the frame from right side so that it is slightly inclined forward.
* Make sure that the starting motor cable is not binding.
* Position the engine bottom hanger correctly before tightening the bolts.
2. Install the engine hanger bolts as shown in the figure below.

Fig. 4-1

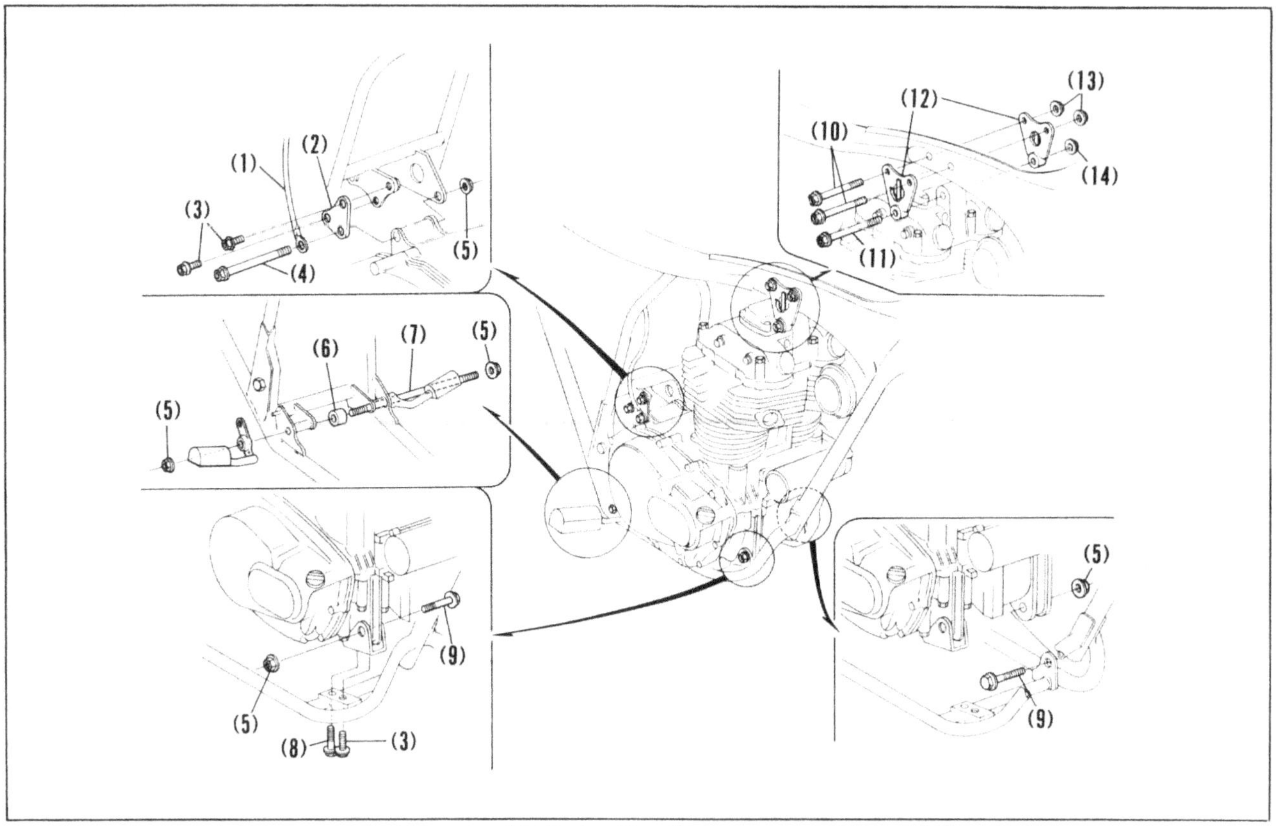

Fig. 4-2 (1) Battery ground cable
(2) Engine hanger plate
(3) 8 x 14 UBS bolt
(4) 10 x 110 UBS bolt
(5) 10 mm UBS nut
(6) Engine side collar
(7) Rear engine lower hanger bolt
(8) 8 x 45 UBS bolt
(9) 10 x 45 UBS bolt
(10) 8 mm UBS bolt
(11) 8 x 85 flanged bolt
(12) Engine upper hanger
(13) 8 mm UBS nut
(14) 8 mm nut

3. The threaded part of each engine rear hanger bolt with which the foot rest is tightened, must be identical in length.

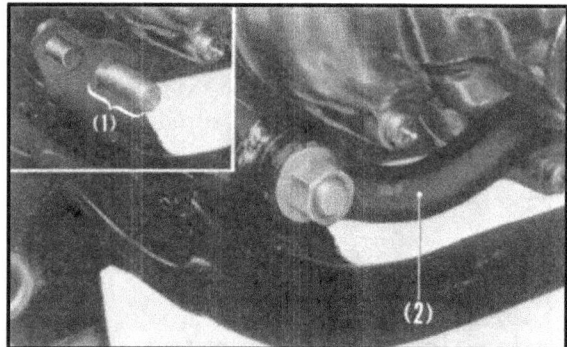

Fig. 4-3 (1) Engine rear hanger bolts (Threaded parts are identical in length.)
(2) Foot rest

IV. ENGINE

4. Route the starting motor cable as shown in Fig. 4-4 and connect it to the starter magnetic switch.

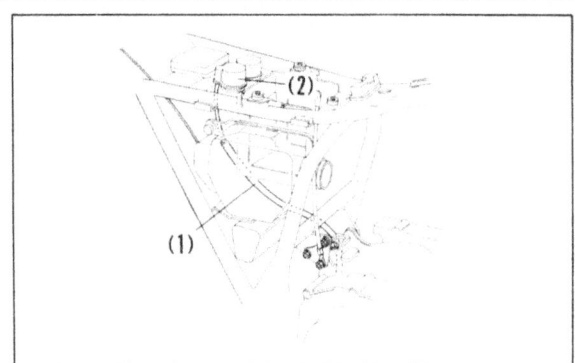

Fig. 4-4 (1) Starting motor cable
(2) Starter magnetic switch

5. Push the carburetor toward the insulator completely and secure it with the connecting tube band.

   NOTE:
   Install the A.C. generator connector before installing the carburetor.

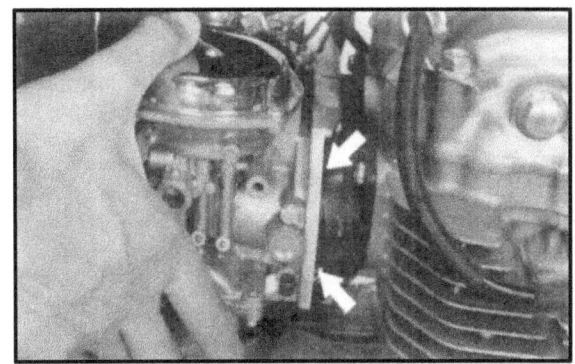

Fig. 4-5

6. Loosen the rear axle nut, chain adjuster lock nut and chain adjuster, and push the rear wheel forward all the way.
7. Install the driven sprocket to the drive chain and then the assembly to the countershaft. Secure the sprocket with the fixing plate and fixing bolts.

Fig. 4-6 Push rear wheel forward all the way

8. Adjust the chain tension.
   * The chain slack should be **20 mm (¾ in)** at the position shown at right.
   * Align the index marks on the right and left adjusters with the reference marks on the side scales.

Fig. 4-7 (1) Chain slack (2) Index and reference marks

IV. ENGINE

9. Making sure that the #10 steel ball is inside the clutch lever as shown, install the left crankcase rear cover.

   CAUTION:
   Missing of the steel ball may cause the clutch to be disengaged improperly.

Fig. 4-8 (1) #10 steel ball
(2) Clutch lever

10. Making sure that wires and leads are not binding, install the fuel tank. Connect the fuel tube from the right carburetor to the rear side of the fuel valve and the fuel tube from the left carburetor to the front side of the fuel valve and secure with the clips.

Fig. 4-9 (1) Fuel valve
(2) Tube from right carburetor
(3) Tube from left carburetor

11. Route the battery overflow tube as shown on the label, taking care not to bend it.

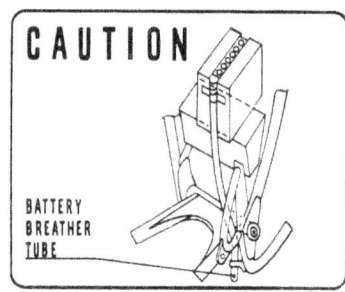

Fig. 4-10 (1) Label

12. When the engine has been reassembled after overhauling, fill with oil and start the engine. Remove the tappet hole caps and check if the oil comes up in about 10 seconds.

Fig. 4-11 Check oil circulation

IV. ENGINE

3. CYLINDER HEAD, CAMSHAFT, CYLINDER AND PISTONS

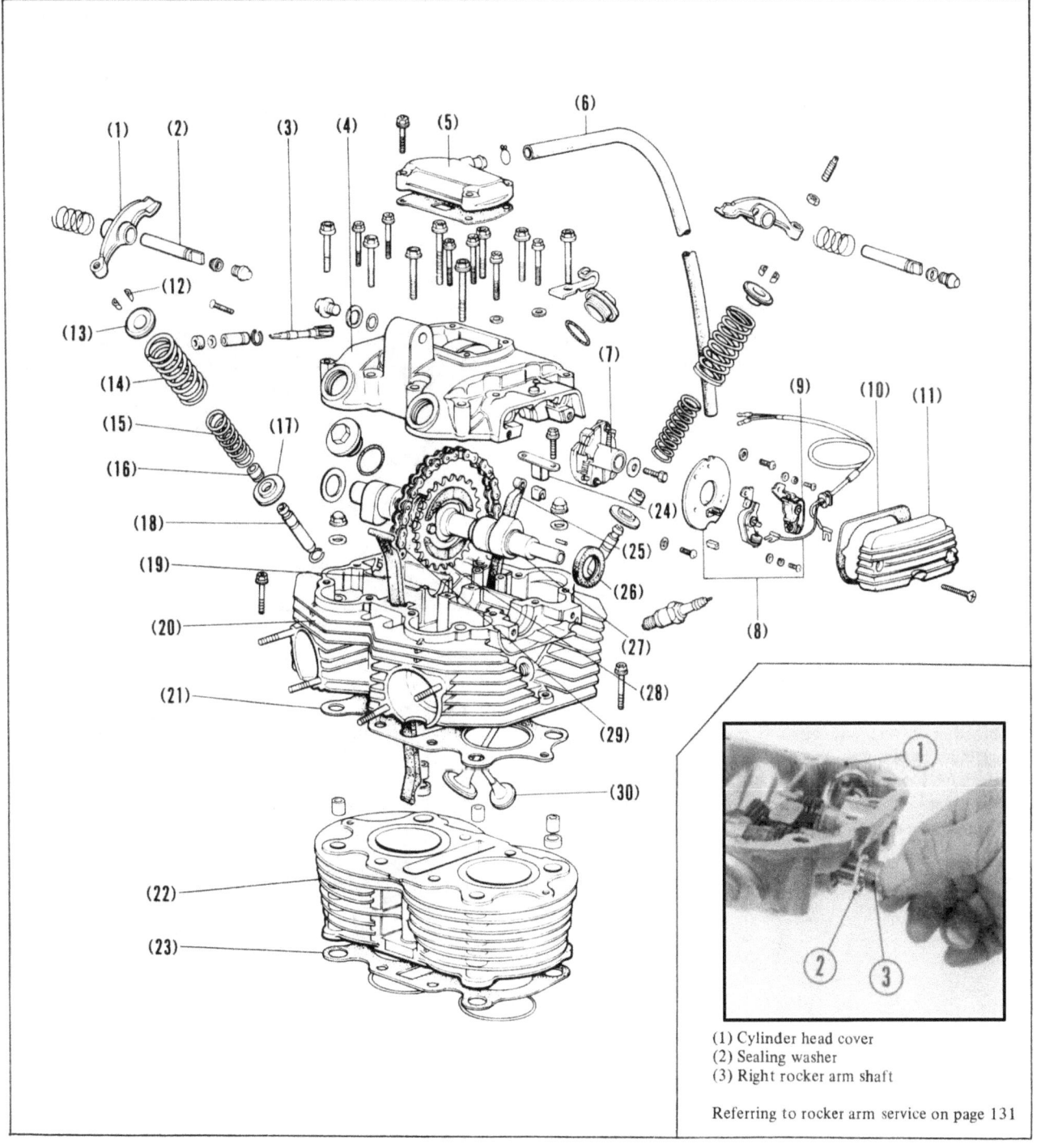

(1) Cylinder head cover
(2) Sealing washer
(3) Right rocker arm shaft

Referring to rocker arm service on page 131

Fig. 4-12
(1) Rocker arm
(2) Rocker arm shaft (L)
(3) Tachometer gear
(4) Cylinder head cover
(5) Breather cover
(6) Breather tube
(7) Spark advancer
(8) Contact breaker assembly
(9) Contact breaker
(10) Point cover gasket
(11) Point cover
(12) Valve cotters
(13) Valve spring retainer
(14) Valve outer spring
(15) Valve inner spring
(16) Valve stem seal
(17) Valve spring seat
(18) Valve guide
(19) Cam chain guide
(20) Cylinder head
(21) Cylinder head gasket
(22) Cylinder
(23) Cylinder gasket
(24) Cam chain tensioner holder
(25) Tensioner slipper
(26) 22 x 35 x 6 oil seal
(27) Camshaft
(28) Cam sprocket
(29) Cam chain
(30) Valve

Disassembly

* Completely remove mud, dust or dirt from around the engine before disassembling.
* Take care not to allow dust and dirt to get inside or to come in contact with the cylinder, crankcase, carburetor and air cleaner.
1. Open the seat and remove the fuel tank.
2. Remove the nuts (1) and remove the engine upper hanger.
3. Remove the bolts (2) and remove the breather cover.
4. Remove the point cover and remove the contact breaker.
5. Remove the spark advancer.

Fig. 4-13 (1) Nuts (2) Bolts (3) Point cover

6. Remove the spark plug caps and remove the spark plugs.
7. Disconnect the tachometer cable and remove the tappet hole caps.
* Leave the tappet adjusting screws loosened.

Fig. 4-14 (1) Spark plug cap
(2) Tappet hole cap
(3) Tachometer cable

8. Remove the six 6 mm bolts (two bolts are inside the breather cover) and eight 8 mm bolts and remove the cylinder head cover.
* Remove the cylinder head cover toward left while inclining it forward.
* Completely remove used sealing agent from the cover.

Fig. 4-15 (1) Cylinder head cover

9. To remove each right rocker arm shaft, first remove the sealing bolt. Then turn the 6 mm screw or bolt in and pull it to remove the shaft.
To remove each left rocker arm shaft, remove the rubber plug and remove the shaft by pulling it with pliers
10. Remove the snap ring and remove the tachometer gear.

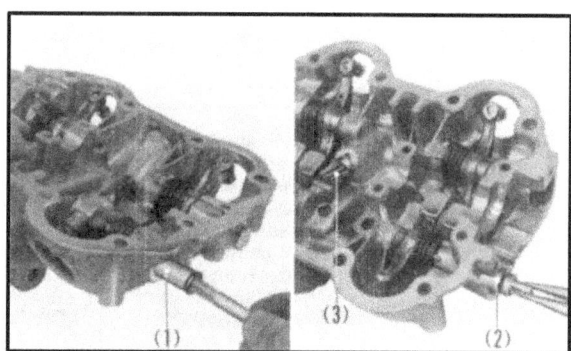

Fig. 4-16 (1) Right rocker arm shaft
(2) Left rocker arm shaft
(3) Tachometer gear

IV. ENGINE

11. Remove the cam chain.
    Remove the generator cover and turn the rotor to allow one fixing bolt to be removed. Then turn the rotor ½ turn more and remove the other fixing bolt.
12. Remove the cam chain tensioner holder.
13. Remove the cam chain guide and tensioner slipper.

Fig. 4-17 (1) Fixing bolt
(2) Cam sprocket
(3) Cam chain tensioner holder
(4) Tensioner slipper

14. Remove the cam sprocket from the camshaft, remove the cam chain and pull out the camshaft.
    NOTES:
    1. Until the cylinder head is removed, hold the cam chain with a screwdriver to prevent it from dropping into the crankcase.
    2. Take care not to drop the thrust washers into the engine room.
15. Remove the right and left mufflers.
16. Remove the carburetor. (See page 32.)

Fig. 4-18 (1) Cam chain
(2) Camshaft
(3) Cam sprocket

17. Remove the eight 8 mm nuts and two 6 mm bolts and remove the cylinder head.
    CAUTION:
    Do not score or scratch the cylinder attaching surface of the cylinder head.

Fig. 4-19 (1) Cylinder head

18. Remove the cylinder.
    * Attempt to position both the pistons on the same level and to prevent damage of the pistons.

Fig. 4-20 (1) Cylinder

19. Remove the piston pin clips and piston pin and remove each piston.

    NOTE:
    When removing the piston pin clips, place a rag over the crankcase to prevent the clips from dropping into the crankcase.

20. Remove the piston rings taking care not to damage the piston.

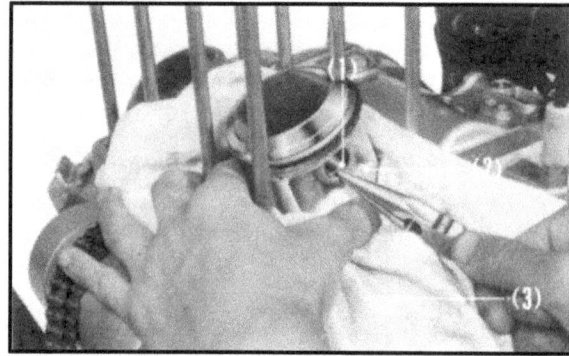

Fig. 4-21 (1) Piston pin clip
(2) Piston
(3) Rag

21. Remove the valves.
    Compress the valve springs using the valve spring compressor (Tool No. 07957-3290000) and remove the valve cotters, springs and valve in this order.
    CAUTION:
    Compress the valve springs with care attention paid not to damage the valve stem seal.

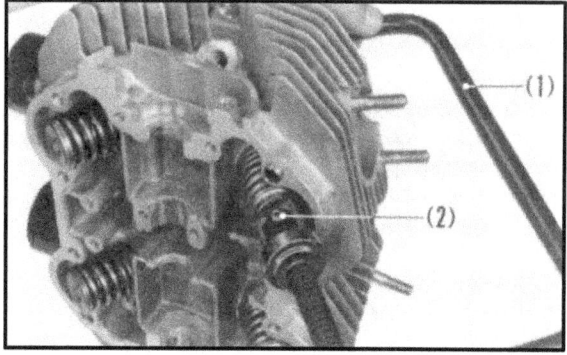

Fig. 4-22 (1) Valve spring compressor
(2) Valve cotters

22. Remove the stem seal and pull out the valve guide using the valve guide driver (Tool No. 07942-6110000)
    CAUTION:
    Do not remove the valve guide except when replacing it, as a rule.

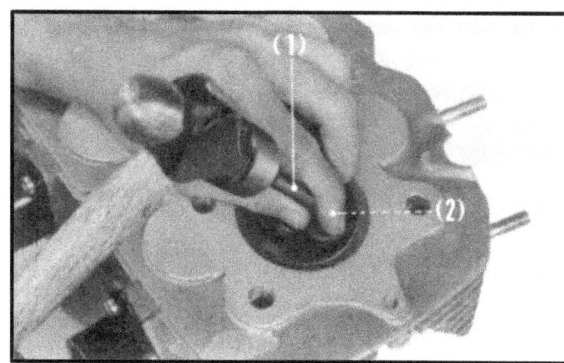

Fig. 4-23 (1) Valve guide remover
(2) Valve guide

Inspection

Refer to service data on page 112.
1. Check the rocker arm-to-shaft clearance.
2. Check the camshaft journals for wear or damage.
3. Check the cam height for wear.

Fig. 4-24 Checking the surface of the camshaft journal

IV. ENGINE

4. Check the valve seat contact width and if necessary recondition.
   Apply a thin coat of red lead to the valve seat surface. Press the valve against the seat and rotate it to check if the contact width is uniform. If not, lap the valve, seat and again check the contact width. If necessary, recondition the valve seat using a valve seat grinder.
   CAUTION:
   Use the valve seat grinder in accordance with the instruction manual.

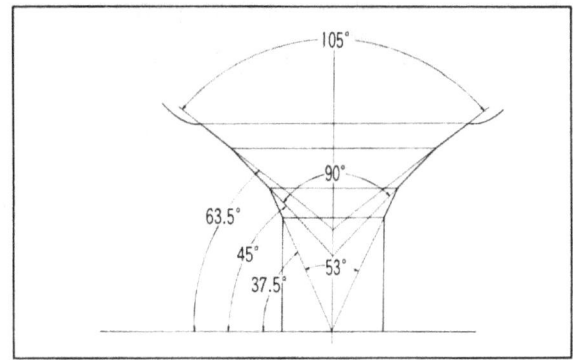

Fig. 4-25

5. Measure the valve-to-guide clearance.
6. Measure the valve spring free length. Also check the installed load.
7. Check the matching surface of the cylinder head for roughness.
8. Measure the cylinder bore.
   Using a cylinder gauge, measure the cylinder bore in the directions X and Y at the upper, middle and lower points.
   If wear is too great so that the service limits are exceeded, the cylinder should be rebored, and oversize piston and piston rings installed. The following four oversize piston and piston rings are available as service parts:

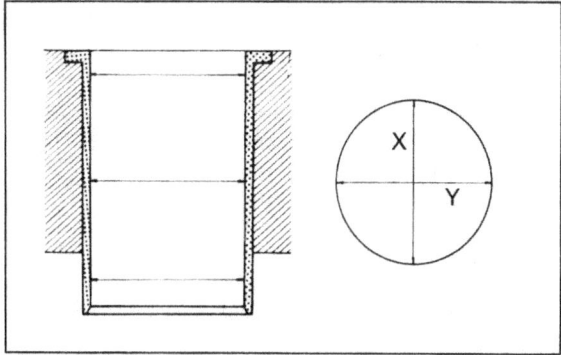

Fig. 4-26 Measure the cylinder bore

Unit: mm (in.)

Oversize piston and ring	Size to which cylinder is to be rebored	
	250 cc	360 cc
0.25	56.26-56.27 (2.2149-2.2153)	67.26-67.27 (2.6480-2.6484)
0.50	56.51-56.52 (2.2248-2.2252)	67.51-67.52 (2.6579-2.6583)
0.75	56.76-56.77 (2.235-2.295)	67.76-67.77 (2.6677-2.6681)
1.00	57.01-57.02 (2.2445-2.2449)	68.01-68.02 (2.6776-2.6780)

9. Measure the piston skirt OD (outside diameter).
10. Measure the piston pin hole diameter.
11. Measure the piston pin OD.
12. Check the side clearance of the piston ring in the groove.
13. Check the piston ring gap.
    Install the ring squarely in the skirt of the cylinder to check the ring gap.

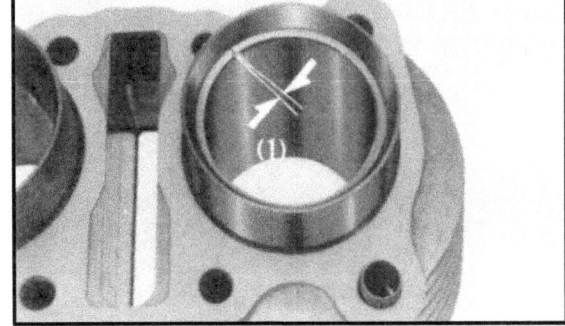

Fig. 4-27 (1) Piston ring gap

Assembly

To assemble, reverse the disassembly procedures paying attention to the following:
1. When the valve guide must be replaced, install it using the valve guide driver (Tool No. 07942-6110000) and finish the inside surface using the valve guide reamer (Tool No. 07984-5900000).

Fig. 4-28 (1) Valve guide remover
(2) Valve guide

2. Assemble the valve so that the smaller pitch side of the valve springs is toward the cylinder head, using the valve spring compressor (Tool No. 07957-3290000).

CAUTION:
Compress the springs with careful attention paid not to break the valve stem seal.

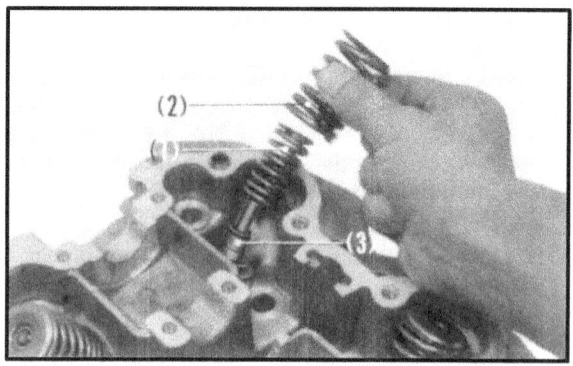

Fig. 4-29 (1) Inner valve spring
(2) Outer valve spring
(3) Valve stem seal

3. Use the piston rings of the same brand in a set. Face the markings on the rings upward when installing them in the grooves in the piston.

CAUTION:
Do not install the top and second rings conversely.

* When using new piston rings, install them in the grooves in the piston and check for proper fit.
4. Each ring gap must be staggered 120° and must not be at right angles to the piston pin.
5. Install the piston with the arrow, if marked, on the head facing front (exhaust side).
* Apply a coat of oil to the piston rings first.

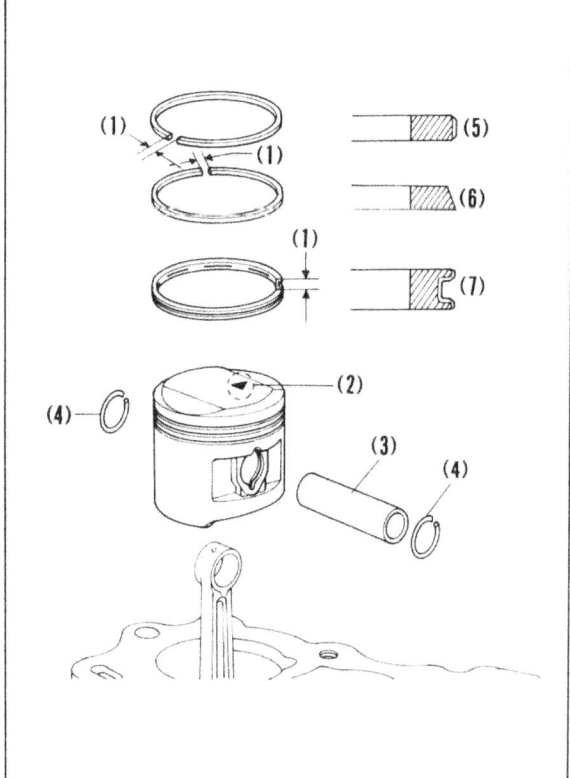

Fig. 4-30 (1) Piston ring gaps (5) Top ring
(2) Mark (6) Second ring
(3) Piston pin (7) Oil ring
(4) Piston pin clips

6. While holding the piston rings with the piston ring compressor (Tool No. 07954-3670000 for 250 model, Tool No. 07954-3690000 for 360 model), carefully install the cylinder.
7. Upon noting that pistons are properly positioned in the cylinder, route the cam chain into the cylinder and install the cylinder securely.

Fig. 4-31 (1) Cylinder
(2) Piston
(3) Piston ring compressor

IV. ENGINE

8. Tighten the cylinder head in the numerical order shown at right.

   Specified tightening torque:
   10 mm bolt: **3.0–3.4 kg·m (21.7–24.6 lbs-ft)**
   6 mm bolt: **0.7–1.1 kg·m (5.1– 8.0 lbs-ft)**

   NOTE:
   1. Apply a coat of oil to the threads.
   2. Take care not to score or scratch the cylinder attaching surface of the head with the cylinder studs.

9. Install the cam chain guide and tensioner slipper securely.

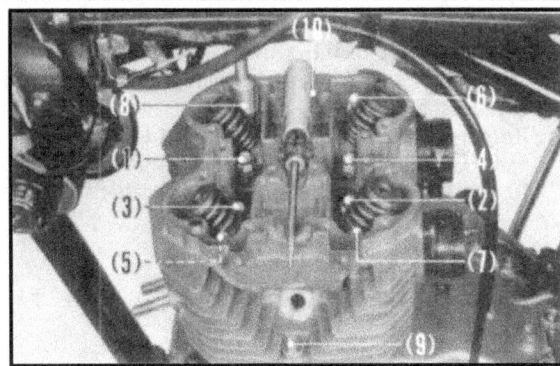

Fig. 4–32

10. Before installing the camshaft, set it to the cylinder head and check the side clearance. If necessary adjust the clearance so that it becomes **0.07 to 0.3 mm (0.003 to 0.012 in.)**, by using the thrust washer below.

    NOTE:
    Insert the washers into the clearance (3) shown in Fig. 4–33. Do not insert them into the clearance on the left side.

Description	Parts No.	Thickness
Thrust washer A	90483-369-000	1.0 mm
Thrust washer B	90484-369-000	1.1 mm

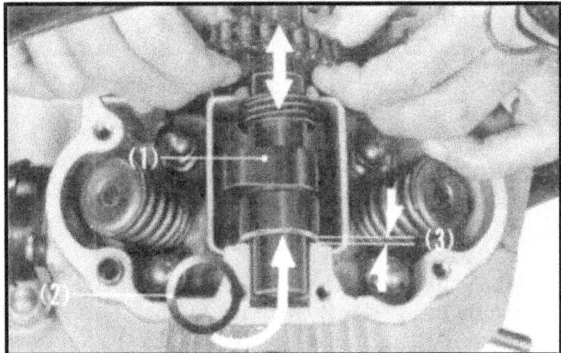

Fig. 4–33 (1) Camshaft
(2) Thrust washer
(3) Camshaft side clearance

11. Install the cam chain and cam sprocket and install the camshaft.

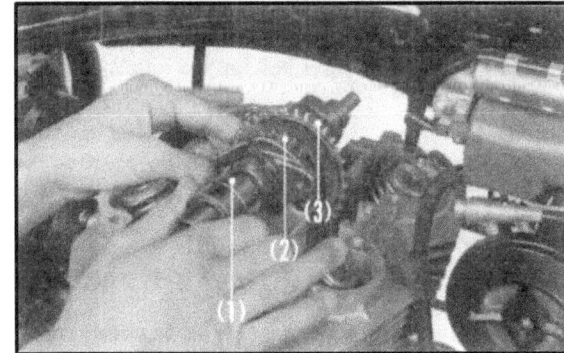

Fig. 4–34 (1) Camshaft
(2) Cam chain
(3) Cam sprocket

12. Rotate the generator rotor in the direction of arrow to align the "LT" mark with the index mark on the stator.

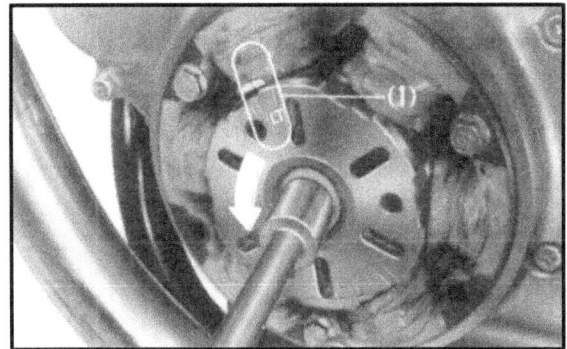

Fig. 4–35 "LT" mark and index mark on stator

13. Under the condition mentioned above, pull the cam chain to align the top of the cylinder head with the matching lines on the cam sprocket. At this time, set the cam sprocket to the camshaft.
14. Rotate the camshaft until the thread holes in the camshaft and cam sprocket are aligned and tighten one fixing bolt. Rotate the crankshaft and tighten the other fixing bolt.

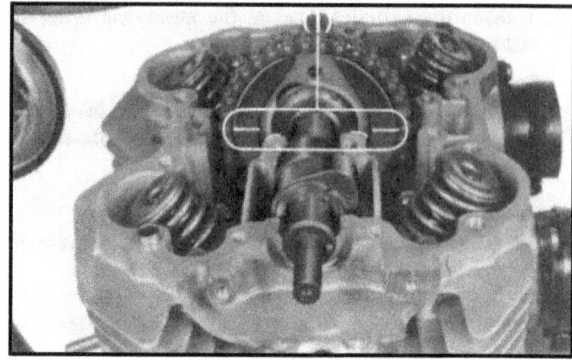

Fig. 4-36 (1) Matching lines on cam sprocket

15. Install the cam chain tensioner holder.
    NOTE:
    Attach the cam chain tensioner holder damper with the narrow side toward the cam sprocket.
16. Fill the cylinder head oil baths with oil. Also apply a coat of oil to the camshaft journals.
17. Apply a coat of oil to the tachometer gear, rocker arm shafts and rocker arms.
18. When installing the cylinder head cover, position the camshaft by slowly rotating so that all cam lobes are towards the bottom to avoid the rocker arms from contacting the cover.

Fig. 4-37 (1) Cam chain tensioner holder
(2) Damper
(3) Oilbath
(4) Camshaft journal

19. Apply a coat of sealing agent to the cylinder head cover. While rotating the camshaft, install the head cover. Slowly tighten the head cover bolts in the numerical order shown at right.
    NOTES:
    1. Take care not to drip excess sealing agent on the other parts.
    2. Use the following bolts:
       (1)–(6): 6 x 45 mm, (3) and (5) need a washer.
       (7), (8), (10), (11), (12): 8 x 45 mm, (12) needs a cable clamper.
       (13)–(14): 8 x 60 mm, (13) needs a cable clamper.

Fig. 4-38 Cylinder head cover tightening sequence

20. Install the spark advancer and contact breaker by fitting the holes onto the camshaft dowel pin.
21. Adjust the cam chain tension.
22. Adjust the tappet clearance.
23. Adjust the ignition timing and point gap.

Fig. 4-39 (1) Dowel pin
(2) Spark advancer

4. A.C. GENERATOR AND STARTING MOTOR

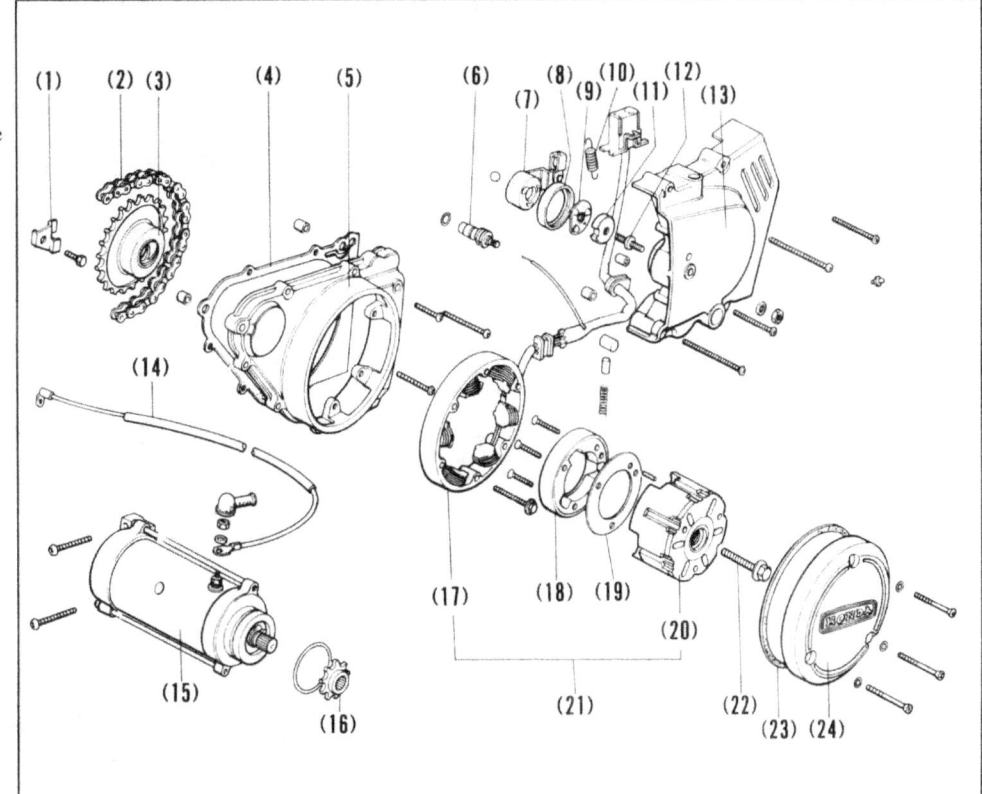

Fig. 4-40
(1) Starting sprocket setting plate
(2) Starting chain
(3) Starting sprocket
(4) Left crankcase cover gasket
(5) Left crankcase cover
(6) Neutral switch
(7) Clutch lever
(8) Dust seal
(9) Clutch ball retainer
(10) Clutch lever spring
(11) Clutch adjusting cam
(12) Clutch lifter adjusting screw
(13) Left crankcase rear cover
(14) Starting motor cable
(15) Starting motor assy.
(16) Starting sprocket
(17) Stator
(18) Starting clutch outer
(19) Starting clutch side plate
(20) A.C. generator rotor
(21) A.C. generator assy.
(22) Rotor setting bolt
(23) Generator cover gasket
(24) Generator cover

Disassembly

1. Remove the gear change pedal.
2. Remove the left crankcase rear cover.

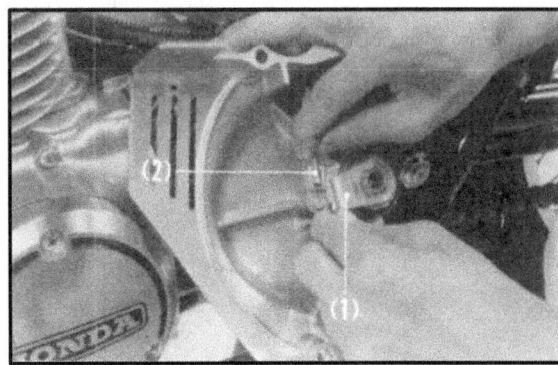

Fig. 4-41 (1) Clutch lever (2) Clutch cable end

3. Remove the A.C. generator connector and disconnect the lead from the neutral switch.
   * It is advisable to remove the carburetor before removing the connector.
4. Remove the left crankcase cover.
5. Remove the three bolts (5) and remove the A.C. generator stator from the left crankcase cover.

Fig. 4-42 (1) Left crankcase cover (3) Neutral switch lead
(2) Stator (4) Generator cable

6. Remove the A.C. generator rotor by removing the rotor setting bolt and screwing in the rotor puller (Tool No. 07933-2160000).

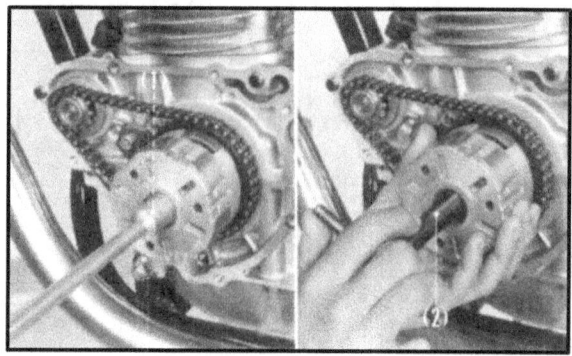

Fig. 4-43 (1) Rotor setting bolt
(2) Rotor puller

7. Remove the starting sprocket setting plate and remove the starting sprocket, starting motor sprocket and starting chain together.

Fig. 4-44 (1) Starting motor sprocket
(2) Starting chain
(3) Starting sprocket

8. Disconnect the starting motor cable from the starting motor. Remove the tightening screws and give a tap to the starting motor to remove it from the crankcase.

Fig. 4-45 (1) Starting motor

Inspection

1. Check the roller, roller cap and clutch outer of the starting clutch (over-running clutch) for damage or abnormal wear.
2. Check the roller and spring for proper movement.
3. For the starting motor, refer to the chapter "ELECTRICAL SYSTEM" on page 103.

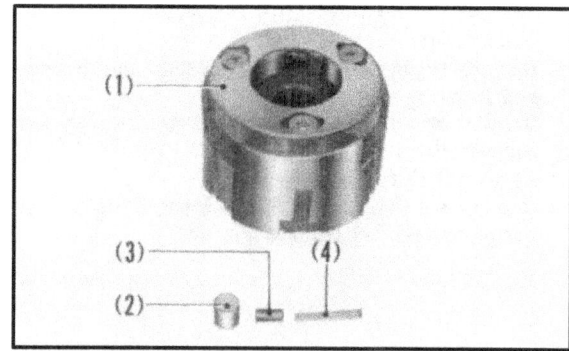

Fig. 4-46 (1) Starting clutch outer (3) Roller cap
(2) Roller (4) Spring

IV. ENGINE

Assembly

To assemble, reverse the disassembly procedures paying attention to the following:
1. Apply a thin coat of oil to the starting motor O-ring and install the motor to the crankcase.
2. Connect the cable to the starting motor.

Fig. 4-47 (1) O-ring
(2) Starting motor

3. Install the A.C. generator rotor.
   Make sure that the starting clutch roller and spring move properly and that the crankshaft woodruff key is not missing. Fit the woodruff key into the keyway in the rotor and push the rotor into position while rotating it.
* With the rotor held, tighten it to the specified torque.
   Specified tightening torque:
     3.0–3.5 kg-m (21.7–25.3 lbs-ft)

Fig. 4-48 (1) A.C. generator rotor

5. RIGHT CRANKCASE COVER AND CLUTCH

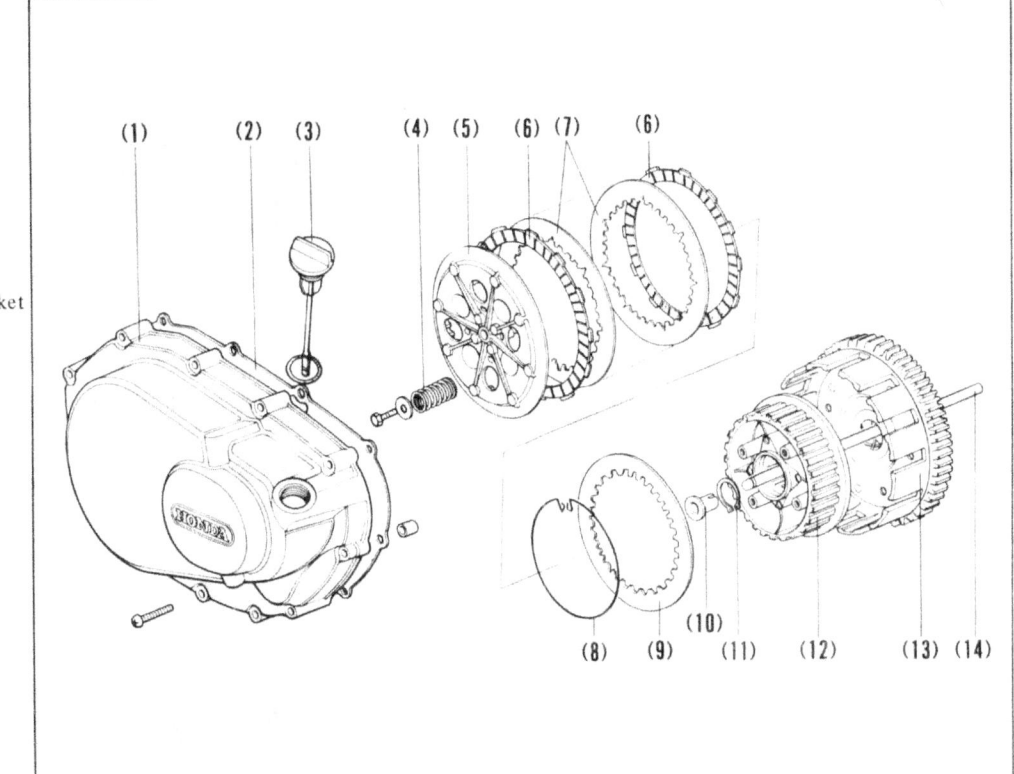

Fig. 4-49

(1) Right crankcase cover
(2) Right crankcase cover gasket
(3) Oil level gauge
(4) Clutch spring
(5) Clutch pressure plate
(6) Clutch friction disc
(7) Clutch plate B
(8) Stopper ring
(9) Clutch plate A
(10) Clutch lifter joint piece
(11) 25 mm snap ring
(12) Clutch center
(13) Clutch outer
(14) Clutch lifter rod

IV. ENGINE

Disassembly

1. Drain the engine.
2. Remove the right exhaust muffler. (On CB type only)
3. Remove the right foot peg.
4. Remove the kick starter pedal.
5. Remove the 6 mm screws and remove the right crankcase cover.
   Place an oil pan in position to collect oil.

Fig. 4-50 (1) Right foot peg
(2) Kick starter pedal
(3) Right crankcase cover

6. Remove the bolts (2) and remove the clutch springs and clutch pressure plate. Then the clutch friction discs and clutch plates B can be removed.

Fig. 4-51 (1) Clutch pressure plate

7. Remove the clutch lifter joint piece and 25 mm external snap ring. Then the clutch center can be removed.

Fig. 4-52 (1) 25 mm external snap ring
(2) Clutch center

8. Remove the clutch outer after removing the oil filter rotor. (See page 50)

Fig. 4-53 (1) Clutch outer

IV. ENGINE

9. Remove the stop ring and clutch plate A from the clutch center.

Inspection

Refer to service data on page 112.
1. Measure the friction disc thickness.
2. Check the clutch plates for face runout.
3. Measure the clutch spring free length. Also check the spring installed load.

Fig. 4-54 (1) Clutch plate A
(2) Clutch center
(3) Stop ring

Assembly

To assemble, reverse the disassembly procedures paying attention to the following:
1. Install the clutch plate A to the clutch center and secure with the stop ring.
* Face the chamfered side of the clutch plate outside.

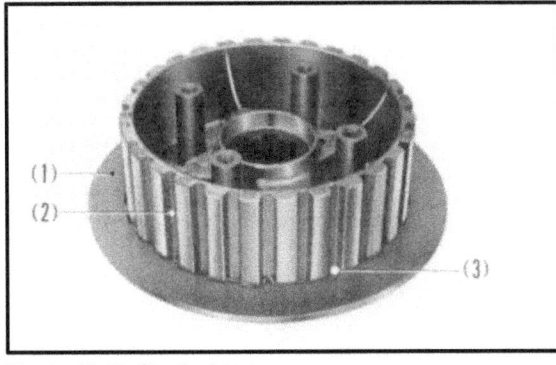

Fig. 4-55 (1) Clutch plate A
(2) Clutch center
(3) Stop ring

2. Install the clutch center to the clutch outer and install the eight friction discs and seven plates B alternatively.
3. Install the clutch assembly to the main shaft and secure with the 25 mm external snap ring.

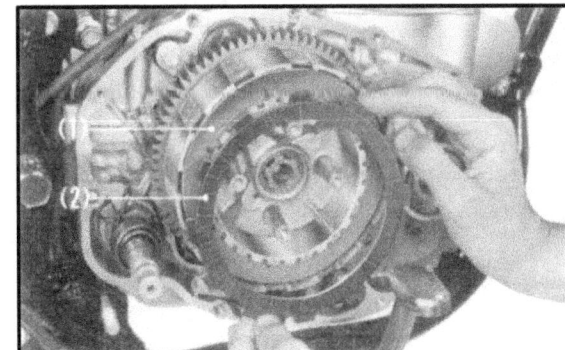

Fig. 4-56 (1) Clutch plate B
(2) Friction disc

4. Make sure that the clutch lifter joint piece is not missing. Install the clutch pressure plate and clutch springs and tighten with the 6 mm bolts.
5. To install the oil filter rotor, see page 51.
6. Adjust the clutch. (See page 22.)

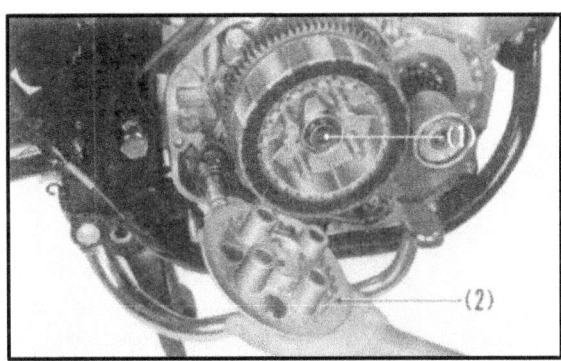

Fig. 4-57 (1) Clutch lifter joint piece
(2) Clutch pressure plate

6. OIL PUMP AND OIL FILTER ROTOR

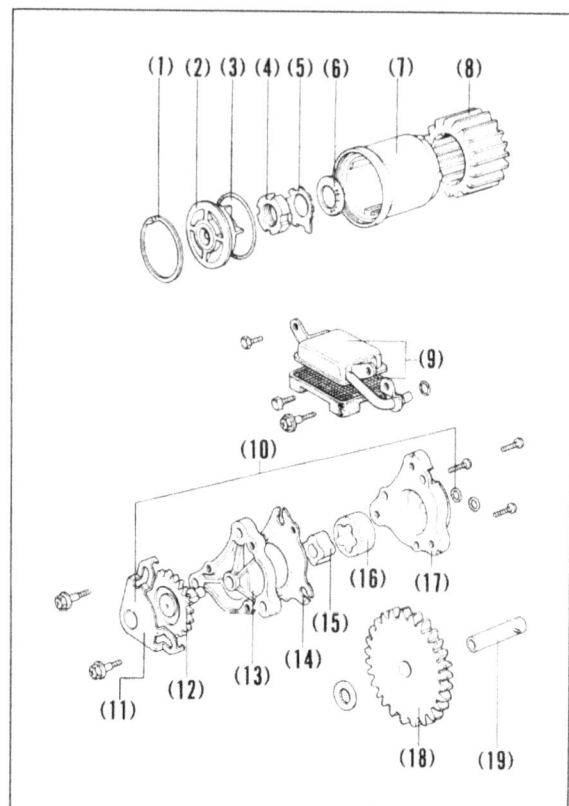

Fig. 4-58
(1) 45 mm internal snap ring
(2) Oil filter cap
(3) 41 x 2 O-ring
(4) 16 mm lock nut
(5) 16 mm lock washer
(6) Oil filter lock washer
(7) Oil filter rotor
(8) Primary drive gear
(9) Oil filter screen
(10) Oil pump assy.
(11) Oil pump setting plate
(12) Oil pump drive gear
(13) Oil pump side cover
(14) Oil pump cover gasket
(15) Oil pump inner rotor
(16) Oil pump outer rotor
(17) Oil pump body
(18) Oil pump idle gear
(19) Oil pump idle shaft

Disassembly

1. Remove the right crankcase cover.
2. Remove the oil pump idle gear by lifting the idle shaft.

Fig. 4-59 (1) Oil pump idle shaft
(2) Oil pump idle gear

3. Remove the bolts (2) and (3) and remove the oil filter screen.

Fig. 4-60 (1) Oil filter screen
(2) Bolt
(3) Bolt

IV. ENGINE

4. Remove the bolts (2) and remove the oil pump assembly.

Fig. 4-61 (1) Oil pump assembly
(2) Bolt

5. Remove the screws (2) and disassemble the oil pump assembly.
   CAUTION:
   Do not disassemble the oil pump assembly unless necessary.

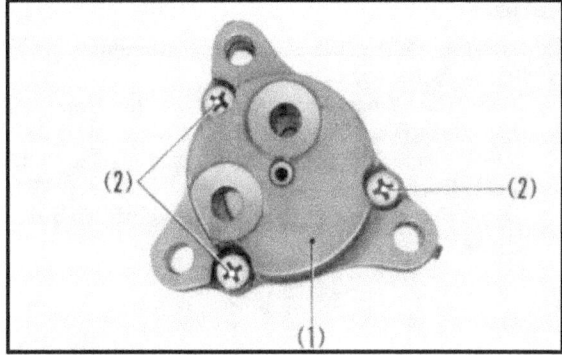

Fig. 4-62 (1) Oil pump body

6. Remove the 45 mm snap ring and remove the oil filter cap. To remove the filter cap, screw a 6 mm screw or bolt in as shown at right and pull it.

Fig. 4-63 (1) 45 mm snap ring
(2) Oil filter cap

7. Straighten the locking lugs of the 16 mm lock washer and remove the 16 mm lock nut using the 16 mm lock nut wrench (Tool No. 07916-2830000). Then the oil filter rotor and primary drive gear can be removed.

Fig. 4-64 (1) 16 mm lock nut wrench

Inspection

Refer to service data on page 112.
1. Check the filter screen for contamination or breakage.
2. Check the inside surface of the oil filter rotor for contamination.
3. Measure the oil pump inner-to-outer rotor clearance and the side clearance.

Fig. 4–65 (1) Primary drive gear

Assembly

To assemble, reverse the disassembly procedures paying attention to the following:
1. Install the primary drive gear so that the larger chamfered side faces toward the crankshaft.
2. Install the lock washer with the side marked "OUTSIDE" facing front.
3. Install the lock nut so that the larger chamfered side toward the oil filter.

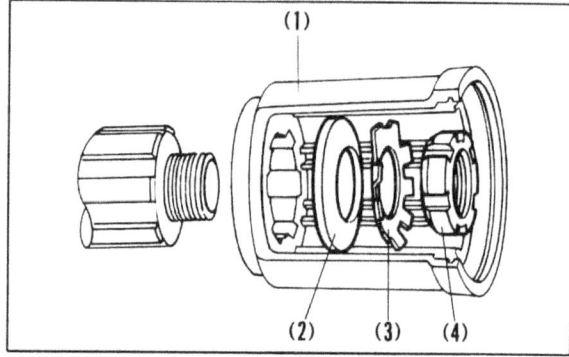

Fig. 4–66 (1) Oil filter rotor (3) 16 mm lock washer
(2) Lock washer (4) Lock nut

4. Tighten the lock nut using the lock nut wrench and bend the locking lugs of the lock washer securely.
   Specified tightening torque:
   4.5–5.5 kg·m (32.6–39.7 lbs-ft)
5. Install the O-ring when installing the oil filter cap. Secure the cap with the snap ring.

Fig. 4–67 (1) Lock nut (3) Oil filter cap
(2) 16 mm lock washer (4) O-ring

6. Install the two O-rings when installing the oil pump.

Fig. 4–68 (1) O-ring

IV. ENGINE

7. Install the filter screen to the oil filter screen and install the assembly to the crankcase.

   CAUTION:
   Do not forget to install the O-ring.

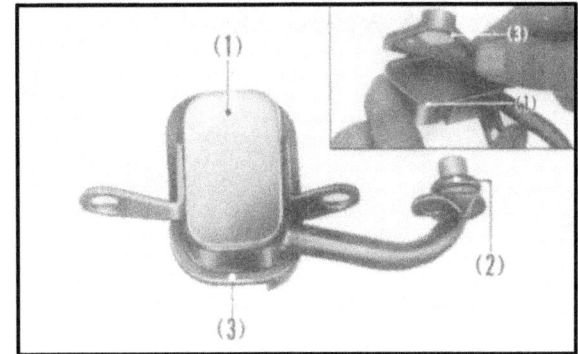

Fig. 4-69 (1) Oil filter screen
(2) O-ring
(3) Filter screen

7. KICK STARTER AND LOWER CRANKCASE

Fig. 4-70
(1) Oil separator setting bar
(2) Oil separator
(3) 18mm washer
(4) 18mm snap ring
(5) Kick starter spring
(6) Kick starter spindle
(7) Kick starter pinion
(8) 20mm thrust washer
(9) Setting spring
(10) Kick starter ratchet
(11) 15mm thrust washer
(12) Ratchet spring
(13) Ratchet guide plate
(14) Thrust washer
(15) 12mm snap ring
(16) Gear shift spindle
(17) Gear shift return spring
(18) Tensioner setting bolt
(19) Oil check bolt
(20) Tensioner outer spring
(21) Tensioner inner spring
(22) Tensioner push bar
(23) Lower crankcase
(24) 14 x 28 x 7 oil seal
(25) Drain bolt

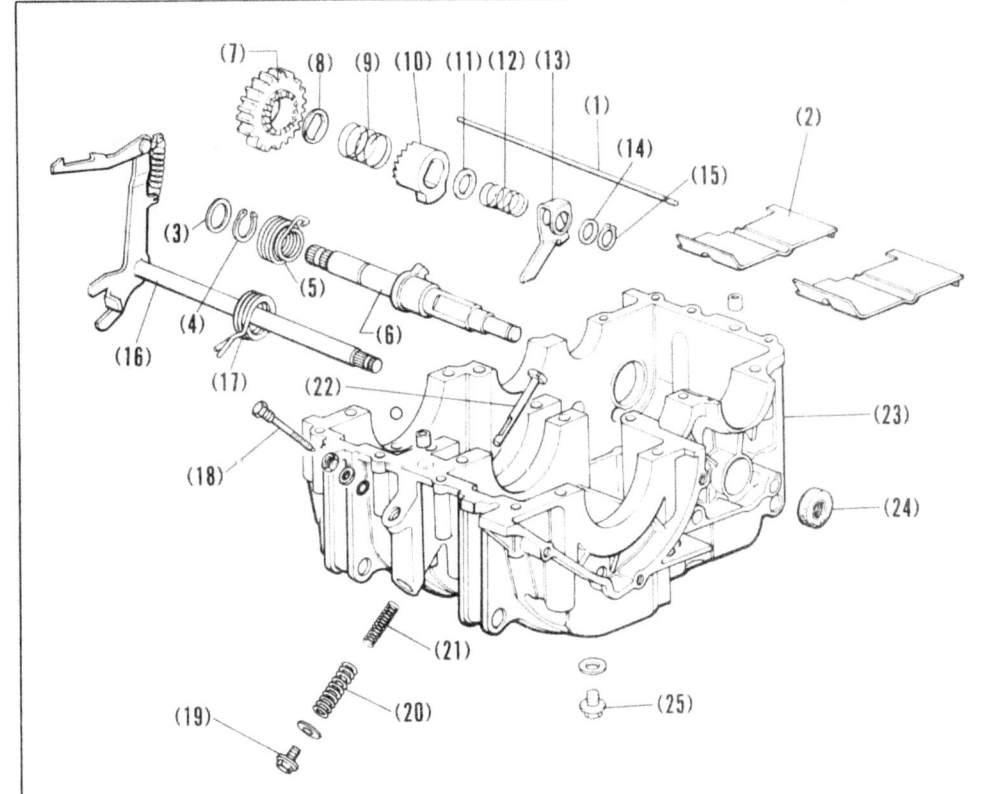

Disassembly

1. Remove the engine. (See pages 31–33)
2. Remove the left crankcase rear cover and left crankcase cover.
3. Remove the right crankcase cover.
4. Remove the upper crankcase tightening bolt.

Fig. 4-71 (1) Upper crankcase tightening bolt

IV. ENGINE

5. Remove the crankcase tightening bolts.

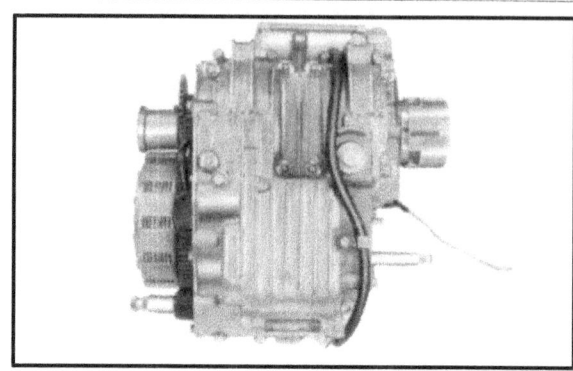

Fig. 4-72

6. Remove the lower crankcase by lifting it.
   The crankcase can be removed without any sign of binding by moving the change arm of the gearshift spindle as shown at right.
   Completely remove sealing agent from the crankcase.
7. Remove the gearshift spindle.

Fig. 4-73 (1) Lower crankcase
(2) Change arm

8. Remove the 18 mm washer and snap ring and remove the kick starter spring.
   Perform this job after removing the right crankcase.

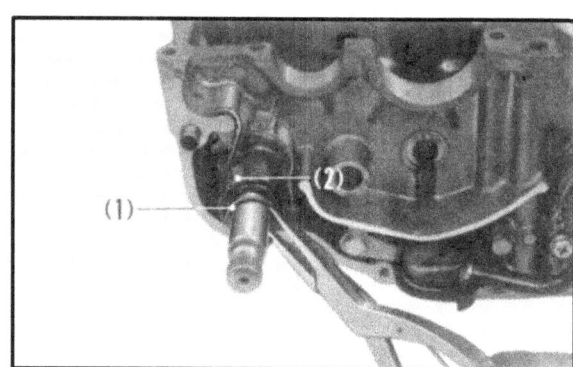

Fig. 4-74 (1) 18mm snap ring
(2) Kick starter spring

9. Remove the 12 mm external snap ring using the snap ring pliers and the ratchet guide plate, kick starter ratchet and kick starter pinion will be removed in this order. Remove the kick starter spindle from the lower crankcase.

Fig. 4-75 (1) Snap ring pliers
(2) 12mm external snap ring
(3) Ratchet guide plate
(4) Kick starter spindle

IV. ENGINE

10. Remove the oil separator setting bar and the oil separators.

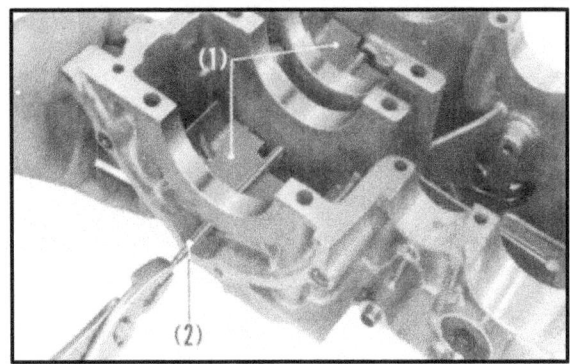

Fig. 4–76 (1) Oil separators
(2) Oil separator setting bar

11. Loosen the tensioner setting bolt and remove the cam chain tensioner push bar and springs.
12. Remove the oil filter and oil pump. (See page 50.)

Inspection

1. Check the mating surface of the crankcase for scores or scratches.
2. Check the kick starter spindle to kick starter pinion clearance.

Fig. 4–77 (1) Tensioner setting bolt
(2) Lock nut
(3) Oil check bolt

Assembly

To assemble, reverse the disassembly procedures paying attention to the following:

1. First tighten the cam chain tensioner setting bolt with the tensioner push bar pushed and the mark facing as shown in Fig. 4–78.
   After assembling the engine, adjust the cam chain. (See page 23)

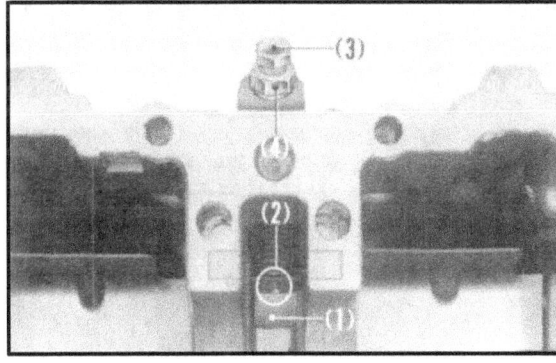

Fig. 4–78 (1) Cam chain tensioner push bar
(2) Mark
(3) Tensioner setting bolt
(4) Lock nut

2. Assemble the kick starter in the numerical order in the Fig. 4–79.

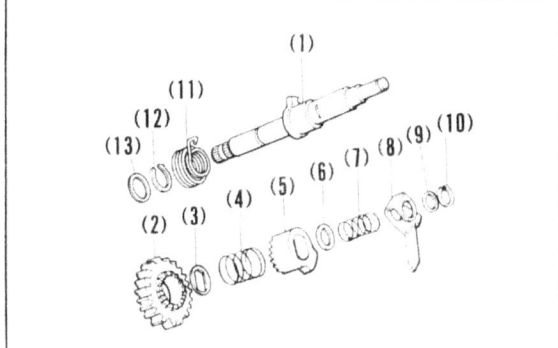

Fig. 4–79

3. Install the kick starter ratchet so that the kick starter spindle is positioned as shown in Fig. 4-80.

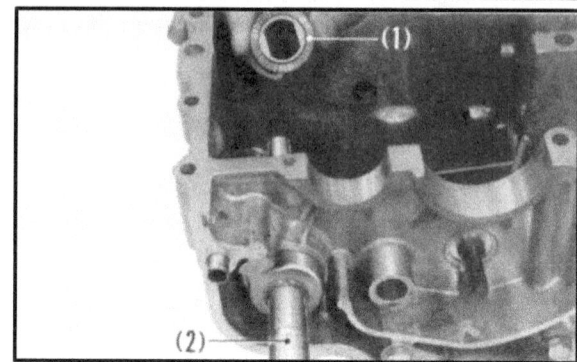

Fig. 4-80 (1) Kick starter ratchet
(2) Kick starter spindle

4. Check the kick starter for proper operation.

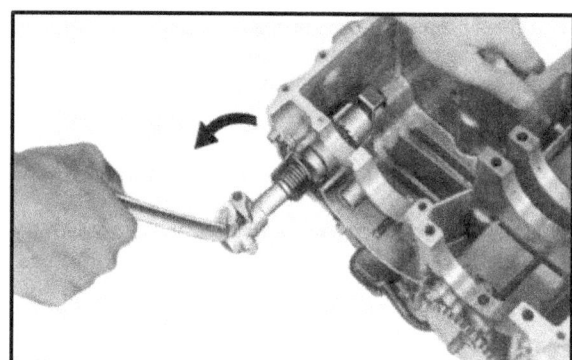

Fig. 4-81

5. Apply a coat of new sealing agent to the lower crankcase. Install the crankcase in such a manner that the gearshift arm comes to the shift drum stopper installation position.

   CAUTION:
   When applying new sealing agent, take care not to allow excess agent to drip on the crankshaft, mainshaft and countershaft bearings or inside the crankcase.

Fig. 4-82 (1) Gearshift arm

6. Install the two starting motor cable clampers as shown, using the bolts of the following length.
   (1) 8 x 150 UBS bolt   (2) 8 x 115 UBS bolt
   (3) 8 x 97 UBS bolt   (4) 6 x 55 bolt
   (5) 6 x 100 UBS bolt   (6) 8 x 50 UBS bolt
   (7) 6 x 35 bolt   (8) 6 x 145 bolt

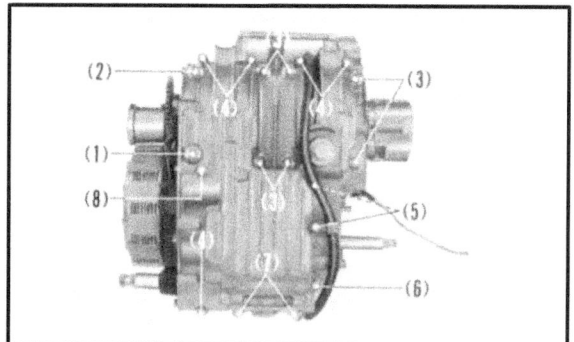

Fig. 4-83

IV. ENGINE

8. GEARSHIFT MECHANISM

Fig. 4-84

(1) Shift drum stopper
(2) Shift drum stopper spring
(3) Shift fork guide shaft
(4) Gear shift fork A
(5) Shift drum guide screw
(6) 12 mm lock washer
(7) Drum stopper cam plate
(8) Gearshift drum
(9) Gearshift fork B
(10) Gearshift spindle
(11) Gearshift return spring

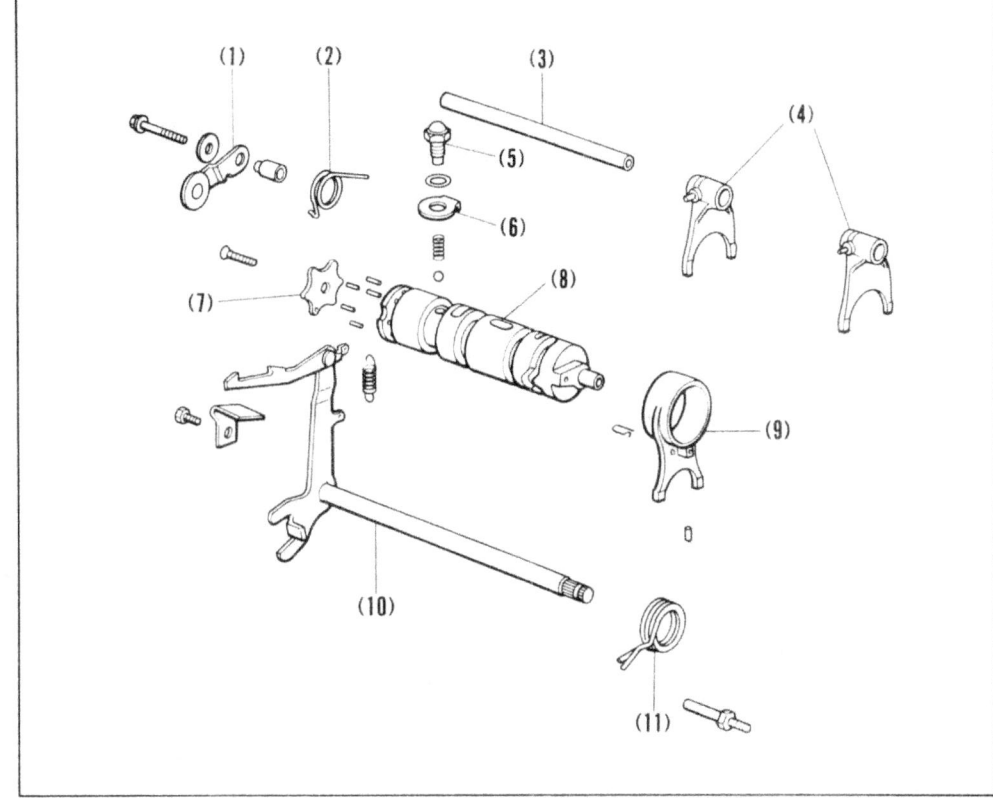

Disassembly

1. Remove the engine.
2. Straighten the locking lug of the 12 mm lock washer and remove the shift drum guide screw. Then remove the neutral stop spring and #10 steel ball.

Fig. 4-85 (1) 12 mm lock washer
(2) Shift drum guide screw

3. Remove the lower crankcase.
   Before performing this job, remove the oil filter rotor (page 50) and clutch assembly (page 47).
4. Remove the transmission mainshaft and countershaft.

Fig. 4-86 (1) Mainshaft
(2) Countershaft

IV. ENGINE

5. Remove the shift drum stopper and shift drum stopper spring and remove the shift fork guide shaft and two gearshift forks A.

Fig. 4–87 (1) Shift drum stopper
(2) Shift drum stopper spring
(3) Shift fork guide shaft
(4) Gearshift fork A

6. Remove the guide pin clip and pull out the guide pin. Then remove the gearshift drum from the upper crankcase and gearshift fork.

Inspection

Refer to service data on page 112.
1. Measure the gearshift fork finger thickness.
2. Measure the shift fork guide shaft OD (outside diameter).
3. Measure the gearshift fork ID (inside diameter).
4. Measure the gearshift drum OD.
5. Check the clearance between the lug of the gearshift fork and the groove in the gearshift drum.

Fig. 4–88 (1) Guide pin clip
(2) Guide pin

Assembly

To assemble, reverse the disassembly procedure paying attention to the following:
1. Set the drum to the gearshift fork B as shown in Fig. 4–89.

Fig. 4–89 (1) Gearshift drum
(2) Gearshift fork B

2. With the gearshift drum in the neutral position, install the #10 steel ball and neutral stopper spring. Tighten the guide screw and bend the locking lug of the lock washer.

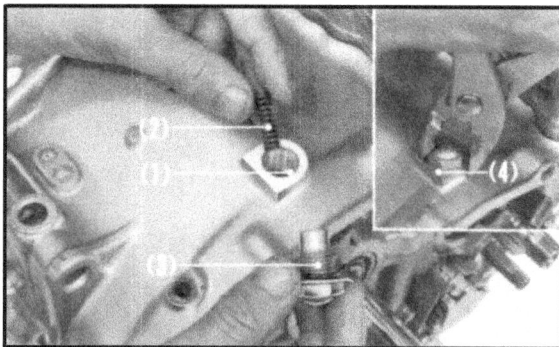

Fig. 4–90 (1) #10 steel ball
(2) Neutral stopper spring
(3) Shift drum guide screw
(4) 12 mm lock washer

3. With the gearshift drum in the neutral position, insert the guide pin into position and install the guide pin clip as shown in Fig. 4-91.
* The gearshift drum in the neutral position can be judged by the state of the points of the neutral switch.

Fig. 4-91 (1) Installation direction of guide pin clip
(2) Neutral position

4. Install the gearshift forks A (the same parts) as shown at right and install the shift fork guide shaft.

Fig. 4-92 (1) Gearshift fork A
(2) Gearshift fork guide shaft

5. Assemble the mainshaft and countershaft as shown in Fig. 4-93.
Replace any deformed snap ring with a new one.
Apply a coat of oil to the rotating and sliding surfaces.

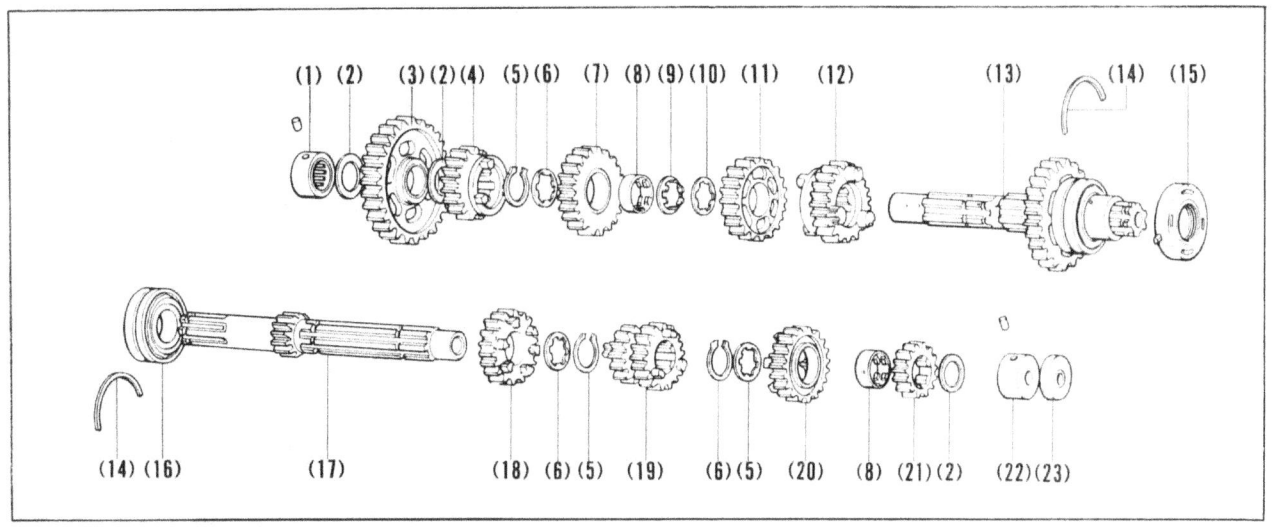

Fig. 4-93
(1) 20 mm needle bearing
(2) 20 mm thrust washer
(3) C-1st. gear
(4) C-5th. gear
(5) 25 mm snap ring
(6) 25 mm thrust washer
(7) C-3rd. gear
(8) 28 mm splined bushing
(9) 25 mm lock washer
(10) 25 mm thrust washer B
(11) C-4th gear
(12) C-6th gear
(13) Transmission countershaft
(14) 52 mm bearing set ring
(15) 34x52x13.5x15.5 oil seal
(16) 5205 HS ball bearing
(17) Transmission mainshaft
(18) M-5th. gear
(19) M-3rd. and 4th. gear
(20) M-6th. gear
(21) M-2nd. gear
(22) 20 mm needle bearing
(23) 8x34x8 oil seal

6. Install the mainshaft.
   Make sure that the bearing set ring and dowel pin are not missing. Securely fit the dowel pin into the hole in the 20 mm needle bearing while rotating.

Fig. 4-94 (1) Dowel pin
(2) Set ring

7. Install the countershaft.
   Similarly as in the mainshaft, make sure that the bearing set ring and dowel pin are not missing and install them into positions. Properly fit the lug of the oil seal into the hole in the upper crankcase.

Fig. 4-95 (1) Dowel pin
(2) Set ring
(3) Lug of oil seal

8. After installing the mainshaft and countershaft, check the gear backlash and the dogs of the gears for proper contact with the transmission in the neutral position.
   Apply a coat of oil to the transmission and crankshaft.
9. Apply a coat of new sealing agent to the lower crankcase and install the crankcase. (See page 56.)
   CAUTION:
   Do not allow excess agent to drip on other parts.

Fig. 4-96

10. Install the shift drum stopper.
    After installing, check the stopper for proper movement.

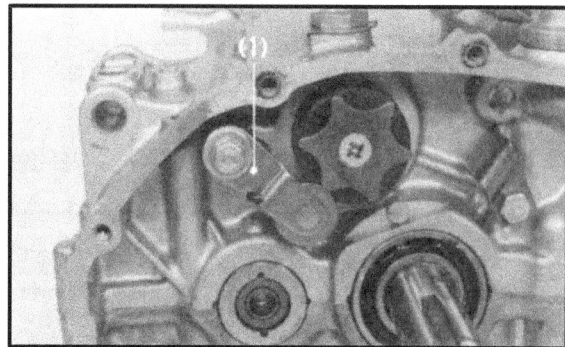

Fig. 4-97 (1) Shift drum stopper

IV. ENGINE

9. CRANKSHAFT AND UPPER CRANKCASE

Fig. 4-98
(1) Cylinder stud bolt B
(2) Cylinder stud bolt A
(3) 6 x 80 flange bolt
(4) Upper crankcase
(5) Cord protector
(6) Crankshaft assembly

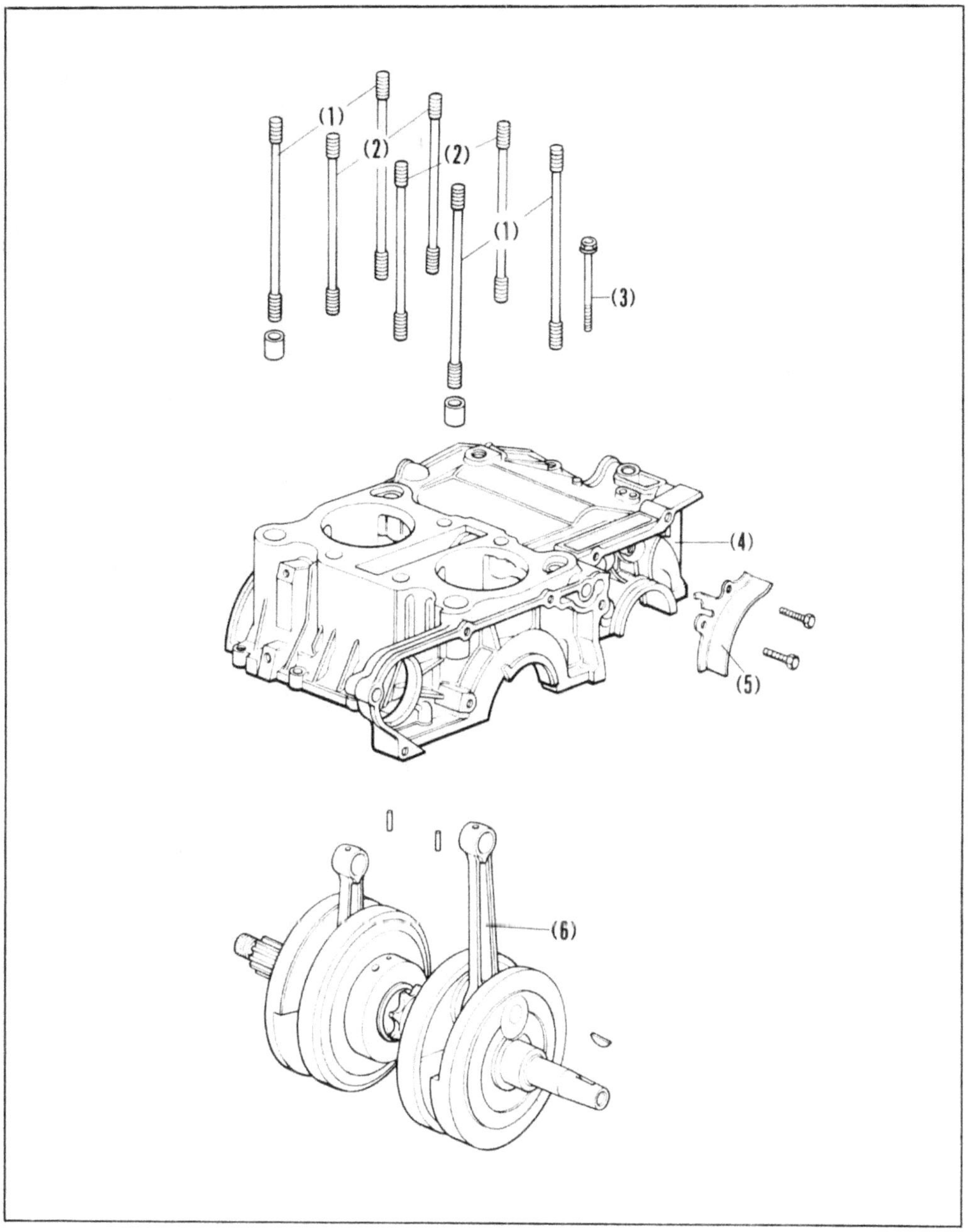

Disassembly

1. Remove the engine.
2. Remove the cylinder and pistons. (See page 37.)
3. Remove the left crankcase and remove the starting motor and related parts. (See page 45.)
4. Remove the right crankcase and remove the oil filter rotor and primary drive gear. (See page 50.)
5. Remove the lower crankcase. (See page 53.)
6. Remove the cam chain tensioner arm.

Fig. 4-99 (1) Cam chain tensioner arm

7. Remove the crankshaft and cam chain together.
8. Remove the transmission and gearshift forks.
   Remove the mainshaft with the clutch assembly.

Fig. 4–100 (1) Crankshaft
(2) Cam chain

Inspection

Refer to service data on page 113.

1. Check the crankshaft runout. Measurements should be taken at several points and by rotating the shaft in V blocks at E and F as shown.

	Standard value
C, D, G and H	0.1 mm (0.004 in.)
A and J	0.05 mm (0.002 in.)
Crankthrow (on machined face)	0.02 mm (0.008 in.)

2. Check the axial and radial clearances of the connecting rod big end.
3. Measure the piston pin hole diameter.
4. Check the crankshaft bearings for excessive looseness or abnormal wear.

Fig. 4–101

Assembly

To assemble, reverse the disassembly procedures paying attention to the following:

CAUTION:
Carefully handle the crankshaft.

1. Properly fit the dowels of the crankshaft bearings into the holes in the crankcase.
   First set the cam chain in position.
2. Apply a coat of oil to the rotating surfaces of the crankshaft.

Fig. 4–102 (1) Dowel pin

IV. ENGINE

10. CARBURETOR

Fig. 4-103
(1) Carburetor assy.
(2) Link set
(3) Jet needle set
(4) Vacuum piston set
(5) Screw set A
(6) Slow jet
(7) Needle jet holder
(8) Main jet
(9) Float valve set
(10) Main nozzle
(11) Primary main jet
(12) Connector joint set
(13) Float set
(14) Float chamber set
(15) Screw set B

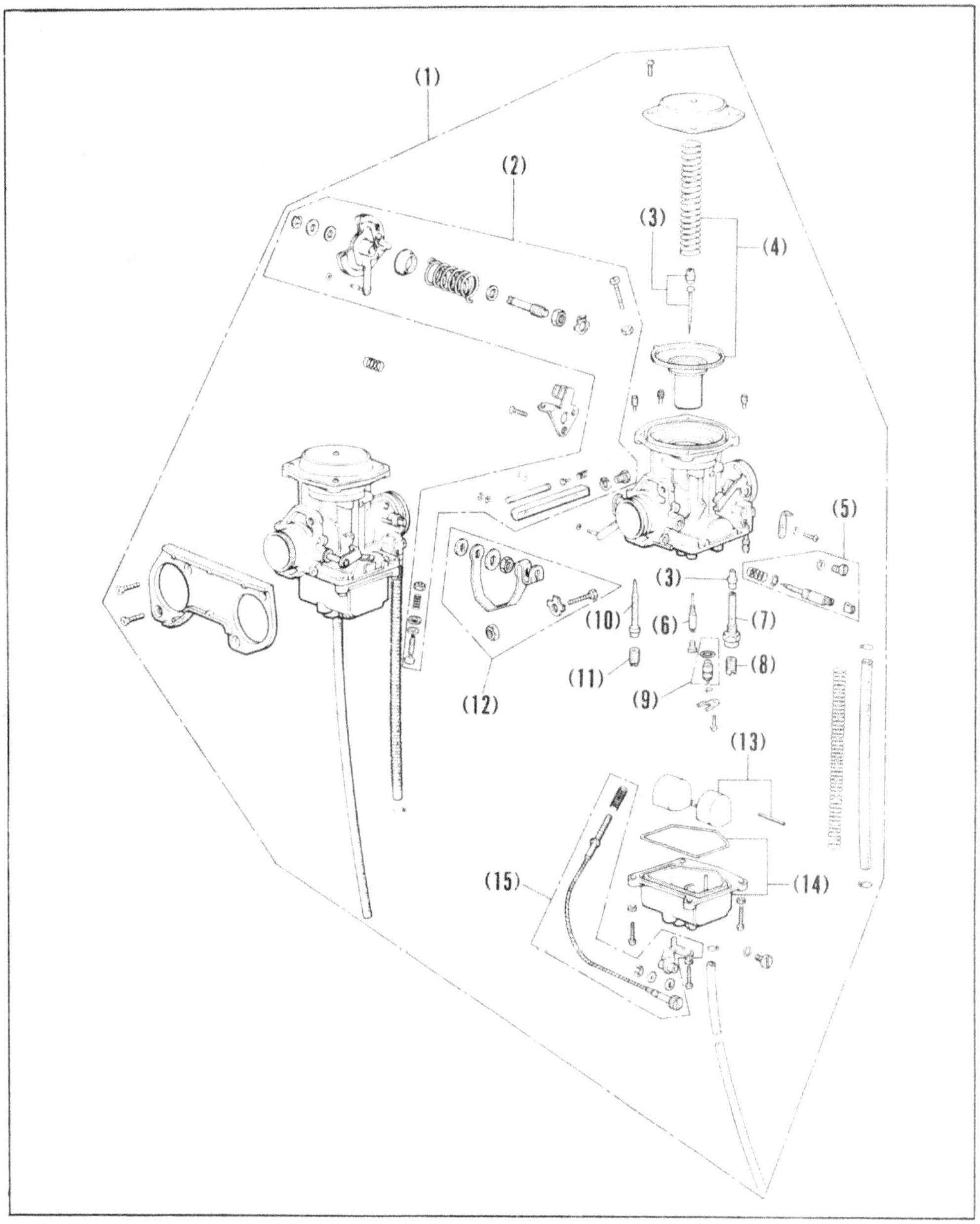

Removal

To remove the carburetor, refer to the "Engine removal" item (page 32.)
 1. Disconnect the throttle cables from the carburetor stay.

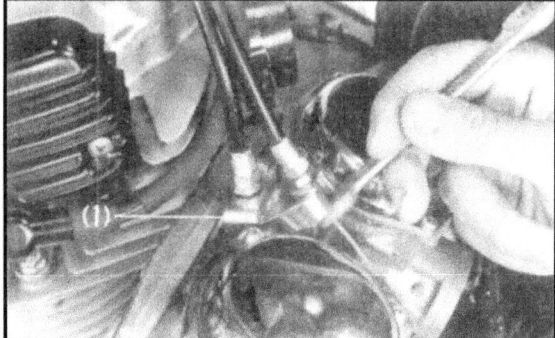

Fig. 4-104 (1) Carburetor stay

2. Straighten the locking lugs of the lock washer and loosen the bolt (2).
   Then remove the connector joint from the left carburetor.
3. Remove the four screws and remove the carburetor assembly from the stay plate.

Fig. 4–105 (1) Connector joint
(2) Bolt

Installation

To install, reverse the removal procedures.
1. Connect the right and left carburetors by the connector joint. Tighten the lock nut and bend the locking lugs of the lock washer securely.

Fig. 4–106 (1) Connector joint

2. Set the throttle lever to the stop screw (1) as shown.
3. Install the coil spring in the position shown and install the carburetor assembly to the stay plate.

Fig. 4–107 (1) Stop screw
(2) Spring

4. Connect the throttle cables with the throttle fully closed. Screw the "closed" side cable in the lower part of the throttle lever. Insert the "open" side cable into the upper part of the lever, adjust the length and lock with the lock nut.

Fig. 4–108 (1) "Closed" side cable   (4) Lock nut
(2) "Open" side cable   (5) Adjusting nut
(3) Throttle lever

IV. ENGINE 65

Disassembly

1. Remove the four screws (1) and remove the top. Then remove the coil spring and vacuum piston.

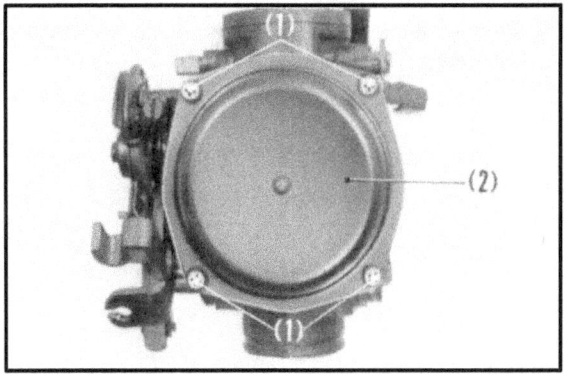

Fig. 4–109 (1) Screws (2) Top

2. Remove the needle jet screw and then the jet needle from the vacuum piston.

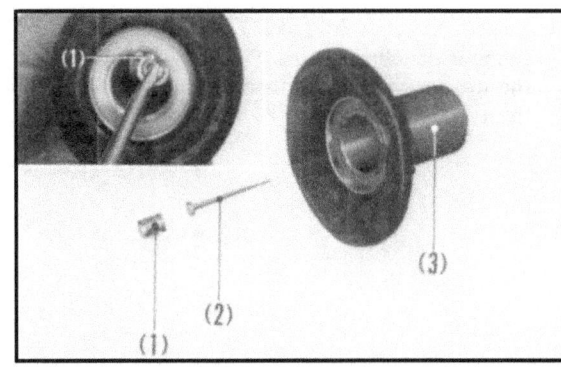

Fig. 4–110 (1) Needle jet screw
(2) Jet needle
(3) Vacuum piston

3. Remove the screws (4) and remove the float chamber body.
4. Pull out the arm pin and remove the float.
 * The float valve is removed together with the float. Take care not to drop it.

Fig. 4–111 (1) Float arm pin
(2) Float
(3) Float chamber body
(4) Screws

5. Remove the primary main jet and main nozzle. Remove the secondary main jet.
Remove the needle jet holder and jet needle.

Fig. 4–112 (1) Needle jet holder
(2) Primary main jet
(3) Secondary main jet

6. Remove the screw (1) and remove the valve seat plate and valve seat.

Fig. 4-113 (1) Screw
(2) Valve seat plate
(3) Valve seat

7. Remove the clips (1) and (2). Straighten the locking lugs of the lock washer and remove the holding bolt. Remove the throttle lever together with the adjusting holder.

Fig. 4-114 (1), (2) Clips
(3) Holding bolt
(4) Throttle lever
(5) Adjusting holder

Inspection

1. Blow the jets to check for clogging.
2. Check the float valve for proper operation.
3. Check the sliding surface of the vacuum piston for scores or scratches.
4. Check the jet needle for wear, scores, or scratches.

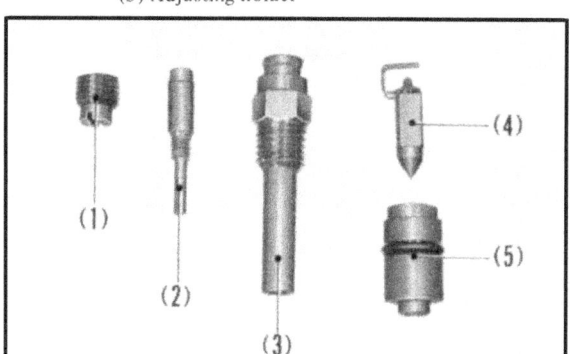

Fig. 4-115 (1) Primary main jet (5) Valve seat
(2) Slow jet
(3) Needle jet holder
(4) Float valve

Carburetor Setting Table

		CB250	CB360	CL360
Setting mark		744B	745B	747B
Main jet	Primary		# 68	
	Secondary	# 95	# 68	
Air jet	Primary		#150	
	Secondary		# 50	
Slow jet			# 35	
Slow air jet			# 85	
Float height			18.5 mm (0.75 in.)	

IV. ENGINE

Assembly

To assemble, reverse the disassembly procedures paying attention to the following:
1. Install the float valve after attaching the special ring in position.
2. Take care not to install the valve seat set plate upside down.

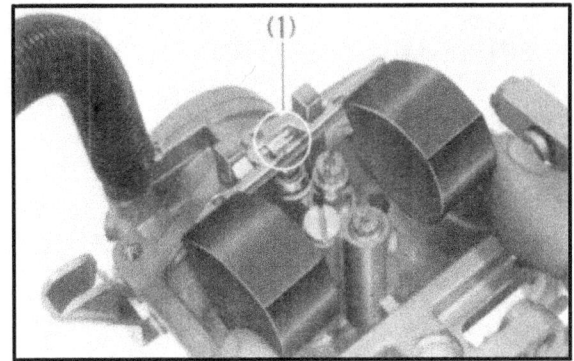

Fig. 4–116 (1) Special ring

3. Use a longer screw for the left carburetor float chamber body tightening screw (2).

Fig. 4–117 (1) Float chamber body
(2) Screw (longer)

4. Correctly set the vacuum piston into position and then install the top.

Fig. 4–118 (1) Matching point

Float level adjustment

Hold the carburetor with its main bore in a vertical position, so the float arm tang will just close the float valve, without compressing the spring loaded plunger in the end of the valve. Measure float height with a float level gauge.

Float height (distance between the carburetor body and the opposite edge of the float) should be **18.5 mm (0.73 in.)** when the float valve just closes.

If adjustment is needed, carefully bend the float arm tang toward or away from the float valve until the specified float height is obtained. Replace any damaged or leaking float.

Fig. 4–119 (1) Float level gauge
(2) Float

V. FRAME

1. FRONT WHEEL AND FRONT BRAKE (DISC BRAKE)

Fig. 5-1
(1) Front wheel axle
(2) 8 x 90 bolt
(3) Speedometer gear box
(4) Gear box retainer cover
(5) Gear box retainer
(6) Retainer O-ring
(7) Tire flap
(8) Wheel tube
(9) Front wheel tire
(10) Front wheel rim
(11) 6302U radial ball bearing
(12) Front axle distance collar
(13) Front wheel hub
(14) Front wheel bearing retainer
(15) Dust seal
(16) Front wheel side collar
(17) Front wheel axle nut
(18) Front brake disc.

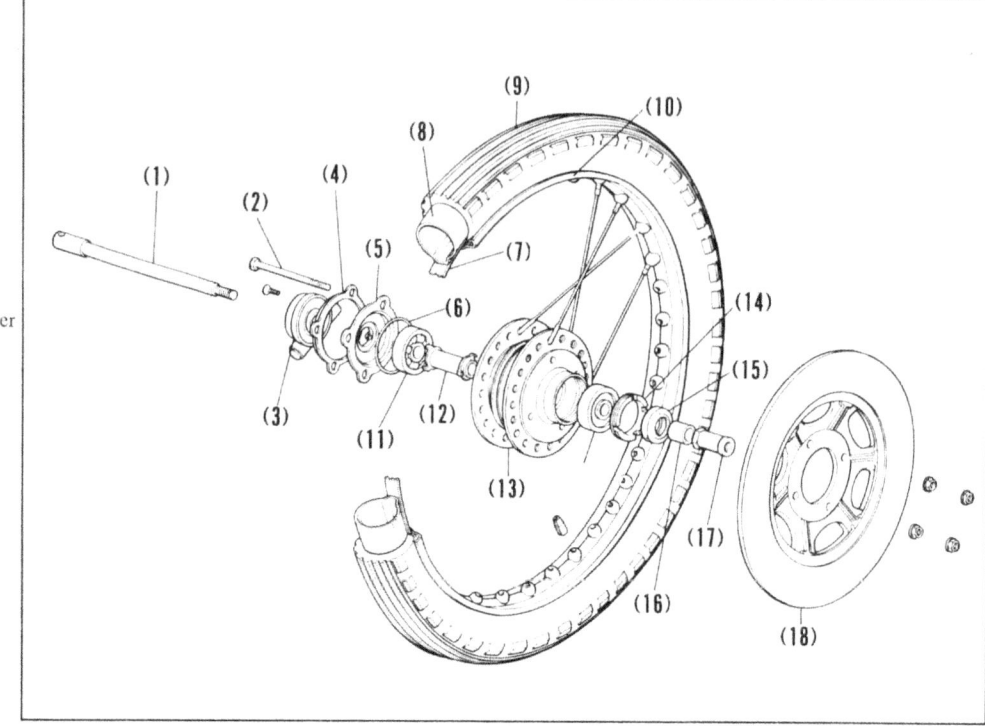

Disassembly

1. Place a stand under the engine to raise the front wheel off the ground.
2. Disconnect the speedometer cable.
3. Remove the nuts (3) and remove the front wheel from the front forks.

   CAUTION:
   Do not operate the front brake lever with the front wheel removed; otherwise, the pads may come out.

Fig. 5-2 (1) Speedometer cable
         (2) Axle holder

4. With the axle nut held in a vice, turn the front wheel axle and remove the axle nut.
5. Pull out the front wheel axle and the speedometer gear box can be removed.

Fig. 5-3 (1) Front wheel axle
         (2) Speedometer gear box

V. FRAME

6. Remove the 8 mm UBS nuts and remove the brake disc.
7. Pull out the bolts (3) and the gear box retainer and cover can be removed.

Fig. 5-4 (1) Brake disc
(2) 8 mm UBS nuts
(3) Bolts

8. Remove the dust seal and remove the bearing retainer using the bearing retainer wrench (Tool No. 07910-3230100).
9. Remove the ball bearings.

CAUTION:
Do not perform the jobs in the steps 8 and 9 above unless necessary.

Fig. 5-5 (1) Bearing retainer wrench

Inspection

Refer to service data on page 113.
1. Check the front wheel axle for bend.
2. Check the ball bearings for looseness.
3. Check the wheel rim for runout or damage.
4. Check the spokes for looseness or bend.
5. Check to see if metal pieces or stones are bitten in the tire tread pattern or wall. Also check the tire for scores, scratches or wear.
6. Check the tire inflation pressure.
Also check for air leakage from the valve.
Specification: 1.8 kg/cm^2 (26 psi)

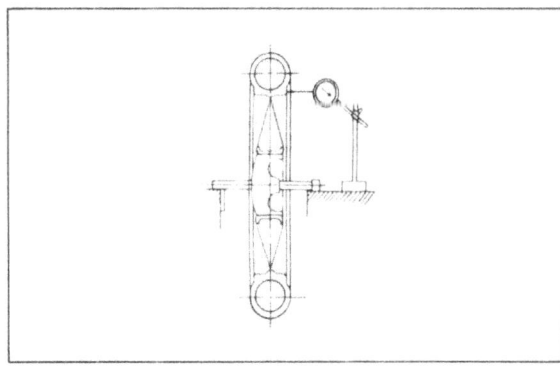

Fig. 5-6 Checking wheel rim for runout

Assembly

To assemble, reverse the disassembly procedures paying attention to the following:
1. Install the ball bearings.
Fill the cavity in each ball bearing and inside the wheel hub with grease.
Install the bearings using the bearing driver attachment (Tool No. 07945-3330100) and driver handle (Tool No. 07949-6110000), taking care not to allow the spacer collar to incline.

Fig. 5-7 (1) Bearing driver attachment
(2) Driver handle

2. After tightening the bearing retainer, stake it at two points using a punch.

Fig. 5–8 (1) Bearing retainer
(2) Stake these points with a punch

3. Make sure that the O-ring is attached to the wheel hub. Install the gear box retainer and cover to the wheel hub using the 8 mm bolts and install the brake disc to the opposite side.

   NOTE:
   The brake disc tightening nuts are 8 mm UBS nuts. Be sure to use the genuine Honda parts. Tighten them to the specified torque.

Fig. 5–9 (1) O-ring
(2) Gear box retainer

4. Install the speedometer gear box to the front wheel. Insert the axle nut.

   NOTE:
   Apply a coat of grease to the speedometer gear box.

Fig. 5–10 (1) Gear box retainer
(2) Speedometer gear box

5. Tighten the front axle holder nuts, beginning with the front one on the disc side, as shown in Fig. 5–11.

   Specified tightening torque:
   2.7–3.3kg·m (19.5–23.8 lbs-ft)

   NOTES:
   1. Secure the axle holders to the front forks tightly at the front.
   2. Use 8 mm UBS nuts. Tighten them to the specified torque.

6. Adjust the front brake caliper. (See page 25)

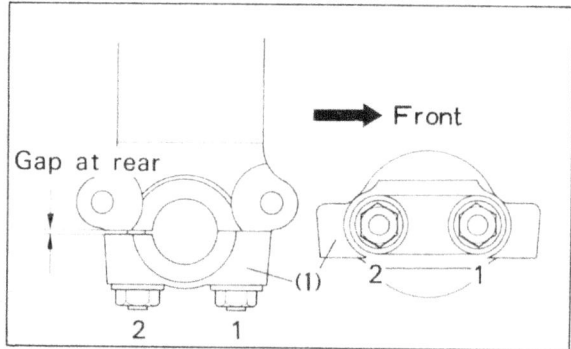

Fig. 5–11 (1) Axle holders

V. FRAME

Fig. 5-12

(1) Front wheel side collar
(2) 26 x 42 x 7 oil seal
(3) 6302 radial ball bearing
(4) Front axle distance collar
(5) Front wheel axle
(6) Front wheel tube
(7) Front wheel tire
(8) Front tire flap
(9) Front wheel rim
(10) Front wheel hub
(11) 6302 radial ball bearing
(12) 54667 oil seal
(13) Speedometer gear
(14) Speedometer gear washer
(15) Wheel balancer
    (5gr, 10gr, 15gr, 20gr)
(16) Front brake cam A and B
(17) Front brake shoes
(18) Front brake shoe springs
(19) 2.0 x 15 cotter pin
(20) Front anchor pin washer
(21) Front brake panel
(22) Front wheel axle sleeve
(23) Brake cam dust seal
(24) 14 mm plain washer
(25) Brake indicator plate
(26) 8 x 28 bolt (U.B.S.)
(27) Front brake stopper arm
(28) Front brake arm return spring
(29) 6 x 36 bolt
(30) Front brake arm A
(31) 6 mm washer
(32) 6 mm nut
(33) 2.0 x 18 cotter pin
(34) Front brake arm A
(35) 6 mm washer
(36) 6 x 36 bolt

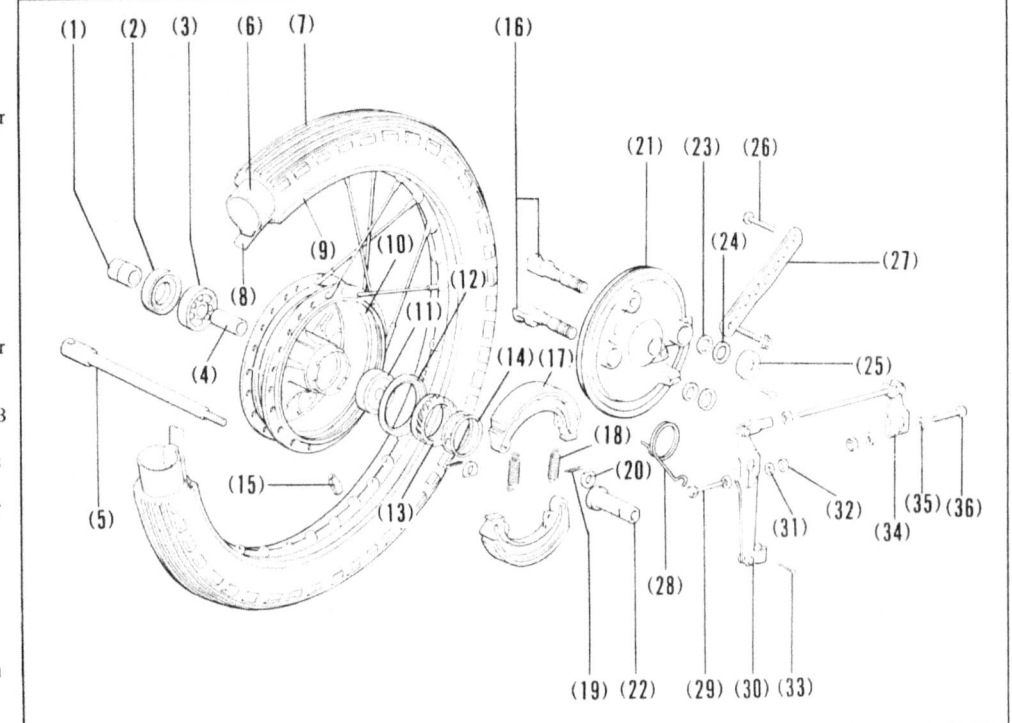

Disassembly

1. Place a suitable block under the engine to raise the front wheel off the ground.
2. Remove the 8 mm bolt (U.B.S) securing the front brake stopper arm in place.

Fig. 5-13 (1) 8 mm bolt (U.B.S.)
(2) Front brake stopper arm

3. Back off the 5 mm screw; pull off the tachometer cable. Disconnect the front brake cable from between the brake arm and brake panel.

Fig. 5-14 (1) 5 mm screw
(2) Tachometer cable
(3) Front brake cable

4. Remove the two 8 mm nuts from the right and left front forks. Remove the axle holders. The front wheel can now be taken out from the motorcycle.

Fig. 5–15 (1) 8 mm nuts
(2) Axle holder

5. Remove the front axle sleeve and withdraw the front wheel axle. Remove the front brake panel from the front wheel.

Inspection

Refer to the service data on page 113.
1. Inspection items on page 69.
2. Measure the inside diameter of the front brake drum.
3. Measure the thickness of the front brake shoe.

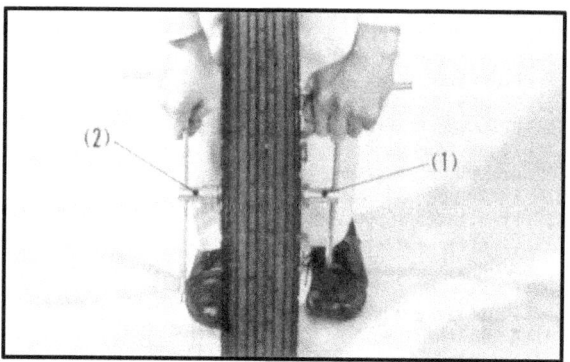

Fig. 5–16 (1) Front axle sleeve
(2) Front wheel axle

Assembly

1. Install the front brake shoes to the brake cams. Install the front anchor pin washers. Secure them with cotter pins.

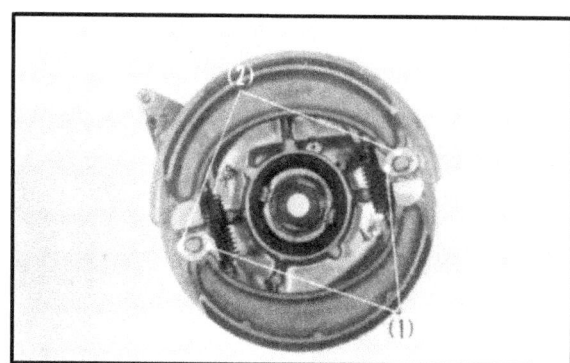

Fig. 5–17 (1) Anchor pin washers
(2) Cotter pins

2. Install the front brake arms "A" and "B", being careful that the marks align.

Fig. 5–18 (1) Front brake arm A
(2) Front brake arm B
(3) Marks

V. FRAME

3. Install the axle holders, tightening the front nut first. Refer to Fig. 5—19.

   Specified tightening torque: 2.7–3.3 kg-m (19.5–23.8 lbs-ft)

Fig. 5–19 (1) Front axle holder
(2) 8 mm nut

2. FRONT DISC BRAKE

Fig. 5—20
(1) Master cylinder assy.
(2) Boot
(3) 18 mm internal snap ring
(4) Piston set
(5) Primary cup
(6) Oil cup cap
(7) Diaphrgam
(8) Master cylinder holder
(9) Oil bolt
(10) Front brake hose B
(11) Front stop switch
(12) Three-way joint
(13) Front brake hose
(14) Front brake pipe
(15) Caliper holder joint
(16) Caliper holder
(17) Caliper assy.
(18) Caliper B
(19) Pad B
(20) Pad A
(21) Piston
(22) Piston seal
(23) Caliper A
(24) Bleeder valve
(25) Brake disc
(26) Caliper holder pin
(27) Disc cover

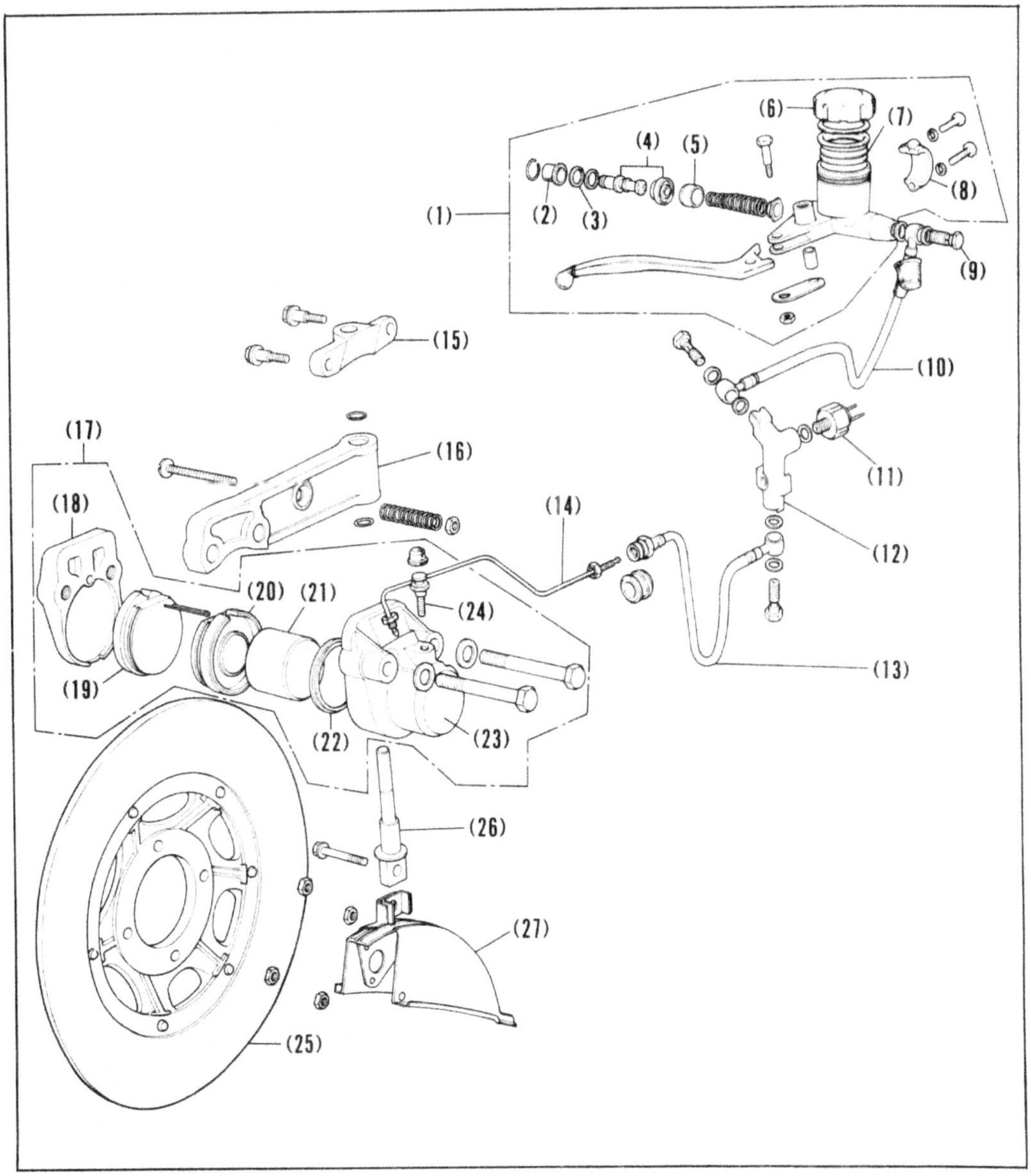

V. FRAME

Removal

1. Disconnect the front brake pipe from the capliper A. Operate the brake lever and remove brake fluid.

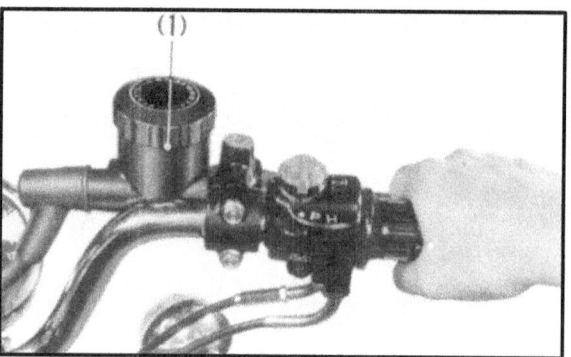

Fig. 5-21 (1) Master cylinder

2. Remove the oil bolt and bolts (3) and remove the master cylinder assembly.

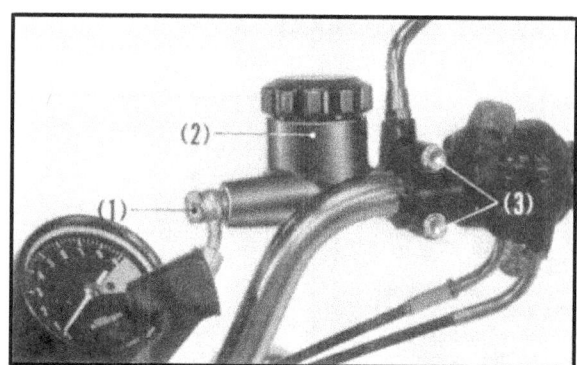

Fig. 5-22 (1) Oil bolt
(2) Master cylinder assembly
(3) Bolts

3. Remove the bolts (1), bolts (2) and adjusting bolt and remove the caliper assembly.

Fig. 5-23 (1), (2) Bolts
(3) Adjusting bolt

4. Remove the front emblem. Remove the bolt (1) and disconnect the front stop switch lead. Remove the three-way joint and disconnect the oil pipe.

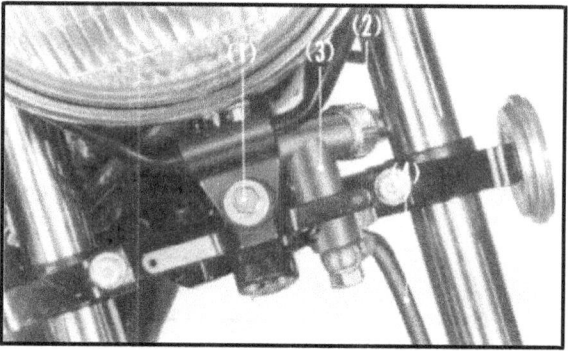

Fig. 5-24 (1) Bolt (3) Three-way joint
(2) Front stop switch (4) Oil pipe

V. FRAME

Installation

To install, reverse the removal procedures paying attention to the following:

1. Connect the pipes as shown in Fig. 5–25.

2. After installing the front disc brake, fill the master cylinder with DOT 3 brake fluid and bleed it completely. (See page 26.)

Fig. 5–25
(1) Front brake hose B
(2) Oil bolt
(3) Three-way joint
(4) Stop switch
(5) Front brake hose A
(6) Oil bolt washer
(7) Three-way joint holder
(8) Oil tube

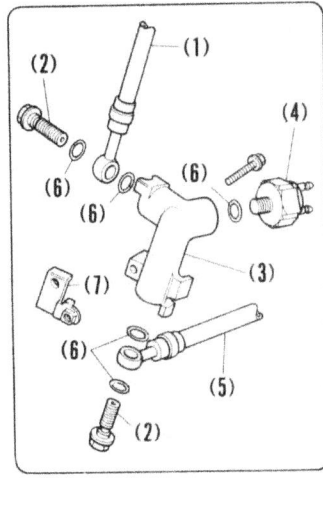

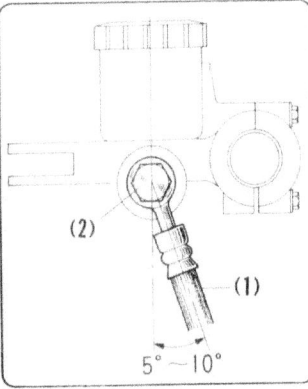

Disassembly

Caliper

1. Remove the caliper assembly.
2. Remove the caliper setting bolts and the caliper assembly can be separated into the calipers A and B.
   (When separating the assembly with it installed to the front wheel, disconnect the oil pipe.)

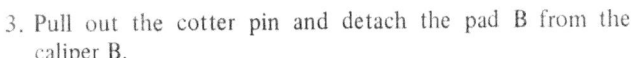

Fig. 5–26 (1) Oil pipe
(2) Caliper setting bolts
(3) Caliper A
(4) Caliper B

3. Pull out the cotter pin and detach the pad B from the caliper B.
4. Give a tap to the head of the caliper A to detach the pad A.

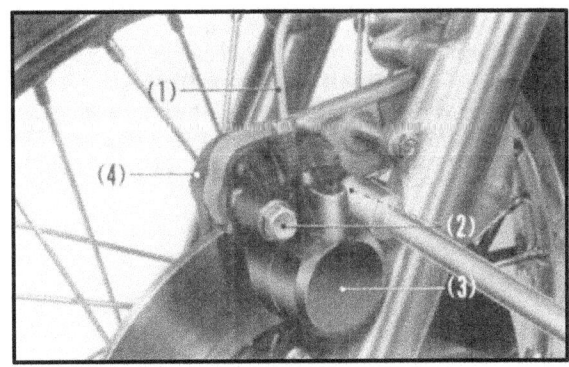

Fig. 5–27 (1) Caliper B
(2) Pad B
(3) Cotter pin

5. Remove the piston using compressed air.

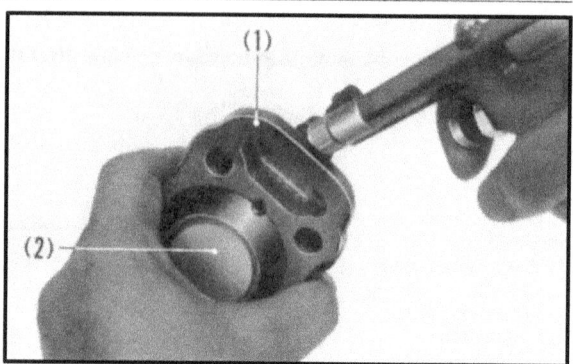

Fig. 5−28 (1) Caliper A
(2) Piston

Master cylinder

1. Remove the master cylinder.
2. Remove the brake lever.
3. Remove the boot and remove the 18 mm internal snap ring using the snap ring pliers (Tool No. 07914−3230000).

   CAUTION:
   Take care not to damage the boot.

Fig. 5−29 (1) Snap ring pliers
(2) Snap ring

4. Remove the piston, check valve and primary cup.
   Remove the primary cup by applying **2 to 3 kg/cm² (28 to 43 psi)** air pressure from the brake hose joint. The cup may also be removed with a tool by which the check valve is not scored or scratched.

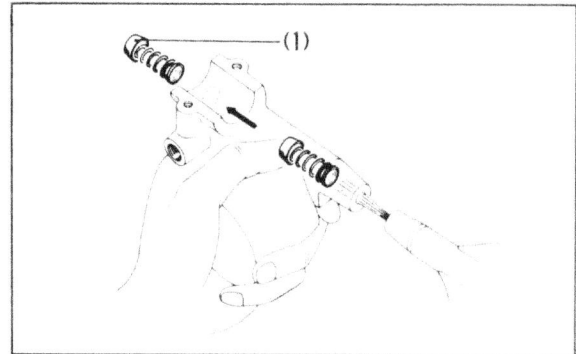

Fig. 5−30 (1) Primary cup

Inspection

Refer to service data on page 113.

1. Check the pads for wear.
   Each pad is marked with the red groove. If the pad wears down to the groove, replace it.
2. Measure the caliper cylinder bore and piston OD. Check them for wear or damage.

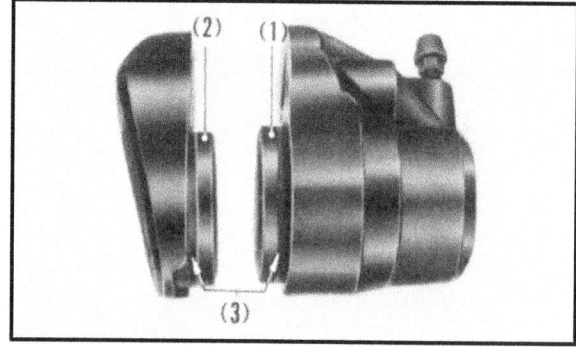

Fig. 5−31 (1) Pad A
(2) Pad B
(3) Red groove

V. FRAME

Assembly

Caliper

1. When attaching the pads, apply a coat of grease to the rear sides. Use silicon sealing grease.

   CAUTIONS:
   1. Do not allow grease to come in contact with the disc attaching surfaces of the pads.
   2. Take care to prevent foreign materials, dust or dirt from getting inside the calipers.

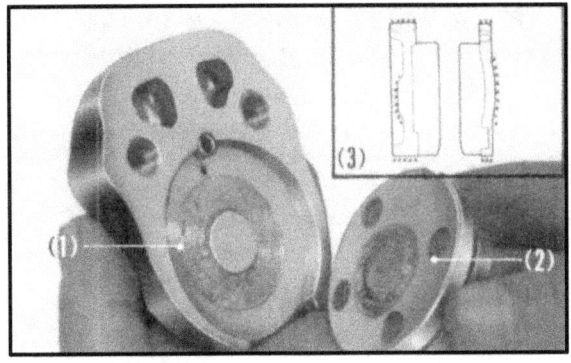

Fig. 5-32 (1) Caliper B
(2) Pad B
(3) Apply grease to part marked (X)

Master cylinder

1. Apply a coat of brake fluid to the inside surface of the cylinder.
2. Install the check valve to the return spring and install them in the cylinder.

   CAUTION:
   When installing the check valve and return spring in the cylinder, make sure that the valve is facing correctly and that the spring is in correct position.

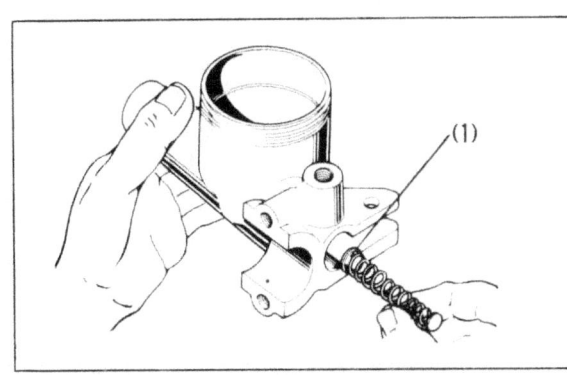

Fig. 5-33 (1) Check valve

3. Apply a thin coat of brake fluid to the outside surface of the primary cup.
   Install the primary cup taking care not to allow dust to attach to it or not to damage it. Make sure that the cup is not inclined or not reversed in the cylinder.

   NOTE:
   When the primary cup has been disassembled, replace it with a new one.

4. Install the 18 mm internal snap ring.
   Turn the snap ring to check for proper fit.

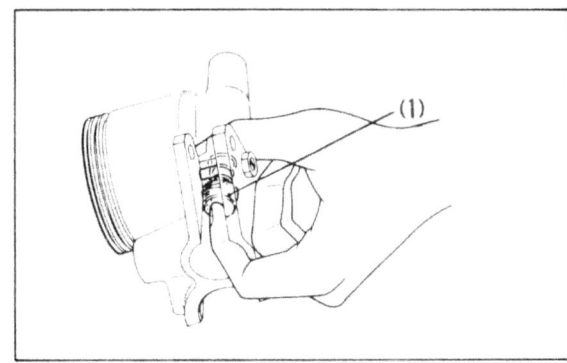

Fig. 5-34 (1) Primary cup

3. REAR WHEEL AND REAR BRAKE

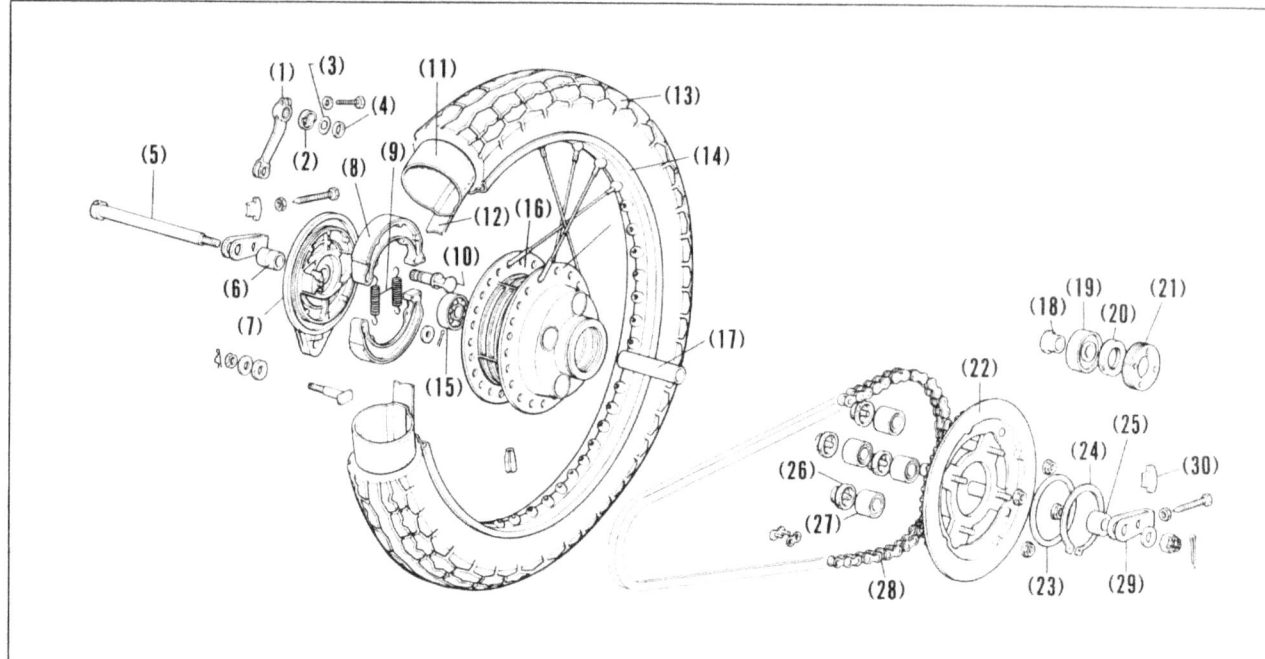

Fig. 5–35
(1) Rear brake arm
(2) Brake indicator plate
(3) 14 mm plain washer
(4) Brake cam dust seal
(5) Rear wheel axle
(6) Rear brake panel side collar
(7) Rear brake panel
(8) Rear brake shoe
(9) Rear brake shoe spring
(10) Rear brake cam
(11) Rear wheel tube
(12) Tire flap
(13) Rear wheel tire
(14) Rear wheel rim
(15) 6303U radial ball bearing
(16) Rear wheel hub
(17) Rear axle distance collar A
(18) Rear axle distance collar B
(19) 6304U radial ball bearing
(20) Dust seal
(21) Bearing retainer
(22) Final driven sprocket
(23) 70 mm washer
(24) 69 mm snap ring
(25) Rear wheel side collar
(26) Rear wheel hub plug
(27) Rear wheel damper bushing
(28) Drive chain
(29) Drive chain adjuster
(30) Chain adjuster stopper

Disassembly

1. Remove the mufflers. (CB type only)
2. Remove the rear brake rod and rear brake stop arm from the brake panel.
3. Loosen the right and left chain adjuster lock nuts and chain adjuster bolts. Pull out the cotter pin and remove the axle nut.

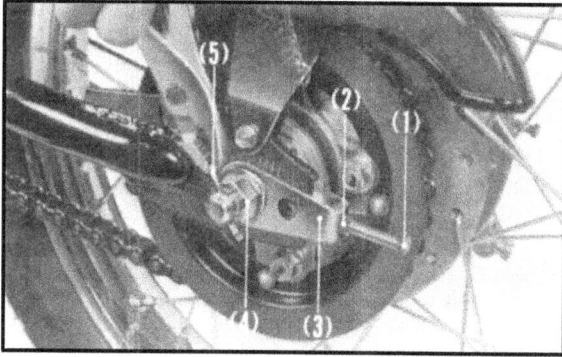

Fig. 5–36 (1) Chain adjuster bolt (5) Cotter pin
(2) Lock nut
(3) Chain adjuster
(4) Axle nut

4. Pull out the rear wheel axle. Remove the drive chain from the final driven sprocket. Remove the rear wheel with the brake panel.

Fig. 5–37

V. FRAME

5. Remove the 69 mm snap ring and remove the final driven sprocket as shown in Fig. 5-38.

   NOTE:
   The **final driven sprocket and fixing** bolt are made in one piece.

Fig. 5-38 (1) Wood block
(2) Final driven sprocket

6. When the ball bearings must be removed for replacement, remove the bearing retainer using the bearing retainer wrench (Tool No. 07910-3290000) and remove the bearings.

   CAUTION:
   Do not remove the ball bearings unless necessary.

Fig. 5-39 (1) Bearing retainer wrench

Rear brake panel

1. Remove the brake shoes.
   Pull the cotter pin out of the anchor pin of the brake panel. While expanding the brake shoes by your hands, remove them together with the shoe springs.
2. Remove the 6 mm bolt and remove the brake arm and brake cam.

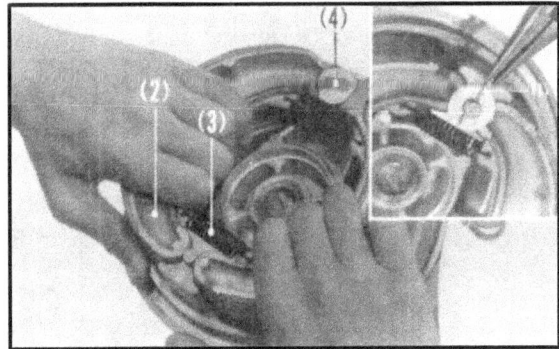

Fig. 5-40 (1) Cotter pin
(2) Brake shoe
(3) Brake shoe spring
(4) Brake cam

Inspection

Refer to service data on page 113.

1. Check the rear wheel axle for bend.
2. Check the ball bearings for looseness.
3. Check the rear wheel rim for runout or damage.
4. Check the spokes for looseness, bend or breakage.
5. Check the final driven sprocket for wear or damage.
6. Check the drive chain for wear, damage, elongation or jamming.
7. Check the tire for scores, scratches or wear.
8. Check the tire inflation pressure.
   Also check for air leakage from the valve.
   Specification: 2.0 kg/cm (28 psi)

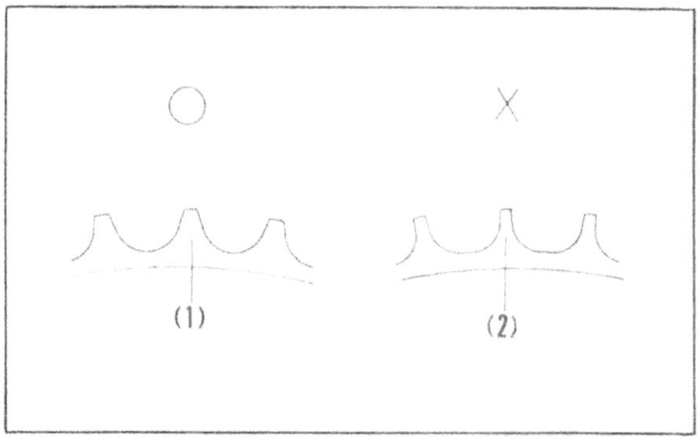

Fig. 5-41 Checking final driven sprocket for wear

9. Check the brake panel for scores, scratches or cracks.
10. Check the wheel hub, brake shoes and brake cam for wear.
11. Check the serrations of the brake arm and brake cam for wear.
12. Check the rear wheel damper bushings for damage.

Assembly

To assemble, reverse the disassembly procedures paying special attention to the following:

CAUTION:
Pay special attention not to allow oil, grease, dust or dirt to get inside the brake shoes and wheel hub.

1. Install the ball bearings.
   Fill the cavity in each ball bearing and inside the wheel hub with grease. Install the bearings using the race driver attachment (Tool No. 07945-3330100) and driver handle (Tool No. 07949-6110000), taking care not to allow the space collars to incline.

Fig. 5-42 (1) Driver handle
(2) Race driver attachment

2. Install and tighten the bearing retainer with the bearing retainer wrench used at the time of removal. After tightening, stake at four points as shown in Fig. 5-43 using a punch.

Fig. 5-43 (1) Stake these points with a punch
(2) Bearing retainer

3. Install the final driven sprocket to the wheel hub squarely as shown in Fig. 5-44.
   After installing, secure with a 70 mm washer and 69 mm snap ring.
   NOTE:
   Use UBS nuts for the 10 mm nuts. Tighten them to the specified torque.
   Specified tightening torque:
      6.0-7.0 kg-m (43.4-50.7 lbs-ft.)

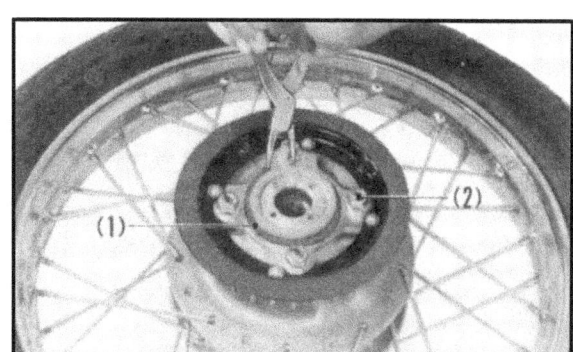
Fig. 5-44 (1) 69 mm snap ring
(2) 10 mm UBS nut

V. FRAME

4. Install the brake cam with the punch mark inside. Apply a coat of grease to the brake shoe attaching surfaces of the anchor pin and cam, brake panel-to-cam contact surface and dust seal.

   CAUTION:
   Do not allow grease to attach to the brake shoes and the inside surface of the wheel hub.

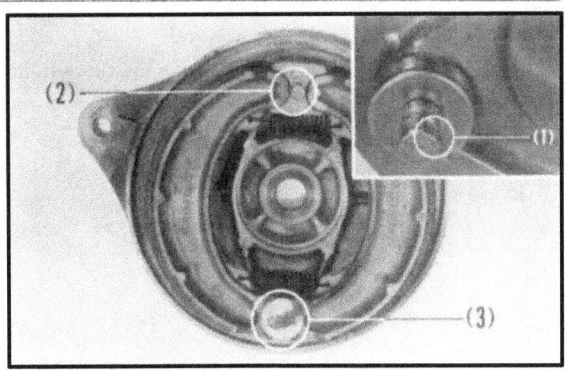

Fig. 5-45 (1) Face the punch mark on brake cam toward the inside
(2) Cam-to-brake shoe contact surfaces
(3) Anchor pin-to-brake shoe contact surfaces

5. Set the brake panel to the wheel hub properly and install the drive chain on the final driven sprocket. Then install the rear wheel to the rear fork with the wheel axle.
6. After assembling, adjust the drive chain and rear brake.

Fig. 5-46 (1) Drive chain

4. STEERING HANDLEBAR

Fig. 5-47
(1) Right grip rubber
(2) Throttle grip pipe
(3) Headlight/ignition switch
(4) Handlebar pipe
(5) Cable holder
(6) Upper holder
(7) Horn/dimmer switch
(8) Left grip rubber
(9) Master cylinder assy.
(10) Throttle cable A
(11) Throttle cable B
(12) Brake hose B
(13) Oil bolt
(14) Clutch cable

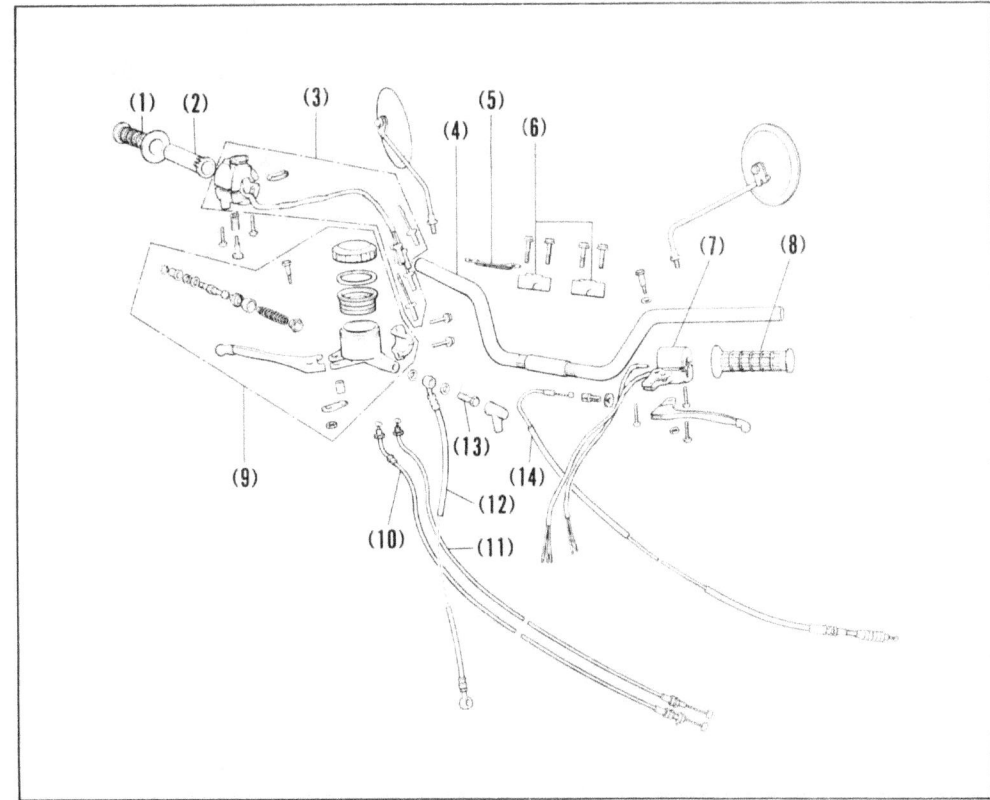

Disassembly

1. Remove the bolts (2) and remove the master cylinder.
   CAUTION:
   Take care not to spill brake fluid.

2. Disconnect the clutch cable.

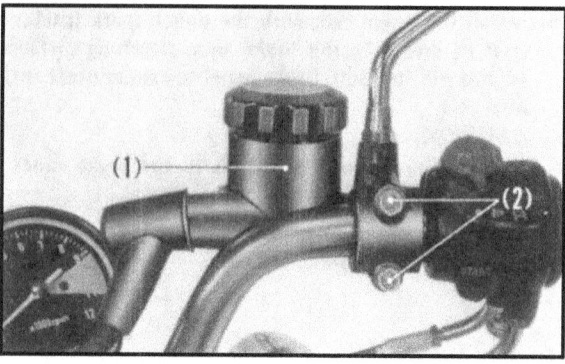

Fig. 5-48 (1) Master cylinder

3. Separate the starter/ignition switch into two parts. Disconnect the ends of the throttle cable wires from the throttle grip pipe and the throttle cables A and B from the starter/ignition switch.

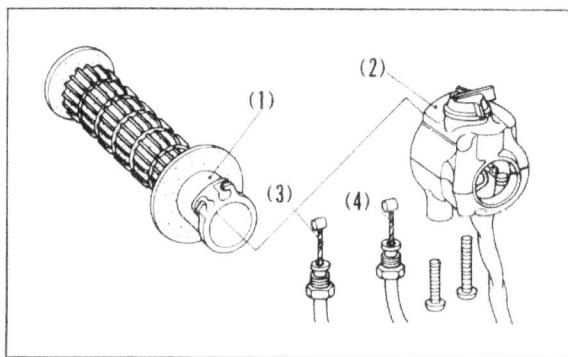

Fig. 5-49 (1) Throttle grip pipe
(2) Headlight/ignition switch
(3) Throttle cable A
(4) Throttle cable B

4. Remove the fuel tank. Disconnect the horn/turn signal dimmer switch, headlight/ignition switch and clutch lever switch leads on the frame from the wire harness.
5. Remove the handlebar upper holders and remove the handlebar pipe.
6. Pull the horn/turn signal dimmer switch and headlight/ignition switch out of the handlebar pipe.
   Attach a wire to the end of each wire and remain the wire in the pipe to facilitate installation.

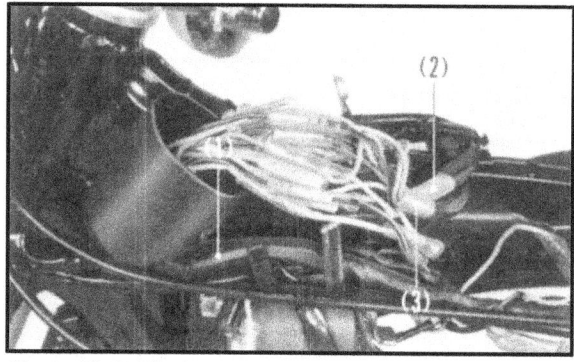

Fig. 5-50 (1) Wire harness
(2) Horn/dimmer switch leads
(3) Headlight/ignition switch leads

Inspection

1. Check the steering handlebar for warpage or breakage.
2. Check the wires for breakage or open circuit.
3. Check the cables for breakage.

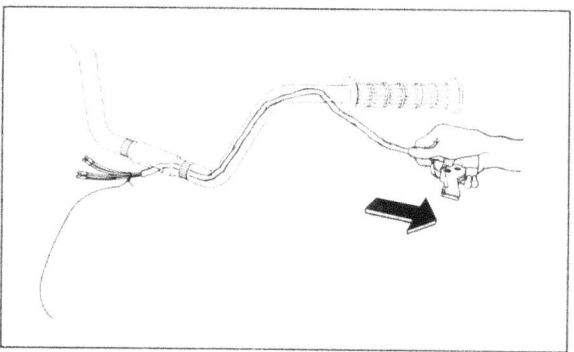

Fig. 5-51 Pulling switch lead

V. FRAME

Assembly

To assemble, reverse the disassembly procedures paying attention to the following:

1. Install the handlebar switches.
   Attach a wire to the end or the wire and route it through the handlebar pipe.
   Similarly install the clutch lever switch.

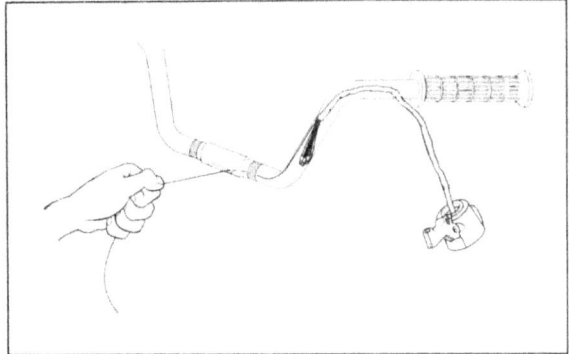

Fig. 5-52 Routing switch lead

2. Install the handlebar pipe.
   Align the punch marks on the pipe with the top of the lower holders.
   Route the front brake pipe, clutch cable and clutch lever switch lead inside the cable holder.
   Specified tightening torque:
   1.8-2.5 kg·m (13.1-18.1 lbs-ft)

   NOTES:
   1. **Face the punch marks on the upper holders toward the front.**
   2. **Tighten the upper holders beginning with the front side. Do not tighten the front side loosely.**

Fig. 5-53 (1) Punch mark on handlebar pipe and top of lower holder
(2) Punch mark on upper holder

V. FRAME

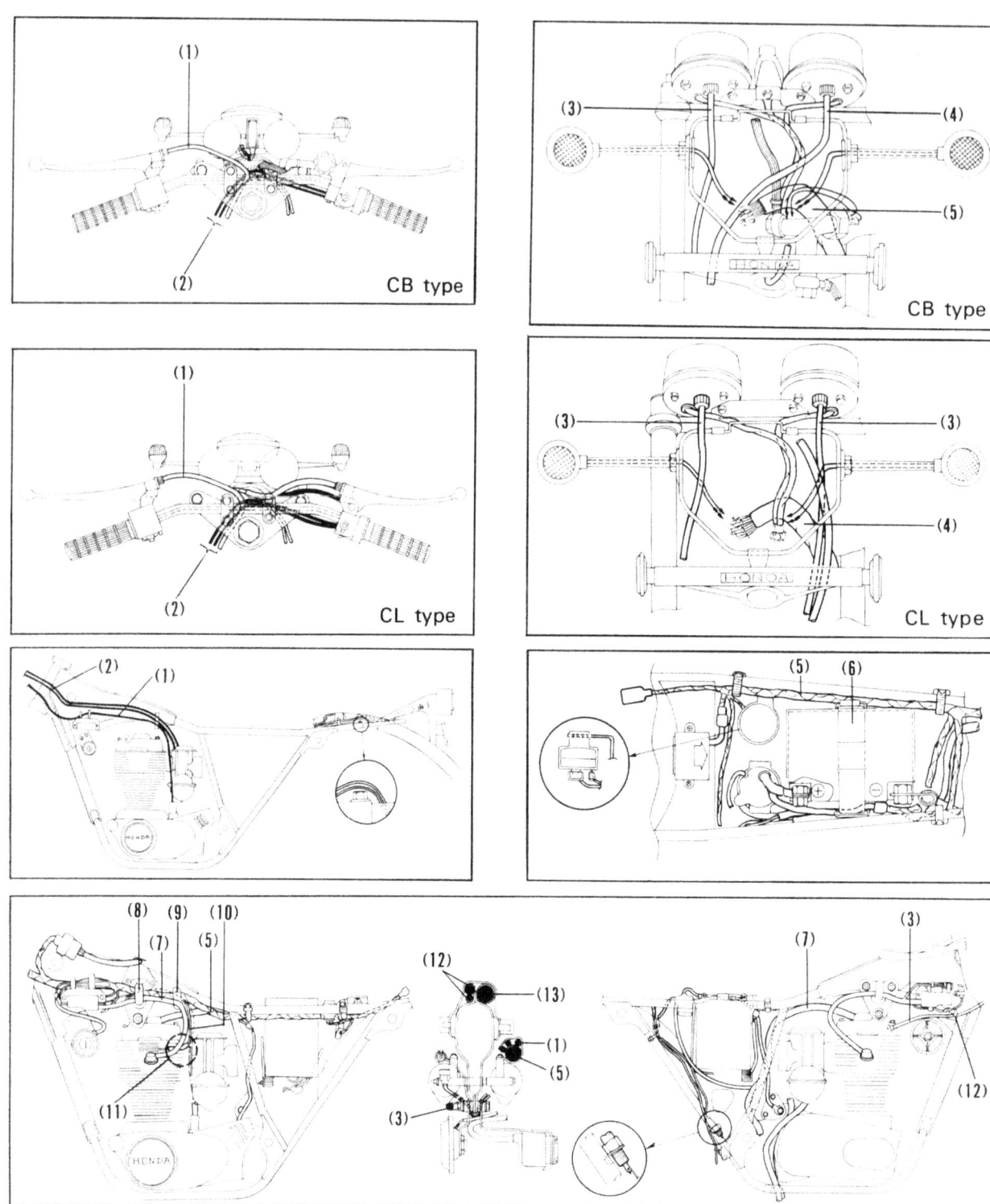

Fig. 5-54
(1) Clutch cable
(2) Throttle cable
(3) Tachometer cable
(4) Speedometer cable
(5) Wire harness
(6) Battery band
(7) High tension cable
(8) This clamper holds wire harness, point lead and high tension cable.
(9) This clamper holds wire harness, point lead and clutch cable.
(10) Point lead
(11) Point lead is located between sixth and seventh fins.
(12) Tachometer cable clip

V. FRAME

5. FRONT SUSPENSION

Fig. 5–55
(1) Front fork assy.
(2) Front fork bolt
(3) O-ring
(4) Front suspension spring
(5) Piston ring
(6) Bottom pipe
(7) Front rebound spring
(8) Front fork pipe
(9) Oil lock piece
(10) Front fork dust seal
(11) Oil seal stopper ring
(12) 33 x 46 x 10.5 oil seal
(13) Front fork bottom case
(14) Oil drain bolt
(15) 8 mm socket bolt
(16) Front axle holder

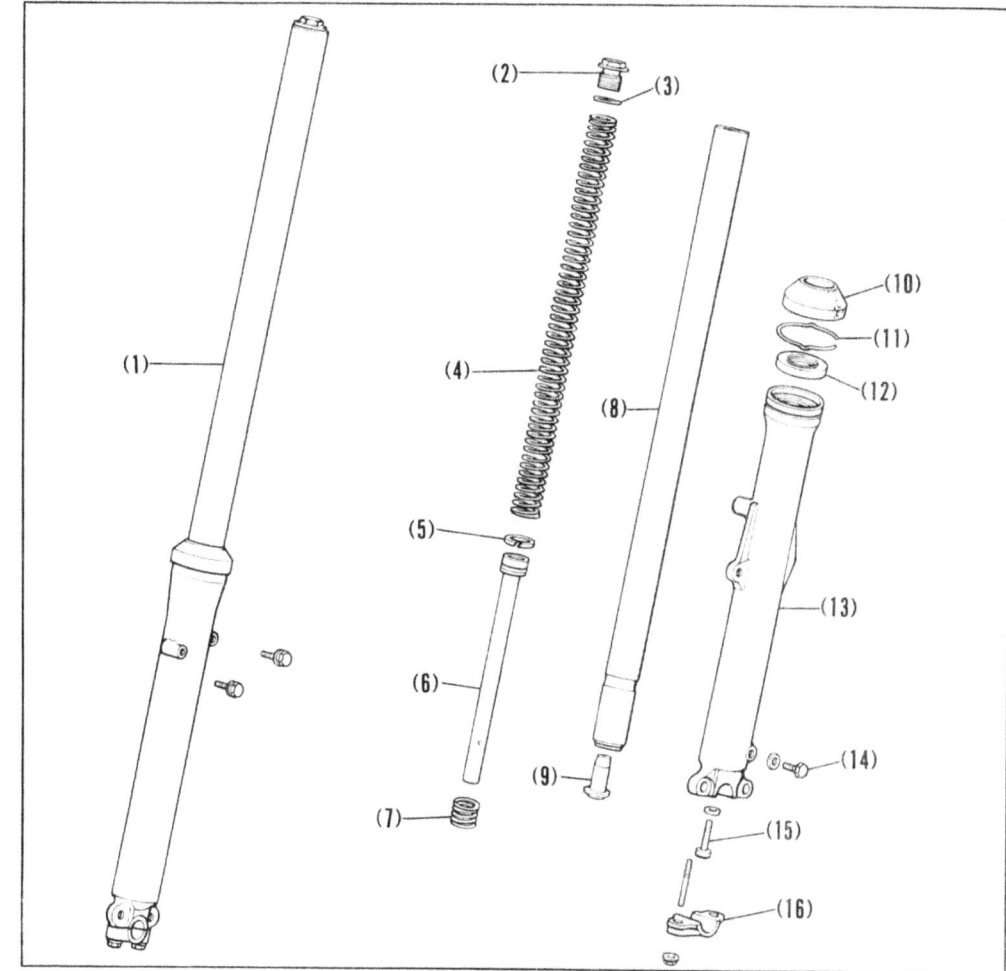

Disassembly

1. Loosen the front fork bolts before removing the forks.
2. Remove the front wheel.
3. Remove the caliper assembly and front fender.
4. Remove the front emblem. Loosen the bolts (4) and pull the front forks downward.

Fig. 5–56 (1) Front fork bolts   (3) Front forks
          (2) Front emblem   (4) Bolts

5. Remove the front fork bolts and drain front shock absorber oil.
6. With each front fork bottom pipe held in a vice, remove the socket bolt using the Allen head wrench (Tool No. 07917-3230000) and separate the pipe from the bottom case.

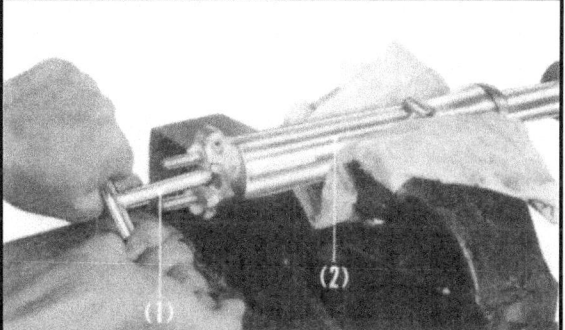

Fig. 5–57 (1) Allen head wrench
          (2) Front fork bottom case

7. Remove the front fork dust seal, 48 mm internal snap ring and oil seal.

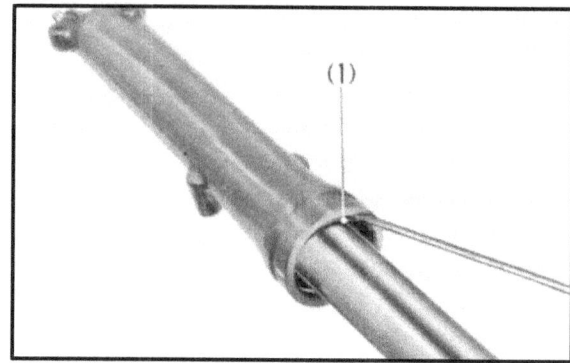

Fig. 5-58 (1) 48 mm internal snap ring

Inspection

Refer to service data on page 113.
1. Measure the front shock absorber spring free length. Check the spring tension.
2. Check the front fork piston rings for wear.
3. Check the front fork pipe-to-bottom case clearance.
4. Check the oil seals for scores, scratches or breakage.
5. Check the sliding surfaces of the front fork pipes for scores or scratches.

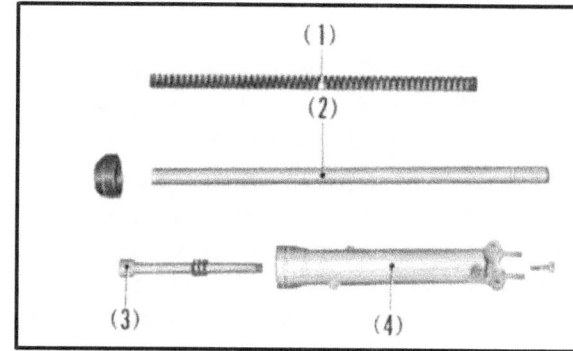

Fig. 5-59 (1) Front shock absorber spring
(2) Front fork pipe
(3) Piston ring
(4) Bottom case

Assembly

To assemble, reverse the disassembly procedures, paying attention to the following:
1. Position each fork pipe in the bottom case. Apply a coat of locking sealant to the socket bolt and tighten it with the Allen head wrench used at the time of disassembly.

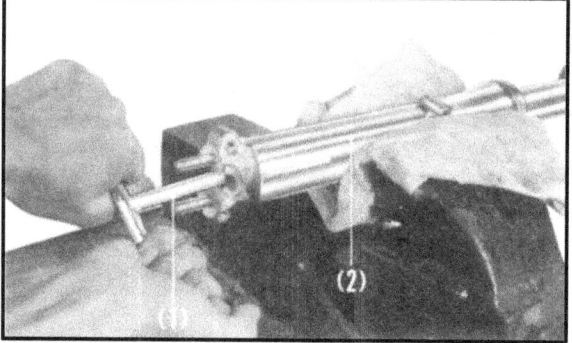

Fig. 5-60 (1) Allen head wrench
(2) Front fork bottom case

2. Apply a coat of high quality ATF to the inside and outside circumferences of the oil seal and install it using the fork seal driver (Tool No. 07947-3330000).

NOTE:
Use a new oil seal.

3. Fill the fork pipes with high quality ATF up to the specified level.
Capacity (each fork pipe):
160~165cc (5.4–5.6 ozs.) at the time of fork disassembly.

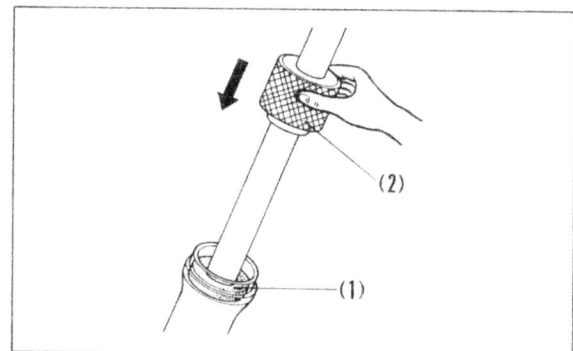

Fig. 5-61 (1) Oil seal
(2) Fork seal driver

V. FRAME

4. Install the front forks so that they are identical in height.

   CAUTION:
   Remove oil, if any, from around the fork pipes.

5. After assembling, check:
   The forks for smooth movement.
   Oil leakage from the oil seals.

Fig. 5-62 Front forks should be identical in height

6. STEERING STEM

Fig. 5-63
(1) Steering stem nut
(2) Steering head top thread
(3) Steering top cone race
(4) #8 steel ball
(5) Steering top ball race
(6) Steering bottom ball race
(7) Steering bottom cone race
(8) Dust seal
(9) Dust seal washer
(10) Fork top bridge
(11) Steering stem

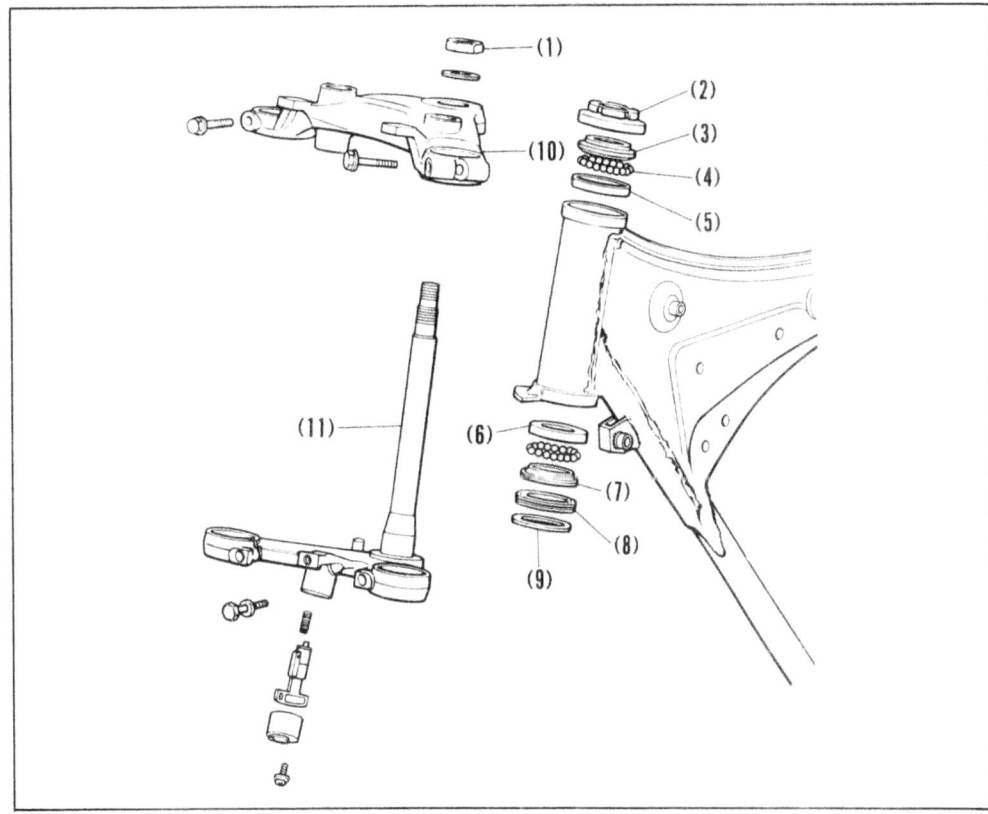

Disassembly

1. Open the headlight case and disconnect the wires inside the case.
2. Disconnect the speedometer and tachometer cables from the meters.
3. Remove the front emblem and remove the three bolts (1). Then the headlight case with the stay and turn signals and the meters with the meter set plate can be removed.

Fig. 5-64 (1) Bolts

V. FRAME

4. Remove the handlebar pipe. (See page 81.)
5. Remove the front wheel and remove the front forks. (See page 85.)
6. Remove the oil pipe and related parts as an assembly.
7. Remove the steering stem nut and remove the fork top bridge.

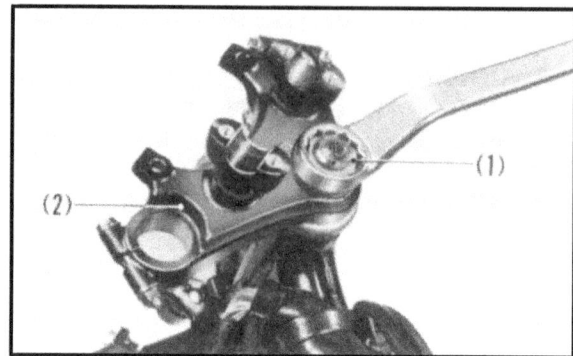

Fig. 5–65 (1) Steering stem nut
(2) Fork top bridge

8. Using the 46 mm pin spanner (Tool No. 07902–2400000) remove the steering head top thread and pull the steering stem downward

   CAUTION:
   Take care not to lose the #8 steel balls.

9. Remove the handlebar lock.

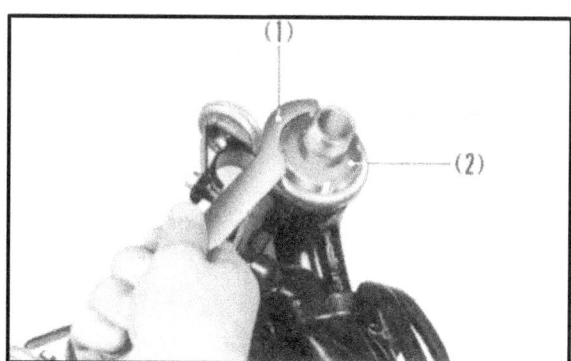

Fig. 5–66 (1) 46 mm pin spanner
(2) Steering head top thread

10. When removing the top and bottom ball races for replacement, remove them from the steering head using the ball race remover (Tool No. 07953–3330000).

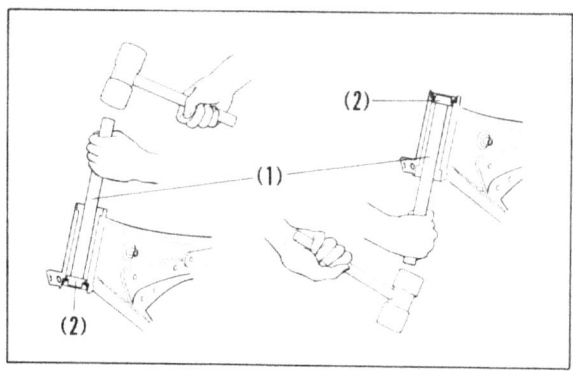

Fig. 5–67 (1) Ball race remover
(2) Ball race

Inspection

1. Check the #8 steel balls for wear or damage. If any one ball is worn or damaged, replace all balls with new ones.
2. Check the contact surfaces of the top and bottom cone races for wear or damage.
3. Check the steering head dust seal for wear.
4. Check the steering stem for bend and the threaded part for wear.
5. Check the stop for deformation or cracks.

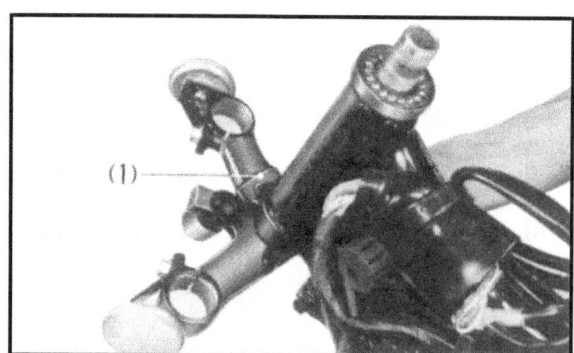

Fig. 5–68 (1) Stop

V. FRAME

Assembly

To assemble, reverse the disassembly procedures, paying attention to the following:

1. When the ball races have been removed, install them squarely using the race driver attachment (Tool No. 07946-3290000).

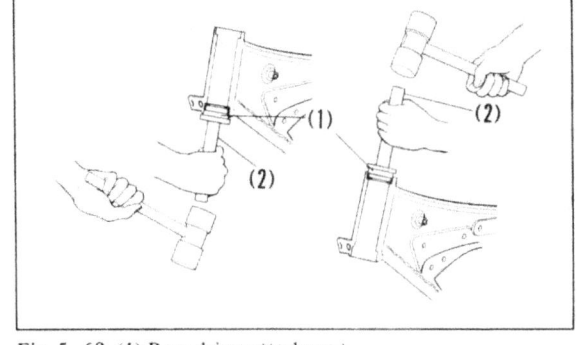

Fig. 5-69 (1) Race driver attachment
(2) Driver handle

2. Apply a coat of grease to the ball races and put the steel balls into them (18 balls into upper race and 19 balls into lower race). Install the steering stem into the head pipe and install the top cone race. While rotating the steering stem, hand tighten the head top thread until it turns freely right and left. Any slightest amount of play in axial direction cannot be tolerated here, until it is turned with reasonable ease.

NOTE:
Wash the cone races, ball races and steel balls and apply a coat of new grease to them.

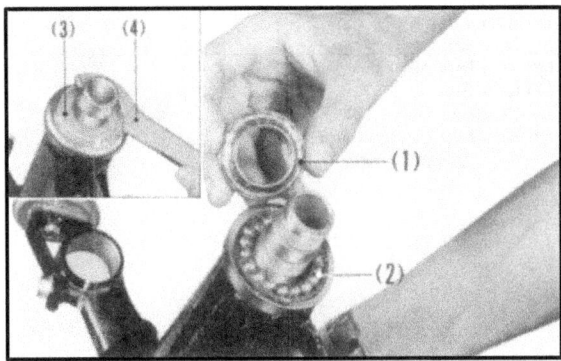

Fig. 5-70 (1) Top cone race
(2) #8 steel ball
(3) Steering head top thread
(4) 46 mm pin spanner

3. Temporarily install the front forks. Install the fork top bridge and tighten the steering stem nut. After tightening, check if the stem moves smoothly by its own weight from the position 5 to 10° from the center. If it will not move, the following causes may be suspected and checked.
* Maladjusted top thread
* Bent stem
* Wrong number of balls
* Abnormally worn races

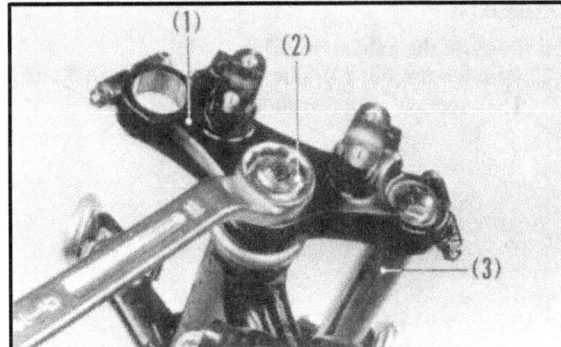

Fig. 5-71 (1) Fork top bridge
(2) Steering stem
(3) Front fork

7. REAR SHOCK ABSORBERS AND REAR FORK

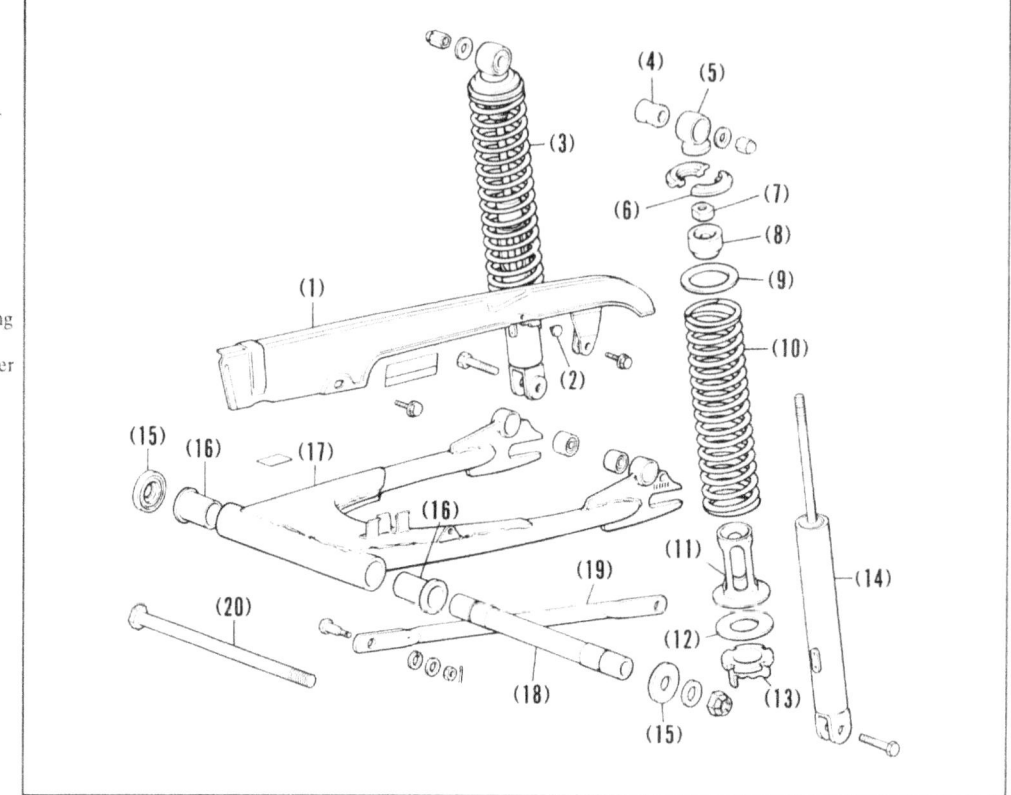

Fig. 5-72
(1) Drive chain case
(2) Chain case plug
(3) Rear shock absorber assy.
(4) Joint rubber
(5) Upper joint
(6) Spring set stopper
(7) 9 mm lock nut
(8) Rear shock absorber stopper rubber
(9) Rear shock absorber spring upper seat
(10) Rear shock absorber spring
(11) Spring guide
(12) Rear shock absorber spacer
(13) Spring adjuster
(14) Rear damper
(15) Dust seal cup
(16) Rear fork pivot bushing
(17) Rear fork
(18) Rear fork center collar
(19) Rear brake stopper arm
(20) Rear fork pivot bolt

Disassembly

1. Remove the exhaust mufflers.
2. Remove the nut (4), side glip (left side only) and bolt (3). Then remove each rear shock absorber.

Fig. 5-73 (1) Rear shock absorber
(2) Side grip (left side only)
(3) Bolt
(4) Nut

3. Remove the bolts (2) and remove the drive chain case.

Fig. 5-74 (1) Drive chain case

V. FRAME

4. Remove the rear fork pivot nut and pull out the pivot bolt. Then remove the rear fork.
5. Remove the rear brake stopper arm from the rear fork.

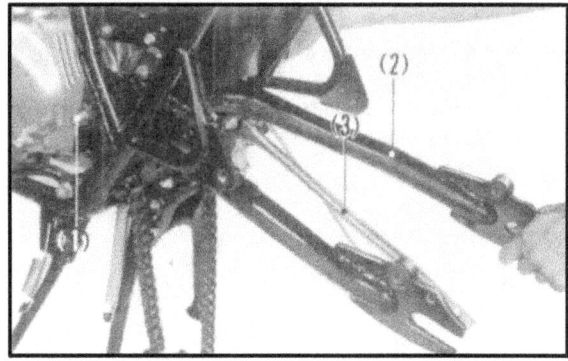

Fig. 5-75 (1) Rear fork pivot bolt (3) Rear brake stopper arm
(2) Rear fork

6. Compress each rear shock absorber using the rear shock absorber compressor (Tool No. 07959-3290000) and remove the spring seat stoppers and rear shock abosorber spring.

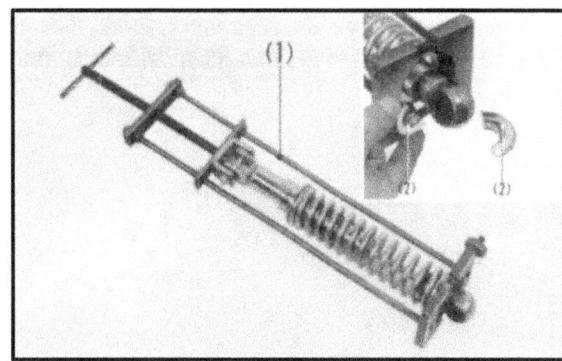

Fig. 5-76 (1) Rear shock absorber compressor
(2) Spring seat stoppers

7. Loosen the 9 mm lock nut and remove the upper joint. Then disassemble each rear shock absorber.

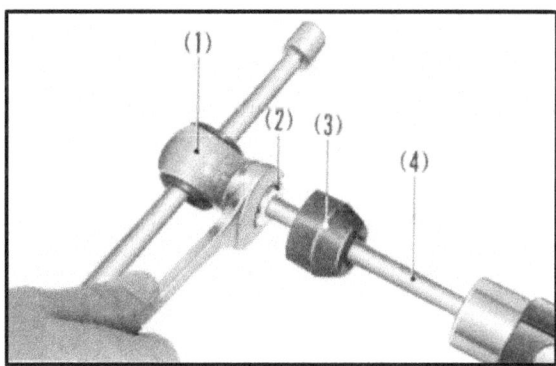

Fig. 5-77 (1) Upper joint (3) Stopper rubber
(2) 9 mm lock nut (4) Rear damper

Inspection

Refer to service data on page 113.
1. Measure the rear shock absorber spring free length. Check the spring tension.
2. Check the rear dampers for deformation or oil leakage and the rods for bend.
3. Check the stop rubbers for breakage.
4. Check the rear fork center collar-to-bushing clearance.
5. Check the holes for the rear axle provided in the rear end of the rear fork for proper alignment.

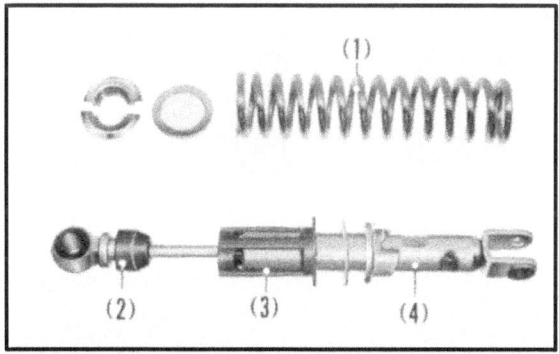

Fig. 5-78 (1) Rear shock absorber spring (3) Spring guide
(2) Stopper rubber (4) Rear damper

V. FRAME

Assembly

To assemble, reverse the disassembly procedures, paying attention to the following:

1. When the upper joints have been removed, apply a coat of thread locking agent to the tapped portion for the rear dampers.

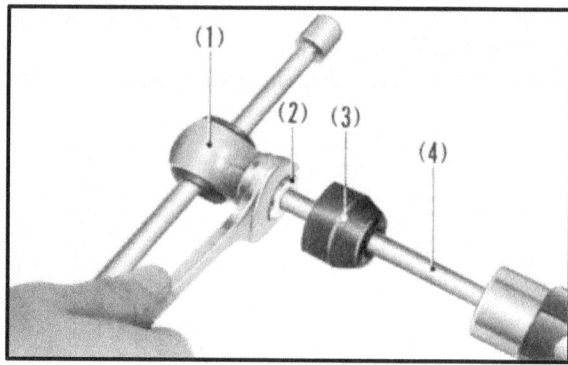

Fig. 5-79 (1) Upper joint
(2) 9 mm lock nut
(3) Stopper rubber
(4) Rear damper

2. Compress each rear shock absorber spring, pull the upper joint upward and secure with the spring seat stops.

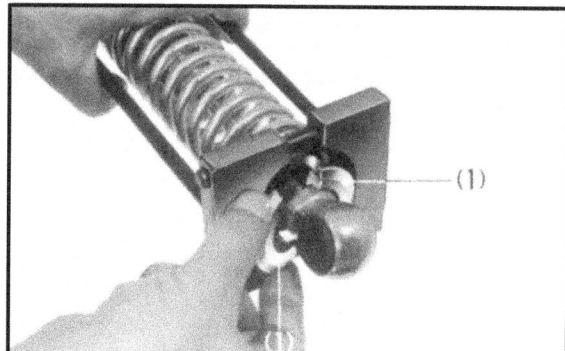

Fig. 5-80 (1) Spring seat stops
(2) Rear shock absorber compressor

3. Apply a coat of grease to the inside and outside of the rear fork center collar and to the inside of the rear fork bushing. Install the right and left dust seal caps and install the rear fork to the frame using the rear fork pivot bolt.
Apply a coat of grease to the rear fork pivot bolt.

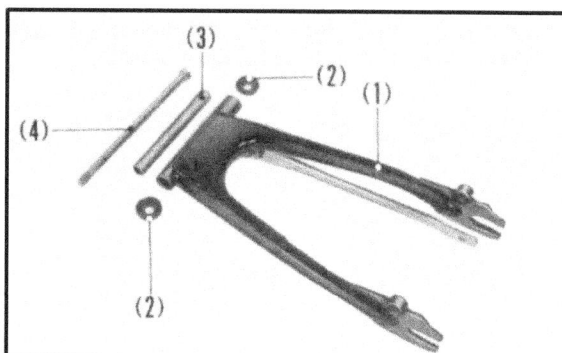

Fig. 5-81 (1) Rear fork
(2) Dust seal caps
(3) Rear fork center collar
(4) Pivot bolt

4. Install the right and left rear shock absorbers so that the adjusters (1) are in the same position. The standard installation position is the 1st groove mark.

Fig. 5-82 (1) Adjuster
(2) Pin spanner

V. FRAME

8. FRAME BODY AND OTHER RELATED PARTS

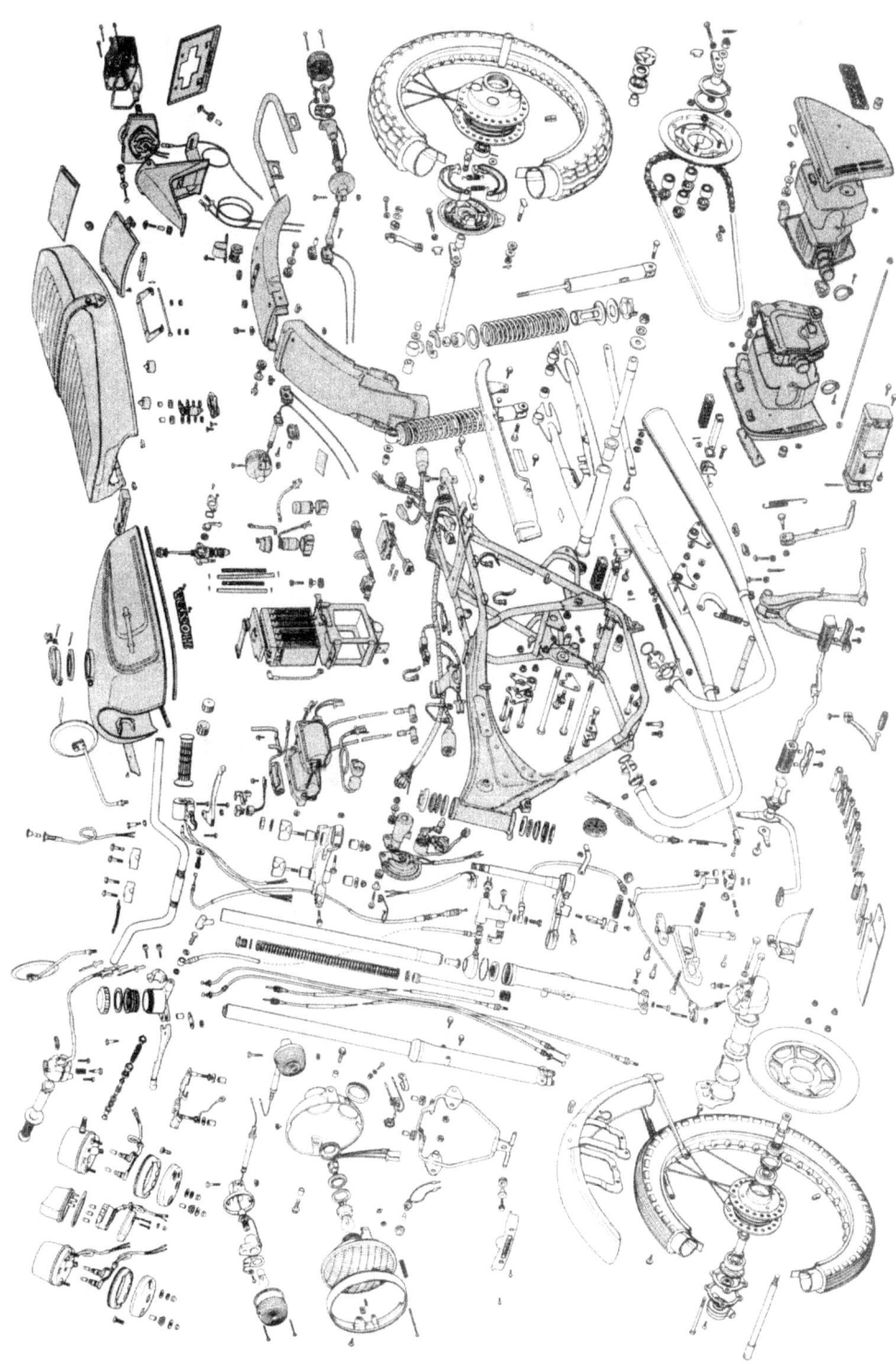

Fig. 5-83

Fuel valve and fuel tank cap

1. Drain the fuel tank and remove it.
2. Remove the fuel strainer cup, O-ring and strainer screen in this order. Remove the 6 mm screw and remove the fuel valve from the fuel tank.
3. Remove the 3 mm screws and remove the fuel valve lever set plate and valve lever.
4. Remove the fuel valve gasket.
5. To install, reverse the removal procedures.
6. Connect the fuel tubes and hold them securely with the clips.
7. Check the following items.
   * Contamination of fuel strainer screen
   * Weakness of fuel valve lever spring
   * Clogging of vent in fuel tank cap

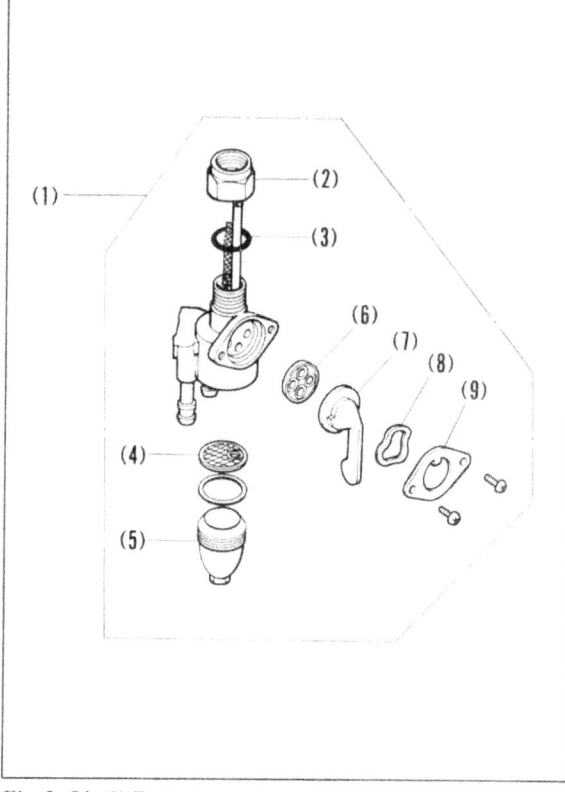

Fig. 5-84 (1) Fuel valve assy.   (6) Valve gasket
         (2) Valve joint nut   (7) Valve lever
         (3) Joint ring   (8) Valve lever spring
         (4) Screen   (9) Valve lever set plate
         (5) Fuel strainer cup

Air cleaner

1. Open the seat and remove the right and left side covers.
2. Remove the nut (2), bolt (3) and screw (4) and remove each air cleaner case.
3. Separate each air cleaner element from the air cleaner case.

Fig. 5-85 (1) Air cleaner case

4. Clean the air cleaner elements.

   Give a light tap to the air cleaner element to remove dirt and dust. If necessary, direct a blast of compressed air at the inner surface to blow off dirt and dust completely.

   CAUTION:
   If the air cleaner elements become oily or if they are broken, replace.

5. To install, reverse the removal procedures.

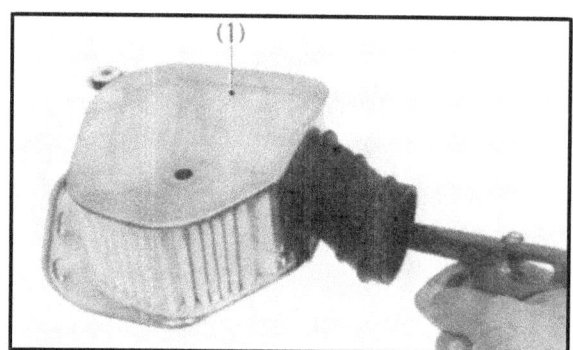

Fig. 5-86 (1) Air cleaner element

V. FRAME

Battery box and tool box

1. Remove the air cleaner assembly.
2. Remove the battery.
3. Disconnect the starting motor cable.
4. Disconnect the electrical part wires at the battery box.
5. Remove the three bolts (2) and the battery box can be removed.
6. Remove the electrical parts.

Fig. 5-87 (1) Battery box   (2) Bolts

7. Remove the four bolts (2) and remove the tool box.
8. To install, reverse the removal procedures.
   Install the electrical parts and connect the wires as shown in Fig. 5-89 below.

Fig. 5-88 (1) Tool box   (2) Bolts

Fig. 5-89
(1) Fuse box
(2) Fuse box leads
(3) Flasher relay
(4) Wire harness
(5) Starting magnetic switch
(6) Starting motor cable
(7) Battery case
(8) Silicon rectifier

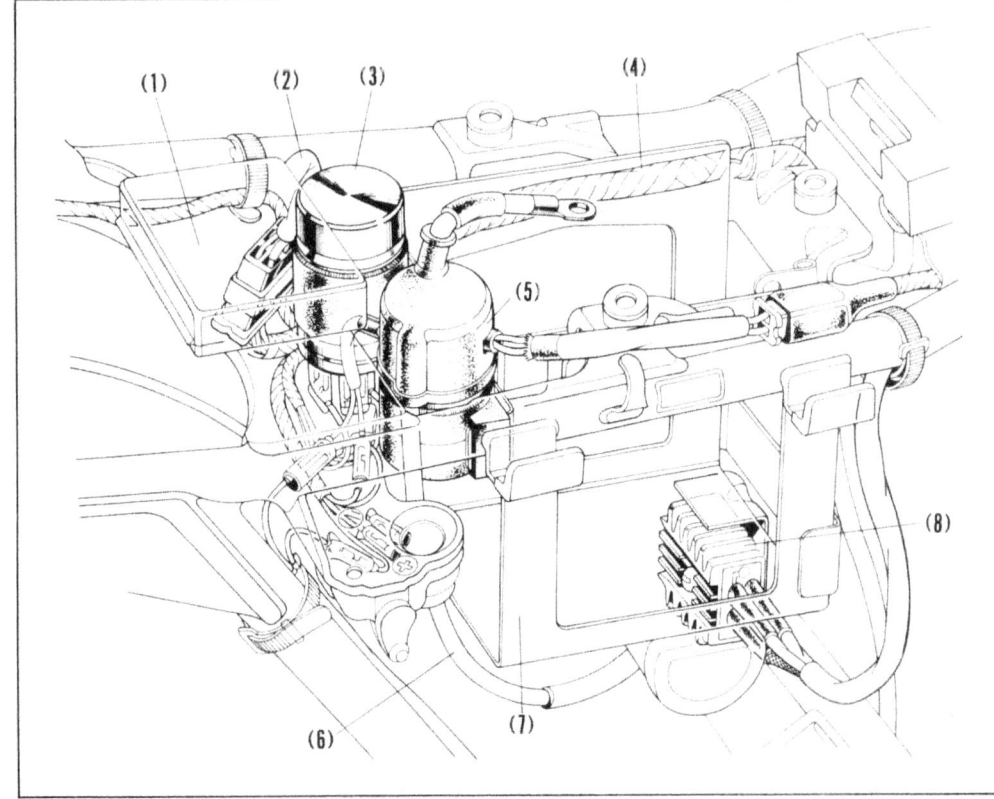

V. FRAME

Wire harness

1. Connect the wire harness as shown below.
   Hold the wire harness with one wire band at the position **20–30 mm (0.8–1.2 in.)** from the rear side of the fuel tank rear stay and with the other band at the position **10–20 mm (0.4–0.8 in.)** from the front side of the upper tube cross plate.

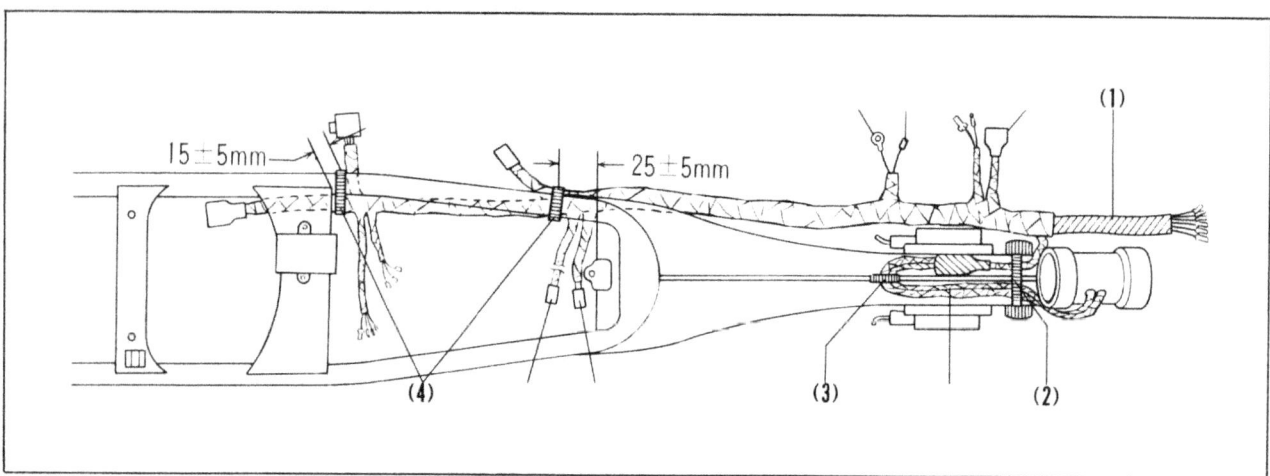

Fig. 5–90   (1) Wire harness   (3) Wire harness clip B
          (2) Wire harness clip A   (4) Wire band

VI. ELECTRICAL SYSTEM

1. CHARGING SYSTEM

The charging system consists essentially of a flywheel type AC generator, a silicon rectifier and a current limiter. Alternating current from the flywheel type rotor installed to crankshaft is converted into direct current (DC) by bridge-type silicon rectifier and then is fed to the battery. Upon battery voltage reaches $15.0 \pm 0.5V$, the regulator begins to actuate in order to bypass a surplus current, reducing the amount of charging current, to prevent the battery from being overcharged.

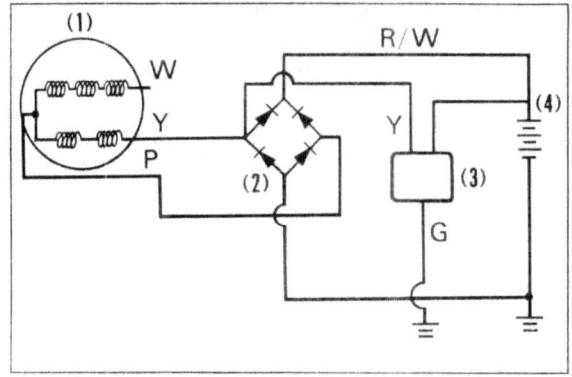

Fig. 6–1 (1) A.C. generator
(2) Silicon rectifier
(3) Regulator
(4) Battery

1. Charging test

1. Check charging current and voltage by means of voltmeter and ammeter.
2. Use a full-charged (12V-12AH) battery
   If the specific gravity is lower than 1.26 (at 20°C or 68°F), recharge battery so that the specific gravity is up to 1.27 ± 0.01 (at 20°C or 68°F).
3. Disconnect the battery cable from the + terminal of the battery, and connect it to the + side of ammeter. Then, connect the − side of the ammeter to the + terminal of battery. Next, connect the − side of voltmeter to the + terminal of battery and consequently + side to the − terminal as shown in Fig. 6–2.
4. Check a reading of ammeter and voltmeter during riding at night and in the day time in accordance with the specifications given below:
   NOTE:
   When checking, disconnect regulator cable.
5. Start the engine. Simulate the nighttime riding and daytime riding conditions and take the ammeter and voltmeter readings at each speed.
   Compare the readings with those in the table below.
   If the actual readings are very different from those in the table, check the generator for condition. The generator output may slightly vary with temperature.

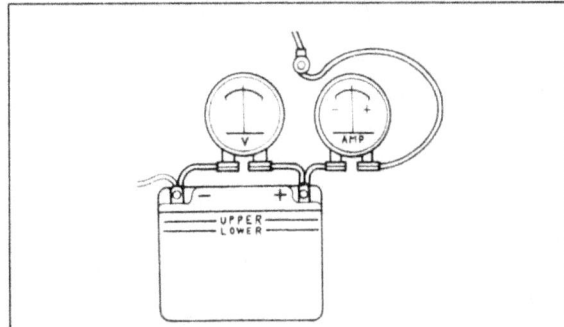

Fig. 6–2 Battery charging test

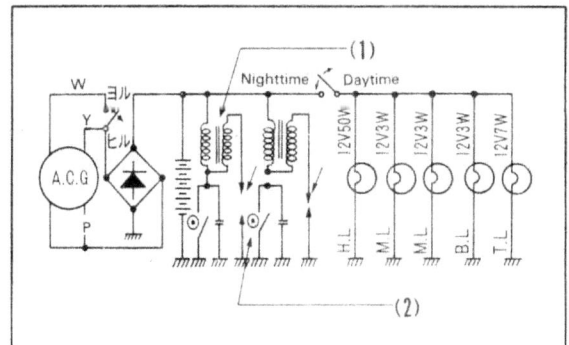

Fig. 6–3 Charging characteristics
(1) Ignition coil
(2) Contact breaker

Charging characteristics (without regulator)

	Load	Beginning of charging (rpm)	5,000 rpm	10,000 rpm
Daytime riding	Battery (12V12 AH) + ignition coil x 2	1,550 max. at battery voltage 12.6V	1.2A, min. at battery voltage 14.8V	4A, max. at battery voltage 15.5V
Nighttime riding	Load in daytime riding + 50W + 7W+3Wx3	2,100, max. at battery voltage 12.6V	1.2A, min. at battery voltage 14.8V	4A, max. at battery voltage 15.5V

2. A-C generator stator continuity test

Using a tester, check for the continuity between:
* White lead and stator
* Yellow lead and stator
* Pink lead and stator

If there is no continuity in any one of the cases above, replace the stator.

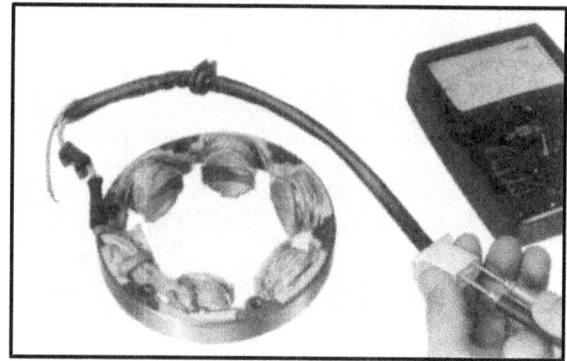

Fig. 6-4 Stator continuity test

Silicon diode rectifier

Check each diode for continuity with a radio tester in high-reading range. If current flows in forward direction (from cathode to anode) only, the diode is normal. Current flow in both directions or no current is a sign of the malfunction of the diode.

To determine that the rectifer is in good condition, follow the instructions given below. Connect the negative probe of the tester to the terminal (1) (green), and positive probe to the terminal (2) (red/white), (3) (yellow) or (4) (pink). If the needle swings, it is an indication that the diode is normal. In like manner as above, connect the positive probe to the terminal (2) (red/white), and negative probe to the terminal (1), (2) or (3). The diode is correct if continuity exists. Continuity should not exist between any terminals or combinations other than those described above.

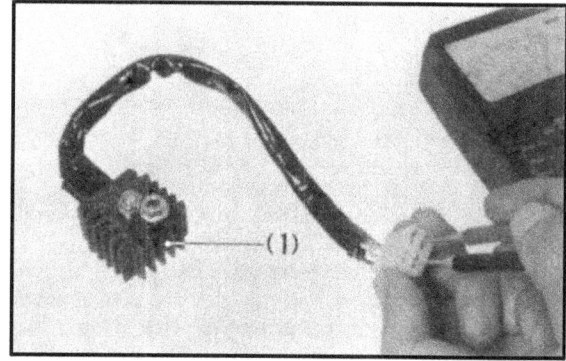

Fig. 6-5 Silicon rectifier

NOTE:
1. Do not use a megger for this test as the megger will generate high voltage to damage the diode.
2. Make sure of proper battery polarity when connecting. Connection in reverse polarity will shorten the battery service life or cause a high current flow throughout the electrical system, resulting in damage to the diodes or burning up the harness.

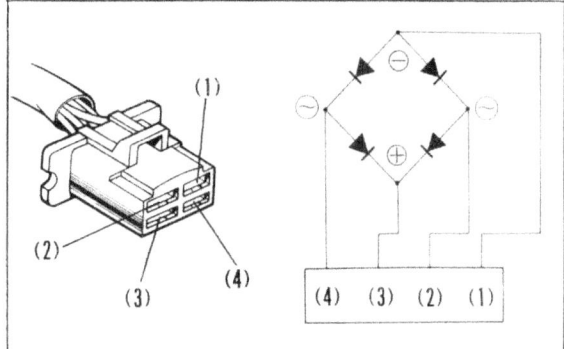

Fig. 6-6 (1) Green lead (3) Yellow lead
(2) Red/white lead (4) Pink lead

4. Battery
1. Specifications

Type	12N12A-4A (Yuasa)
Voltage	12V
Capacity	12AH

Fig. 6-7 (1) 12N12A-4A battery

VI. ELECTRICAL SYSTEM

2. Rate of charge

Use a suction type hydrometer. Place the glass tube vertical and slowly suck the electrolyte until it rises. Take the reading at the uppermost height of the electrolyte. If the specific gravity is below **1.200 (at 20 C or 68 F)**, recharge the battery.

3. Inspection and servicing
   a. Check the electrolyte level in each cell. If it is below the lower level mark, add the distilled water up to the upper level mark.
   b. Periodically measure the specific gravity of the electrolyte.
      When the distilled water has been added, thoroughly stir the electrolyte before measuring the specific gravity.
   c. Thoroughly check for poor contact due to the corroded connector and terminals, falling-off of the cell plates and sulphation which may be the major causes of the battery troubles.

4. Charging

Precautions for charging:
1. Try to avoid boost-charging the battery; otherwise, the service life of the battery may be shortened excessively. If the battery must be boost-charged, the charging current should not exceed 2.0A.
   Standard charging current 1.2A
   When recharging the battery with it mounted on the frame, remove the rectifier connector first.
2. While charging the battery, keep out of fire since hydrogen gas is emitted.
3. After charging, thoroughly wash out spilled electrolyte. Apply a coat of grease to the battery terminals.

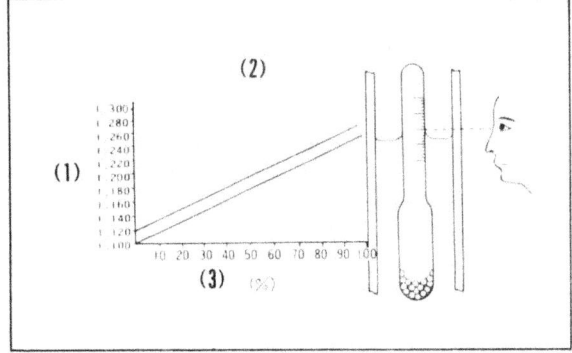

Fig. 6-8 (1) Specific gravity of electrolyte
(2) Relation between state of charge and specific gravity of electrolyte
(3) State of charge (%)

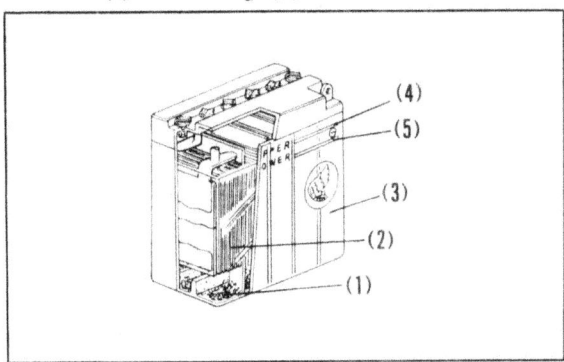

Fig. 6-9 (1) Sediment   (5) Lower level mark
(2) Plate
(3) Battery case
(4) Upper level mark

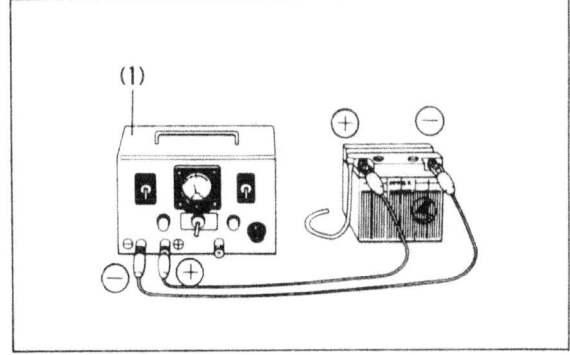

Fig. 6-10 (1) Charger

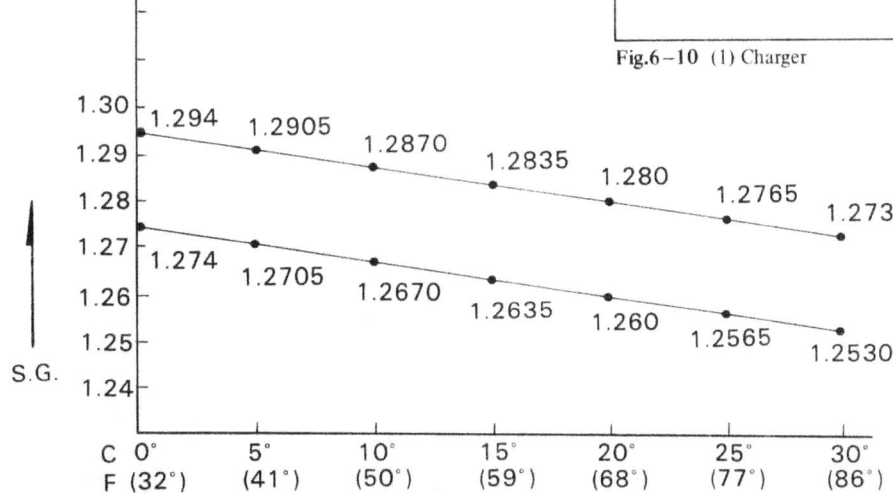

Relationship between atmospheric temperature and specific gravity

2. IGNITION SYSTEM

1. Ignition coil

Continuity test

(1) Primary winding

Check for the continuity between the attaching stay and primary winding (black/white lead) using a tester with the knob in the Ω range.

(2) Secondary winding

Check for the continuity between the attaching stay and high-tension cable using a tester with the knob in the ohm range.

If there is no continuity in the above tests, open circuit is in the ignition coil. Replace the coil.

Performance test

Even if there is a continuity in the ignition coil, the long use of the coil may result in the poor performance. If the engine fails to start, check the spark plugs, points, condenser, etc. for condition.

(1) Use a fully charged battery and service tester, and connect them.

(2) Turn the service tester selector knob to COIL TEST.

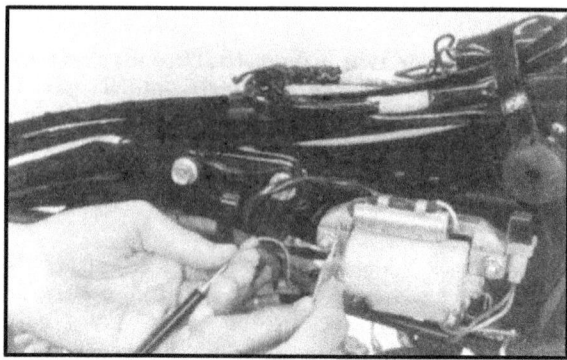

Fig. 6-11 Ignition coil continuity test

Fig. 6-12 Performance test

(3) Observing the spark jumping across a 3-point spark gap, turn the knob and measure the maximum jumping distance.

Specification: **7 mm (0.27 in.)**, min. If the spark appears in the form B in Fig. 6-13, connect the high-tension cable to the tester in the reverse direction and measure the jumping distance with the spark in the form A.

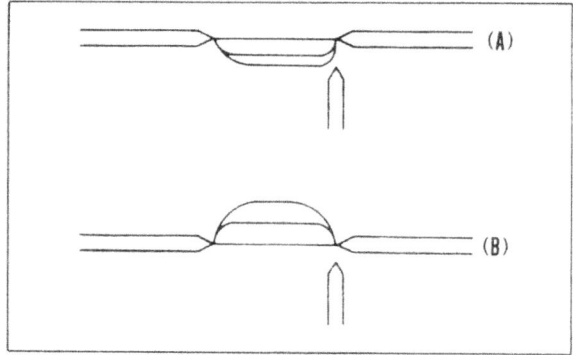

Fig. 6-13 Measuring distance of spark jumping across 3-point spark gap

2. Condenser

Using a service tester, measure the condenser capacity. Also check for short circuit. If the capacity or the insulation resistance is too small, replace the condenser.

Capacity: 0.25μF
Insulation: 10MΩ (by 1,000V megger)

Fig. 6-14 Condenser checking

VI. ELECTRICAL SYSTEM

3. Contact breaker

Check the points for wear or burning.

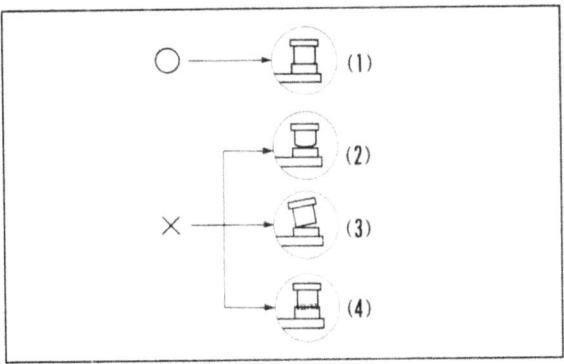

Fig. 6-15 Checking the contact breaker points
(1) Normal (3) Partial wear
(2) Wear   (4) Fouling

4. Spark advancer

1. Remove dust and foreign materials from the sliding surface and check for smooth operation.
2. Check the advance pin for wear.

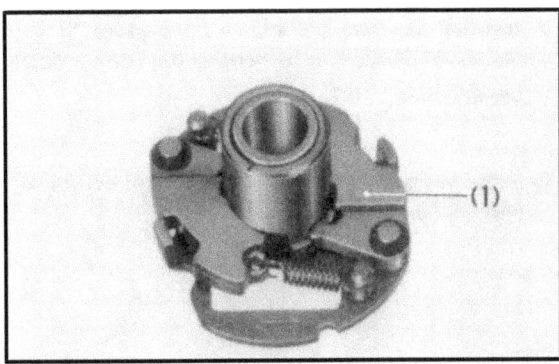

Fig. 6-16 (1) Spark advancer

3. Check the advance angle.
   Using a stroboscopic timing light, measure the speeds (in rpm) at the beginning and end of advance. (See page 18).

Fig. 6-17 (1) Timing light

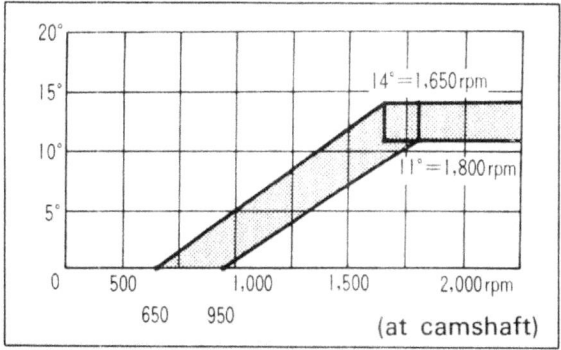

Fig. 6-18 Timing advance chart

VI. ELECTRICAL SYSTEM

5. Spark plugs

Check the spark plug electrodes for wear, improper gap and fouling. Also check the insulator of each plug for breakage.

1. Clean the plugs, if foul, with a plug cleaner or a wire brush.

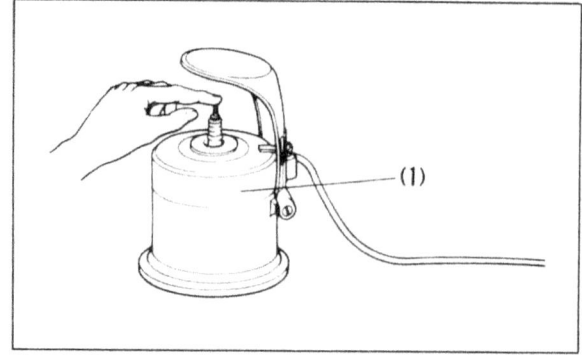

Fig. 6-19 (1) Plug cleaner

2. Measure the plug gap with a feeler gauge. If it is out of specification, adjust it by bending the side electrode.

   Specification: **0.7–0.8 mm**
   (0.028–0.032 in.)

3. If the insulators or gaskets are broken or deformed, replace.
   Specified plug: B8ES (NGK)
   W24ES (ND)

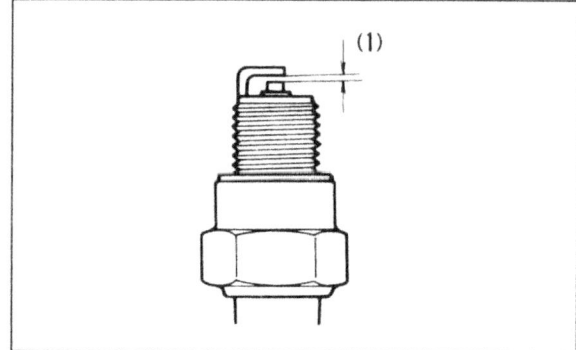

Fig. 6-20 (1) Plug gap

VI. ELECTRICAL SYSTEM

3. STARTING SYSTEM

When the starter switch on the right side of the handlebar is pressed, the starter magnetic switch is actuated to permit current of about 120A to flow from the battery into the starting motor.

1. Starting motor
   Specifications and characteristics

Rated voltage	12V
Rated output	0.45 KW
Rated hours	30 seconds

	Under no load	Under load	When locked
Voltage	9V	11V	5V
Current	35A	120A	280A
Torque	—	0.7 kg-m (5.061 lb-ft)	1.8 kg-m (13.0 lb-ft)
Speed	1,700 rpm	5,000 rpm	—

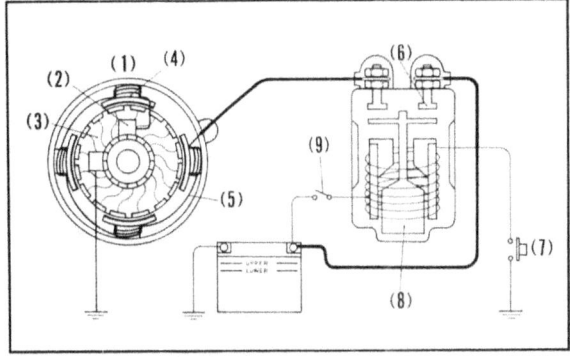

Fig. 6-21　(1) Starting motor　(6) Starting magnetic switch
　　　　　(2) Brushes　　　　(7) Starter button
　　　　　(3) Armature　　　 (8) Plunger
　　　　　(4) Poles　　　　　(9) Main switch
　　　　　(5) Field coil

Inspection

1. Carbon brushes

Check the brushes for wear, roughness of the contact surfaces or spring tension and replace if necessary.

	Standard	Service limit
Brush length	11.0–11.5 mm (0.43–0.45 in.)	Below 5.0 mm (0.20 in).
Brush spring tension	0.5–0.6 kg (1.10–1.32 lb)	Below 0.4 kg (0.88 lb)

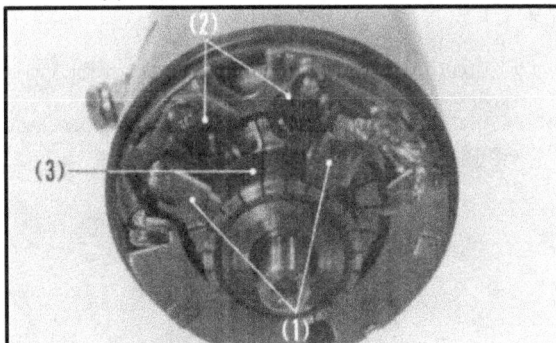

Fig. 6-22　(1) Carbon brush
　　　　　(2) Brush spring
　　　　　(3) Commutator

2. Commutator

Check the commutator surface for contamination. If necessary, recondition it with a fine emery paper and then clean.

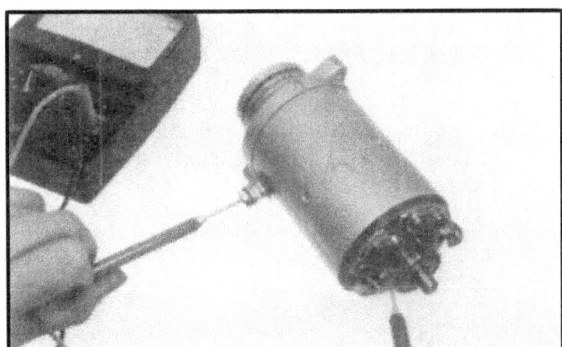

Fig. 6-23　Checking stator coil

3. Starter magnetic switch

The starting motor, because of its characteristics, draws a large current (above 100A) that exceeds the capacity of the starter switch. This needs thick wires to reduce the resistance in the starter circuit and the contact surface of the switch controlling such a large current must also be increased in area. If a large current is suddenly cut off, spark will be given out and some amount of resistance may also be applied to the circuit due to the pressure of the contact surface of the switch. This is the reason why an electromagnetic switch is provided in the circuit and thus the stater circuit is remote-controlled with a small current.

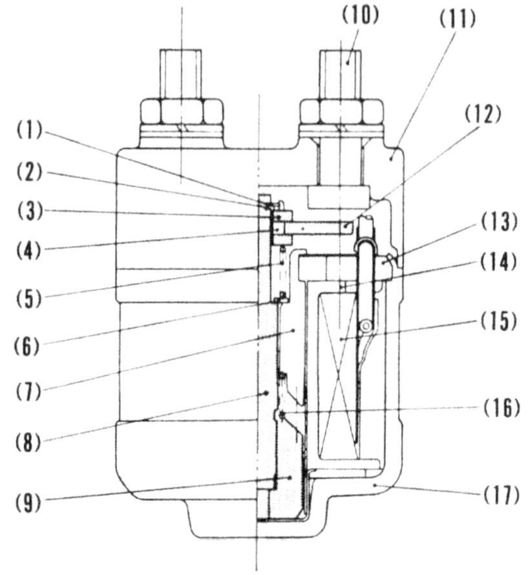

Fig. 6–24
(1) Stopper
(2) Stopper holder
(3) Washer
(4) Roller A
(5) Contact spring
(6) Flat washer
(7) Plunger holder
(8) Plunger shaft
(9) Plunger
(10) Contact bolt
(11) Case
(12) Contact plate
(13) Yoke
(14) Coil bobbin
(15) Coil
(16) Return spring
(17) Body

Inspection

1. Check the primary coil for continuity.
   If there is no continuity, the primary coil has an open circuit.
   If the coil clicks when 12 volts are applied across both terminals, it is in good condition.

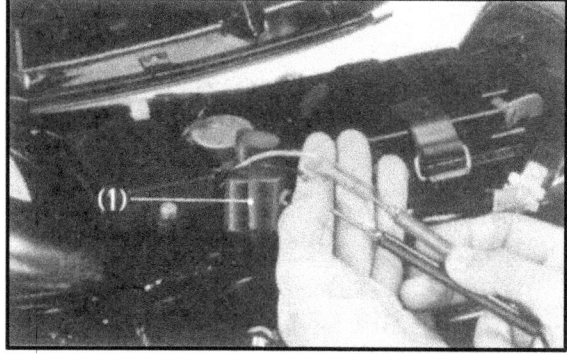

Fig. 6–25 (1) Starter magnetic switch

2. When the magnetic switch is used for a long time of period, the contact surfaces may be burnt to increase the resistance, preventing current from flowing.
   With 12 volts applied across the terminals of the primary coil, turn on the switch and check the terminals for continuity. If there is no continuity, the magnetic switch is defective.

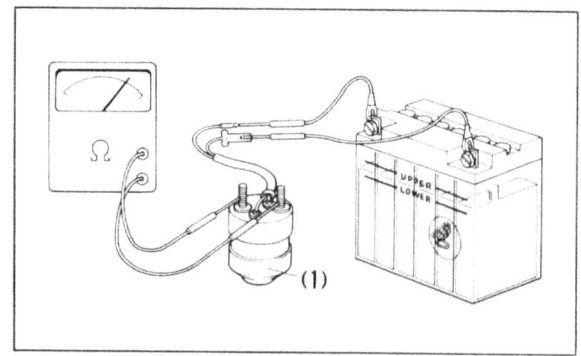

Fig. 6–26 (1) Starter magnetic switch

VI. ELECTRICAL SYSTEM

4. OTHER ELECTRICAL PARTS

1. Main switch

Check the switch for continuity at the key positions (ON and OFF). If there is a continuity between o—o in the table below, the switch is in good condition.

If there is no continuity or if there is a continuity between the other parts than o—o, the switch is defective.

	IG	B	TL1	TL2
OFF				
I	o—	—o	o—	—o
II		o—	—	—o
Leads color	Black	Red	Brown/white	Brown

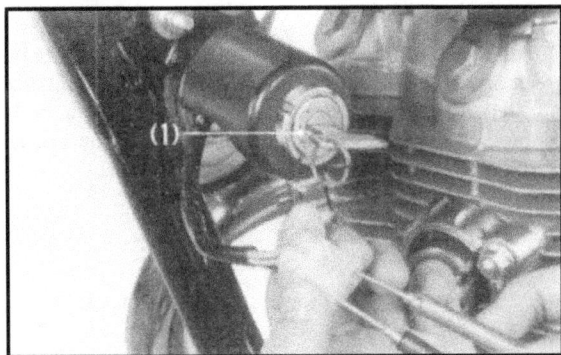

Fig. 6-27 (1) Main switch

2. Front stop switch

Attach the probes of a tester to the switch and check for continuity with the brake lever operated. The stop light should come on when the lever moves **5 to 10 mm (0.20 to 0.4 in.)** as measured at the tip of the lever.

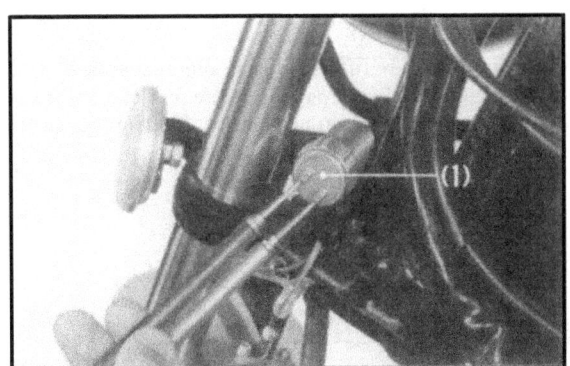

Fig. 6-28 (1) Front stop switch

3. Rear stop switch

Pull the rear stop switch spring to the end of the rear stop switch and check for continuity between the black and green/yellow leads. If there is no continuity, replace the switch. After checking, adjust the rear stop switch by turning the adjusting nut so that the stop light comes on when the brake pedal is depressed and moves about **20 to 30 mm (0.8 to 1.2 in.)** as measured at the tip of the pedal.

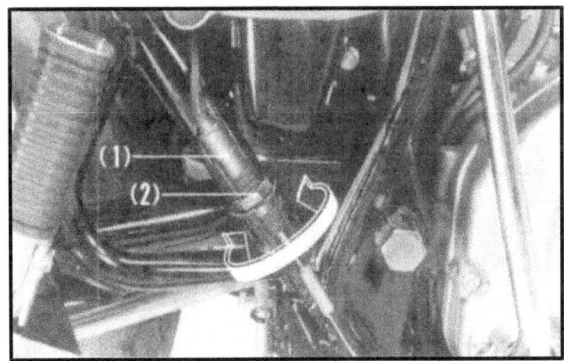

Fig. 6-29 (1) Rear stop switch
(2) Adjusting nut

4. Horn

Disconnect the leads inside the headlight case. Connect a 12V battery to the leads on the horn side and check for proper sound. If no abnormal conditions are found, check the horn button switch for condition.

Fig. 6-30 (1) Horn
(2) Horn leads

VI. ELECTRICAL SYSTEM

5. Horn button switch

Disconnect the horn/turn signal dimmer switch leads (yellowish green and green) from the frame and check for continuity using a tester. If there is a continuity only when the horn button is pushed, the switch is in good condition. If the switch has an open circuit or is broken, replace it.

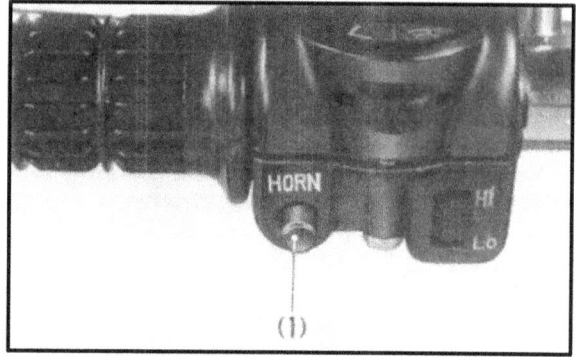

Fig. 6-31 (1) Horn button

6. Turn signal switch

Disconnect the horn/turn signal dimmer switch leads (gray, orange and sky-blue) from the frame and check for continuity at each knob position using a tester. If there is a continuity as shown below, the switch is in good condition.

	W	B	L	R
L2	O—	—O—	—O	
L1	O—	—	—O	
N				
R1	O—	—	—O	
R2	O—	—O—	—	—O
Leads color	Gray		Orange	Sky-blue

Fig. 6-32 Turn signal switch

7. Dimmer switch

Disconnect the horn/turn signal switch leads (blue/white, blue and white) from the frame and check for continuity at each knob position using a tester. If there is a continuity as shown below, the switch is in good condition.

	P	HL	Hi	Lo
Hi		O—	—O	
(N)	O—	—O—	—O—	—O
Lo	O—	—O—	—	—O
Leads color		Black/Yellow	Blue	White

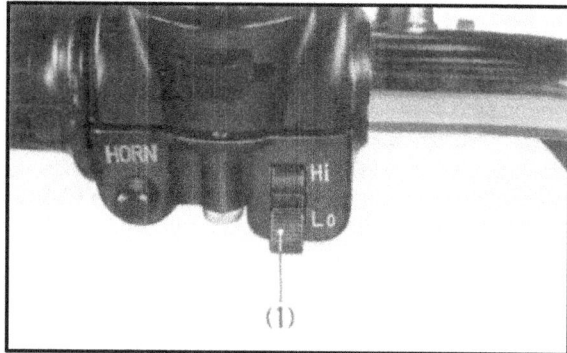

Fig. 6-33 (1) Dimmer switch

VI. ELECTRICAL SYSTEM

8. Ignition switch

Disconnect the ignition switch leads and check the leads on the switch side for continuity using a tester.
If there is a continuity as shown below, the switch is in good condition.

IG	KIL
Black	Black/white

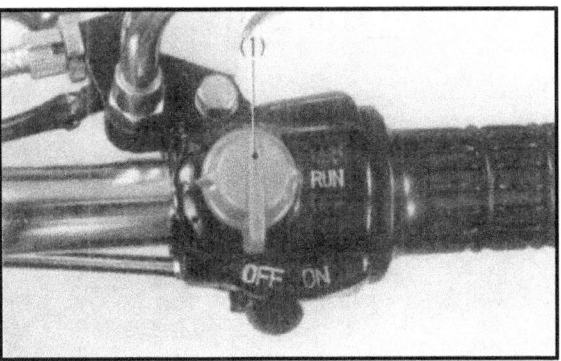

Fig. 6-34 (1) Ignition switch

9. Headlight switch

Disconnect the lighting switch leads from the frame and check the leads on the switch side for continuity at each knob position using a tester. If there is a continuity as shown below, the switch is in good condition.

	IG	TLI	HL	DY	SE
OFF					
ON	O—	—O—	—O	O—	—O
Leads color	Black	Brown/blue	Black/red	Yellow/white	Yellow

Fig. 6-35 (1) Headlight switch

10. Neutral switch

With the transmission in the neutral position, remove the left crankcase cover and check for continuity between the switch and crankcase using a tester. If there is a continuity in the neutral position only, the switch is in good condition.

VII. SERVICE DATA

1. SPECIAL TOOLS

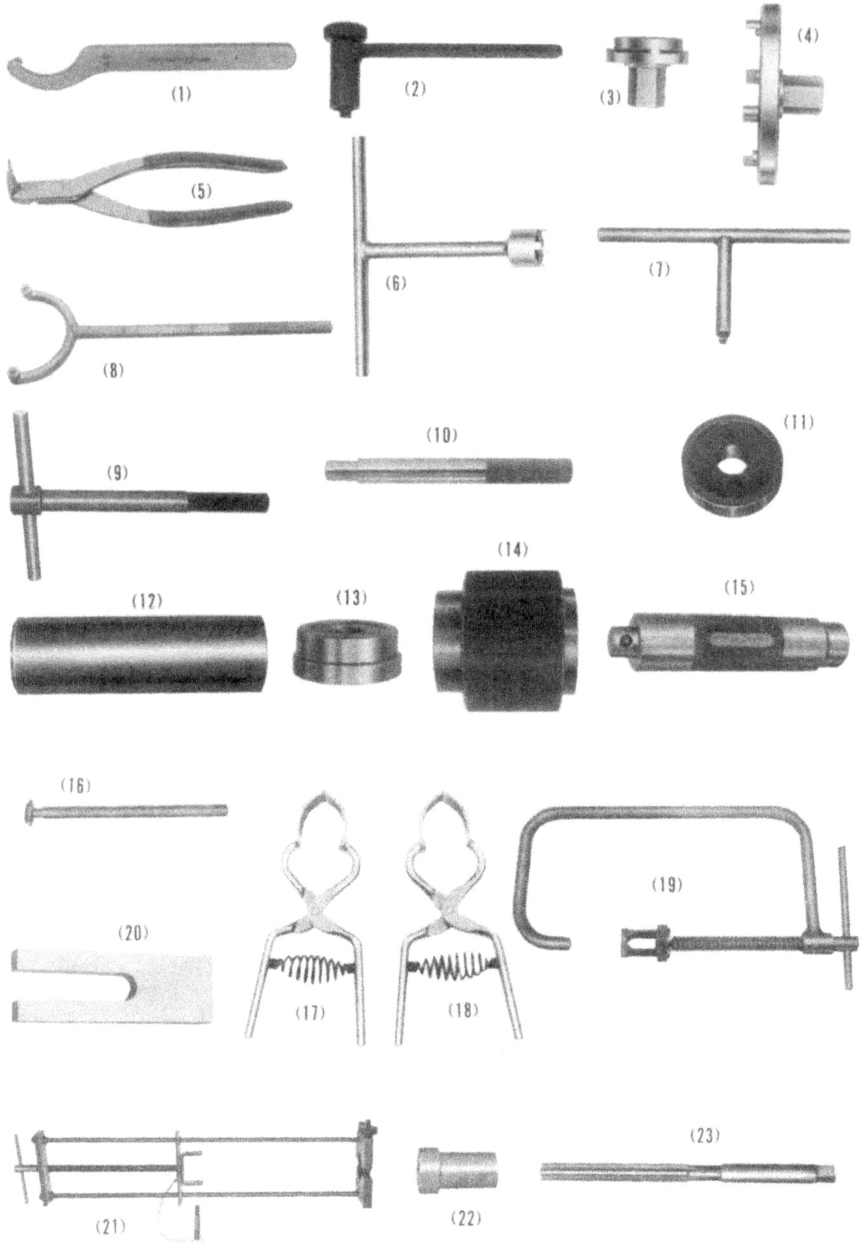

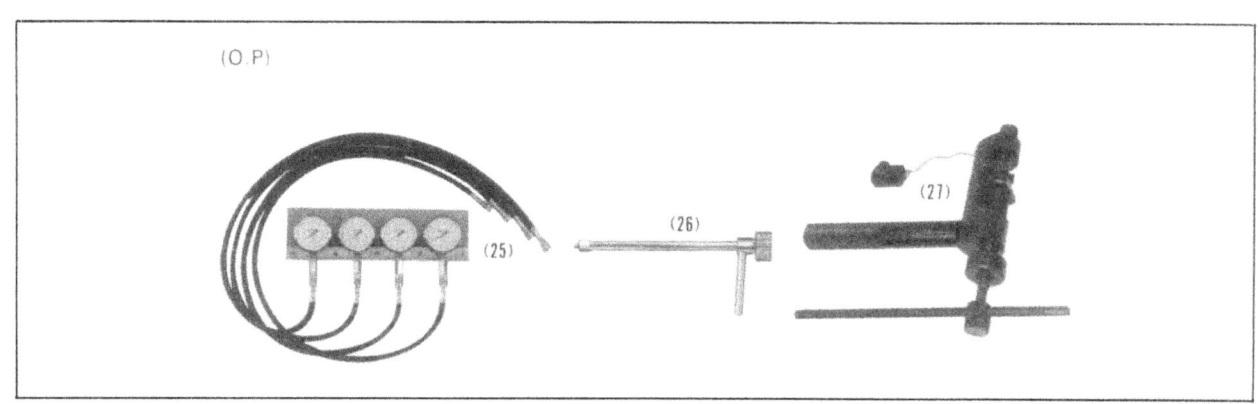

VII. SERVICE DATA

Ref. No.	Tool Part No.	Tool Name	Remarks
①	07902-2400000	Pin spanner, 46 mm	
②	07908-3230000	Tappet adjust wrench	
③	07910-3290000	Wrench, retainer (rear)	
④	07910-3230100	Wrench, retainer (front)	
⑤	07914-3230000	Pliers, snap ring	To disassemble and assemble master cylinder piston
⑥	07916-2830000	Wrench, lock nut, 16 mm	Oil filter rotor
⑦	07917-3230000	Wrench, set, hollow, 6 mm	To disassemble and assemble front fork
⑧	07922-3000000	Holder, drive sprocket	
⑨	07933-2160000	Puller, rotor	
⑩	07942-6110000	Driver, valve guide	To install and remove valve guide
⑪	07945-3330100	Attachment, driver	Wheel bearing (6302, 6303)
⑫	07945-3330200	Attachment, driver	Transmission bearing inner
⑬	07946-3290000	Driver, ball race	
⑭	07947-3330000	Driver, fork seal	
⑮	07949-6110000	Driver handle	For ⑪, ⑫ and ⑬
⑯	07953-3330000	Remover, ball race	
⑰	07954-3670000	Compressor, piston ring	For 250 cc
⑱	07954-3690000	Compressor, piston ring	For 360 cc
⑲	07957-3290000	Valve spring compressor	
⑳	07958-2500000	Piston base	
㉑	07959-3290000	Disassembler, rear shock absorber	
㉒	07974-3230200	Guide, piston cup	
㉓	07984-5900000	Valve guide reamer	
㉔	07797-2920300	Tool case	
OPTIONAL			
㉕	07504-3000100	Vacuum gauge set	For carburetor adjustment
㉖	07908-3690000	Wrench, carburetor	With ㉕
㉗	07975-3000001	Tool, drive chain	Drive chain
㉘	07510-3690100	Attachment, vacuum gauge	With ㉕

VII. SERVICE DATA

2. MAINTENANCE SCHEDULE

MAINTENANCE SCHEDULE This Maintenance Schedule is based upon average riding conditions. Machines subjected to severe use, or ridden in unusually dusty areas, require more frequent servicing.	INITIAL SERVICE PERIOD	REGULAR SERVICE PERIOD Perform at every indicated month or mileage interval, whichever occurs first.			
	500 miles	1 month 500 miles	3 months 1,500 miles	6 months 3,000 miles	12 months 6,000 miles
ENGINE OIL—Change.	●		○		
CENTRIFUGAL OIL FILTER—Clean.					○
OIL FILTER SCREEN—Clean.					○
SPARK PLUG—Clean and adjust gap or replace if necessary.				○	
*CONTACT POINTS AND IGNITION TIMING—Clean, check, and adjust or replace if necessary.	●			○	
*VALVE TAPPET CLEARANCE—Check, and adjust if necessary.	●			○	
*CAM CHAIN TENSION—Adjust.	●			○	
PAPER AIR FILTER ELEMENT—Clean.	(Service more frequently if operated in dusty areas)			○	
—Replace.					○
*CARBURETOR—Check, and adjust if necessary.	●			○	
THROTTLE OPERATION—Inspect cable. Check, and adjust free play.	●			○	
FUEL FILTER SCREEN—Clean.				○	
FUEL LINES—Check.				○	
*CLUTCH—Check operation, and adjust if necessary.	●			○	
DRIVE CHAIN—Check, lubricate, and adjust if necessary.	**●	○			
BRAKE FLUID LEVEL (only disc type)—Check and add fluid if necessary.	●			○	
*BRAKE SHOES/PADS—Inspect, and replace if worn.				○	
BRAKE CONTROL LINKAGE—Check linkage, and adjust free play if necessary.	●			○	
*WHEEL RIMS AND SPOKES—Check, tighten spokes and true wheels, if necessary.	●			○	
TIRES—Inspect and check air pressure.	●	○			
FRONT FORK OIL—Drain and refill.	***●				○
FRONT AND REAR SUSPENSION—Check operation.	●			○	
REAR FORK BUSHING—Grease, check for excessive looseness.				○	
*STEERING HEAD BEARINGS—Adjust.					○
BATTERY—Check electrolyte level, and add water if necessary.	●		○		
LIGHTING EQUIPMENT—Check and adjust if necessary.	●	○			
ALL NUTS, BOLTS, AND OTHER FASTENERS—Check security and tighten if necessary.	●	○			

Items marked * should be serviced by an authorized Honda dealer, unless the owner has proper tools and is mechanically proficient. Other maintenance items are simple to perform and may be serviced by the owner.

** Initial service period 200 miles.

*** Initial service period 1,500 miles.

VII. SERVICE DATA

3. TIGHTENING TORQUE STANDARD

Engine

Item	Size (mm)	Torque kg-m	Torque lbs-ft
R.L. crankcase cover bolt	6	0.7–1.1	5.1–8.0
Cylinder head hold-down bolt	10	3.0–3.4	21.7–24.6
Cylinder head insulator bolt	6	0.7–1.1	5.1–8.0
Camshaft sprocket fixing bolt	7	1.8–2.2	13.1–15.2
A.C. generator mounting bolt	8	3.0–3.5	21.7–25.3
Oil filter lock nut	16	4.5–5.5	32.6–39.7
Crankcase mounting bolt	6	0.9–1.2	6.5–8.7
	8	2.0–2.3	14.5–16.6

Frame

Item	Size (mm)	Torque kg-m	Torque lbs-ft
Steering stem nut	24	7.0–9.0	50.7–65.1
Fork bolt	27	2.5–3.0	18.1–21.7
Handlebar holder attaching bolt	8	1.8–2.5	13.1–18.1
Front fork bottom bridge	8	1.8–2.5	13.1–18.1
Spoke		0.15–0.20	1.1–1.5
Rear fork pivot bolt	14	5.5–7.0	39.7–50.7
Front fork axle nut	12	5.5–6.5	39.7–47.0
Front fork under holder	8 UBS	2.7–3.3	19.5–23.8
Engine hanger bolt	8 UBS	2.7–3.3	19.5–23.8
Engine hanger bolt	10 UBS	4.0–5.5	29.0–39.7
Rear axle	16	8.0–10.0	57.9–72.3
Final driven sprocket	10 UBS	6.0–7.0	43.4–50.7
Brake arm	8	1.8–2.5	13.1–18.1
Rear brake stopper arm	8	1.8–2.5	13.1–18.1
Rear shock absorber	10	3.0–4.0	21.7–29.0
Foot rest	10 UBS	4.0–5.5	29.0–39.7
Change pedal	6	0.8–1.2	5.8–8.7
Seat band	6	0.8–0.95	5.8–6.9
Kick arm	8	2.5–3.0	18.1–21.7

4. MAINTENANCE STANDARDS

Engine

Unit: mm (in.)   [ ]: 360 cc only

Items to be inspected		Standard	Service Limit
Rocker arm-to-rocker arm shaft clearance		0.016–0.061 (0.0006–0.0024)	0.1 (0.0039)
Cam lift	IN.	40.314 (1.5872)	40.1 (1.5787)
	EX.	40.339 (1.5882)	40.1 (1.5787)
Camshaft side clearance		0.07–0.3 (0.0028–0.0118)	Above and below standards
Valve seat width		1.0–1.3 (0.0394–0.0512)	2.0 (0.0787)
O.D. of valve stem	IN.	6.975–6.990 (0.2746–0.2752)	6.93 (0.2728)
	EX.	6.955–6.970 (0.2738–0.2744)	6.93 (0.2728)
Valve-to-valve guide clearance	IN.	0.01–0.035 (0.0004–0.0014)	6.93 (0.2728)
	EX.	0.03–0.05 (0.0012–0.0020)	0.09 (0.0035)
Valve spring tension/ as compressed length	INNER	30.5–35.1 kg/31 (67.24–77.38 lbs/1.2205)	—
	OUTER	62.6–72.0 kg/31 (138.01–158.73 lbs/1.2205)	—
Free length of valve spring	INNER	39.8 (1.5669)	39.3 (1.5709)
	OUTER	49.0 (1.9291)	47.8 (1.8819)
Transverse warpage on cylinder head mating face		—	0.3 (0.0118)
I.D. of cylinder		56.01–56.02 (2.2051–2.2055) [67.01–67.02 (2.6382–2.6386)]	56.1 (2.2087) [67.1 (2.6417)]
O.D. of piston at skirt		55.97–55.99 (2.2036–2.2043) [66.97–66.99 (2.6366–2.6374)]	55.85 (2.1988) [66.85 (2.6319)]
Piston pin hole I.D.		15.002–15.008 (0.5906–0.5909) [16.002–16.008 (0.6300–0.6302)]	15.05 (0.5925) [16.05 (0.6319)]
O.D. of piston pin		14.994–15.00 (0.5903–0.5906) [15.994–16.00 (0.6297–0.6299)]	14.9 (0.5866) [15.9 (0.6260)]
Piston ring-to-ring groove clearance	TOP	0.02–0.06 (0.0008–0.0024)	0.15 (0.0059)
	SECOND	0.015–0.045 (0.0006–0.0018) [0.02–0.04 (0.0008–0.0016)]	0.15 (0.0059) [0.15 (0.0059)]
	OIL	0.010–0.045 (0.0004–0.0018)	0.15 (0.0059)
Piston ring end gap	TOP	0.15–0.35 (0.0059–0.0138) [0.2–0.4 (0.0079–0.0157)]	0.75 (0.0295) [0.8 (0.0315)]
	SECOND	0.15–0.35 (0.0059–0.0138)	0.75 (0.0295)
	OIL	0.2–0.4 (0.0079–0.0157)	0.8 (0.0315)
Oil pump outer rotor-to-pump body clearance		0.15–0.21 (0.0059–0.0083)	0.35 (0.0138)
Radial clearance of oil pump outer rotor		0.02–0.08 (0.0008–0.0032)	0.1 (0.0039)
Thickness of clutch friction disc		2.62–2.78 (0.1031–0.1095)	2.3 (0.9055)
Transverse warpage on clutch plate		0.1 (0.0039)	0.2 (0.0079)
Clutch spring tension		25/21.8–23.2 kg (0.984/48.06–51.15 lbs)	—
Free length of clutch spring		31.25 (1.2305)	29.7 (1.1693)
Gear shift fork width, A and B		5.93–6.00 (0.2335–0.2362)	5.5 (0.2165)
O.D. of gear shift guide shaft		12.957–12.984 (0.5101–0.5112)	12.9 (0.5079)

VII. SERVICE DATA

Items to be inspected	Standard	Service Limit
I.D. of gear shift fork A	13.000–13.018 (0.5118–0.5125)	12.95 (0.5098)
O.D. of gear shift drum	39.950–39.975 (1.5374–1.5384)	39.9 (1.5709)
I.D. of gear shift fork B	40.000–40.025 (1.5748–1.5758)	40.075 (1.5798)
Kick starter pinion-to-shaft clearance	0.04–0.082 (0.0016–0.0032)	0.1 (0.0039)
Gear shift fork-to-drum clearance (A and B)	0.05–0.22 (0.0020–0.0087)	0.3 (0.0118)
Thickness of cam chain tensioner slipper (at center)	4.0 (0.1575)	3.0 (0.1181)
Thickness of cam chain guide (at center)	6.1–6.3 (0.2402–0.2480)	5.0 (0.1969)
Crankshaft runout (See Fig. 4-101 on page 62)	———	Below 0.1 (0.0039)
I.D. of connecting rod small end	15.016–15.034 (0.5912–0.5919) [16.016–16.034 (0.6306–0.6313)]	15.07 (0.5933) [16.07 (0.6327)]
Connecting rod big end side clearance on pin	0.07–0.33 (0.0028–0.0130)	0.60 (0.0236)
Connecting rod big end radial clearance on pin	0.004–0.012 (0.0002–0.0005)	0.05 (0.0020)

Frame

Items to be inspected	Standard	Service Limit
Wheel rim surface runout	0.5 (0.0197) max.	2.0 (0.787)
Wheel bearing axial play	0.07 (0.0276) max.	0.1 (0.0039)
Wheel bearing radial play	0.03 (0.0012) max.	0.05 (0.0020)
Front axle bend	0.01 (0.0004)	0.2 (0.0079)
Transverse warpage on front brake disc	0.05 (0.0020)	0.3 (0.0118)
Thickness of front brake disc	6.9–7.1 (0.2717–0.2795)	6.0 (0.2362)
I.D. of caliper cylinder	38.18–38.20 (1.5032–1.5039)	38.215 (1.5045)
O.D. of caliper piston	38.115–38.18 (1.5006–1.5032)	38.105 (1.5002)
I.D. of master cylinder	14.000–14.043 (0.5512–0.5529)	14.055 (0.5534)
O.D. of master cylinder piston	13.957–13.984 (0.5495–0.5506)	13.940 (0.5488)
Rear axle bend	0.01 (0.0004)	0.2 (0.0079)
Thickness of brake lining	4.9–5.0 (0.1929–0.1969)	2.5 (0.098)
I.D. of rear brake drum	160.0–160.3 (6.2992–6.3110)	161 (6.3386)
Free length of front suspension spring	478.6 (18.843)	468.0 (18.425)
I.D. of front fork bottom case	33.025–33.064 (1.3002–1.3017)	33.139 (1.3047)
O.D. of front fork pipe	32.97–32.985 (1.2980–1.2986)	32.25 (1.2697)
Free length of rear suspension spring	207.6 (8.1732)	
O.D. of rear fork center collar	21.427–21.460 (0.8436–0.8449)	21.46 (0.8449)
I.D. of rear fork bushing	21.5–21.552 (0.8465–0.8485)	21.70 (0.8543)

VII. SERVICE DATA

5. TROUBLE SHOOTING

Engine

Trouble	Probable cause	Remedy
Engine does not start	1. Insufficient compression pressure	
	1) Incorrect tappet adjustment	Adjust
	2) Worn valve guide or improper valve seating	Replace or repair
	3) Incorrect valve timing	Adjust
	4) Worn piston rings	Replace
	5) Worn cylinder	Replace
	2. No sparking at spark plug and contact point	
	1) Dirty spark plug	Clean
	2) Wet spark plug	Clean
	3) Dirty contact breaker point	Clean
	4) Improper point gap	Adjust
	5) Incorrect ignition timing	Adjust
	6) Defective ignition coil	Replace
	7) Disconnection or short circuit of ignition cord	Replace
	8) Short circuit in condenser	Replace
	3. Fuel does not flow to carburetor	
	1) Clogged vent hole in tank cap	Clean
	2) Clogged fuel valve	Clean
	3) Defective carburetor float valve	Replace
	4) Clogged fuel feed pipe	Clean
Engine stalls soon	1. Dirty spark plug	Clean
	2. Dirty contact breaker point	Clean
	3. Incorrect ignition timing	Adjust
	4. Clogged fuel feed pipe	Clean
	5. Clogged carburetor jet	Clean
	6. Incorrect tappet adjustment	Adjust
Noisy engine	1. Noisy tappet	
	1) Large tappet clearance	Adjust
	2) Loss of valve spring tension	Replace
	2. Piston knocking	
	1) Worn piston ring or cylinder	Replace
	2) Carbon accumulated in combustion chamber	Clean
	3) Worn piston pin or connecting rod small end	Replace
	3. Cam chain	
	1) Stretched cam chain	Replace or adjust cam chain tensioner
	2) Worn cam sprocket or timing sprocket	Replace
	4. Noisy clutch	
	1) Loose clutch center spline	Replace
	2) Excessive clearance between clutch friction disc and teeth of clutch outer housing	Replace
	3) Warped friction disc or clutch plate	Replace or repair
	5. Crankshaft	
	1) Worn crankshaft bearing	Replace
	2) Worn connecting rod big end	Replace
	6. Noisy gear	
	1) Worn transmission gear or interference between gears	Replace
	2) Worn spline	Replace
	3) Worn primary gear or interference between gears	Replace

VII. SERVICE DATA

Trouble	Probable cause	Remedy
Clutch slips	1. Improper clutch adjustment (no play in clutch lever) 2. Weak clutch pressure plate spring 3. Worn or warped pressure plate 4. Warped clutch plate 5. Worn or warped friction disc	Adjust Replace Replace Replace Replace
Clutch will not be disengaged	1. Improper clutch adjustment (excessive play of clutch lever) 2. Weak or non-uniform tension of clutch springs 3. Warped clutch plate	Adjust clutch lever Replace weak spring Replace
Difficult gear shifting	1. Deformed shift drum stopper 2. Broken gear shift drum 3. Deformed gear shift fork	Repair or replace Replace Repair or replace
Change gear slips out position	1. Worn shifting gears on main shaft and countershaft 2. Worn or bent gear shift fork 3. Weak shift drum stopper spring	Replace Repair or replace Replace
Engine idling is not stable	1. Improper tappet adjustment 2. Improper seating of cylinder head valve 3. Defective valve guide 4. Incorrect ignition timing 5. Faulty contact breaker point 6. Excessive spark plug gap 7. Weak ignition spark (defective condenser or ignition coil) 8. Improper carburetor float level 9. Incorrect carburetor air screw adjustment	Adjust Replace or repair Replace Adjust Repair Repair Replace Adjust Adjust
Engine high speed running is not stable	1. Weak valve spring 2. Incorrect valve timing 3. Insufficient spark plug gap 4. Retarded ignition timing 5. Weak point arm spring 6. Defective ignition coil 7. Improper carburetor float level adjustment (low level) 8. Clogged air cleaner element 9. Insufficient fuel in carburetor	Replace Adjust Adjust Adjust Replace Replace Adjust Clean Clean or supply fuel
Exhaust smoke from muffler	1. Excessive engine oil 2. Worn cylinder and piston rings 3. Worn valve guide 4. Defective cylinder	Adjust oil level Check with level gauge Replace Replace Replace
Loss of power	1. Incorrect tappet adjustment 2. Loss of valve spring tension 3. Incorrect valve timing 4. Worn cylinder and piston 5. Improper valve seating 6. Incorrect ignition timing 7. Defective contact breaker point 8. Incorrect spark plug gap 9. Clogged carburetor main or slow jet nozzle 10. Improper float level adjustment 11. Clogged air cleaner	Adjust Replace Adjust Replace Replace Adjust Repair or replace Repair Clean Adjust Clean

Trouble	Probable cause	Remedy
Engine overheating	1. Heavy carbon deposit on cylinder head 2. Insufficient engine oil 3. Defective oil pump, or clogged oil passage 4. Too lean gas mixture 5. Advanced ignition timing (knocking)	Decarbonize Supply to normal level Clean Adjust Adjust

Frame

Trouble	Probable cause	Remedy
Hard steering	1. Over-tightened steering stem 2. Damaged steering stem steel balls 3. Bent steering stem 4. Low tire inflation pressure 5. Over-tightened steering cone race	Adjust Replace Replace Adjust Adjust
Motorcycle pulls to one side	1. Unequal tension of left and right suspension springs 2. Bent front fork 3. Bent front axle, or incorrect alignment of wheel	Replace Repair or replace Replace or repair
Front wheel wobbles	1. Deformed rim 2. Worn front wheel bearings 3. Loose spoke 4. Defective tire 5. Loose front axle 6. Improper balance	Replace Replace Retighten Replace Retighten Rebalance
Soft front suspension	1. Loss of spring tension 2. Insufficient damper oil	Replace Add oil
Hard front suspension	1. High viscosity of damper oil 2. Excessive damper oil	Change Adjust
Noisy front suspension	1. Interference between shock absorber case and spring 2. Damaged shock absorber stopper rubber 3. Insufficient damper oil	Replace Replace Adjust
Rear wheel wobbles	1. Distorted rim 2. Worn rear wheel bearings 3. Loose spoke 4. Defective tire	Replace Replace Retighten Replace
Soft rear suspension	1. Loss of spring tension 2. Improper rear shock absorber adjuster adjustment	Replace Adjust
Hard rear suspension	Improper rear shock absorber adjuster adjustment	Adjust
Noisy rear suspension	1. Interference between shock absorber case and spring 2. Loose installation	Replace Retighten
Poor braking	1. Poor contact of brake shoe 2. Brake lining is contaminated with oil or grease 3. Loose brake cable or worn brake pedal shaft 4. Improper brake adjustment	Replace or repair Replace Repair or adjust Adjust
No adjusting allowance	1. Worn brake shoe 2. Worn brake shoe cam 3. Improperly engaged brake arm serration 4. Worn brake cam	Replace Replace Replace Replace
Brake squeals when applied	1. Worn brake shoe 2. Foreign matter sticking to brake shoe surface 3. Hardened brake shoe surface 4. Bent or twisted brake shoe	Replace Clean or replace Replace Replace

VII. SERVICE DATA

Electrical

Trouble	Probable cause	Remedy
No or poor sparking	1. Defective ignition coil 2. Defective spark plug	Replace Replace
Burned contact breaker point	Defective condenser	Replace
Spark plug electrode fouled with carbon	1. Too rich gas mixture 2. Poor quality of gasoline 3. Clogged air cleaner 4. Use of cold spark plug	Adjust carburetor Change Clean Use proper heat range plug
Spark plug electrode fouled with oil	1. Worn piston rings 2. Worn piston or cylinder 3. Excessive clearance between valve guide and valve	Replace rings Replace piston or cylinder Replace
Spark plug electrode overheated or burnt	1. Use of hot spark plug 2. Engine overheating 3. Incorrect ignition timing 4. Loose spark plug 5. Too lean gas mixture	Use proper heat range plug Adjust Retighten Adjust carburetor
No charging	1. Broken wire or shorted or loose connection 2. Defective generator coil due to short circuit, or grounding 3. Defective silicon diode 4. Shorted or broken lead wire of regulator	Repair or replace Replace Replace Repair or replace
Insufficient charging	1. Wiring · Broken or shorted wire, or loose connection 2. Generator · Shorting across layers in stator coil · Open circuit in stator coil · Defective silicon diode 3. Regulator · Voltage below specified value at no load · Coil or resistor internally shorted 4. Battery · Low electrolyte level · Defective battery plates	Repair or retighten Replace Replace Replace Replace Replace Add distilled water to normal level
Excessive charging	1. Battery internally shorted 2. Regulator · Excessive voltage at no load · Improper grounding · Broken coil lead wire	Repair Replace Ground properly Repair or replace
Unstable charging voltage	1. Wire shorting intermittently under vibration 2. Generator layer shorting 3. Regulator · Intermittent open circuit in coil · Improperly adjusted voltage · Defective key switch · Dirty points	Repair or replace Repair or replace Repair or replace Replace Replace Clean

VII. SERVICE DATA

6. SPECIFICATIONS

Item	CB250 (General type)		
DIMENSION			
Overall length	2,040 mm (80.3 in.)		**2,085 mm (82.1 in.)
Overall width	775 mm (30.5 in.)	* 800 mm (31.5 in.)	** 800 mm (31.5 in.)
Overall height	1,125 mm (44.3 in.)	*1,070 mm (42.1 in.)	**1,070 mm (42.1 in.)
Wheel base	1,345 mm (53.0 in.)		
Seat height	810 mm (31.9 in.)		
Ground clearance	160 mm (6.3 in.)		
Dry weight	162 kg (357 lbs)	*165 kg (364 lbs)	**165 kg (364 lbs)
FRAME			
Type	Semi-double cradle		
F. suspension, travel	Telescopic fork, 114.5 mm (4.5 in.)		
R. suspension, travel	Swing arm, 77.6 mm (3.1 in.)		
F. tire size, pressure	3.00-18-4PR, 1.8 kg/sq. cm (26 psi)		
R. tire size, pressure	3.50-18-4PR, 2.0 kg/sq. cm (28 psi)		
F. brake	Internal expanding shoes/Disc brake		
R. brake	Internal expanding shoes		
Fuel capacity	11.0 lit. (2.7 U.S. gal., 2.2 Imp. gal.)		
Fuel reserve capacity	2.5 lit. (0.7 U.S. gal., 0.6 Imp. gal.)		
Caster angle	62.5°		
Trail length	92 mm (3.6 in.)		
ENGINE			
Type	Air cooled, 4-stroke, O.H.C. engine		
Cylinder arrangement	Vertical, twin parallel		
Bore and stroke	56.0 × 50.6 mm (2.204 × 1.992 in.)		
Displacement	249 cc (15.2 cu. in.)		
Compression ratio	9.5 : 1		
Valve train	Chain driven over head camshaft		
Oil capacity	2.0 lit. (2.1 U.S. qt., 1.8 Imp. qt.)		
Lubrication system	Forced and wet sump		
Intake valve — Opens	At 5° (before top dead center)		
Intake valve — Closes	At 40° (after bottom dead center)		
Exhaust valve — Opens	At 40° (before bottom dead center)		
Exhaust valve — Closes	At 5° (after top dead center)		
Valve tappet clearance	IN : 0.05 mm (0.002 in.), EX : 0.08 mm (0.03 in.)		
Idle speed	1,200 rpm		
DRIVE TRAIN			
Clutch	Wet, multi-plate type		
Transmission	6-speed, constant mesh		
Primary reduction	3.714		
Gear ratio I	2.500		
Gear ratio II	1.750		
Gear ratio III	1.375		
Gear ratio IV	1.111		
Gear ratio V	0.965		
Gear ratio VI	0.866		
Final reduction	2.375		
Gear shift pattern	Left foot operated return system		
ELECTRICAL			
Ignition	Battery and ignition coil		
Starting system	Starting motor and kick starter		
Alternator	A.C. generator, 0.13 kW/5,000 rpm		
Battery capacity	12V-12AH		
Spark plug	NGK B 8ES, ND W 24ES		

* Indicates specification of U.K. type.

** Indicates specification of European type.

VII. SERVICE DATA

Item		CB360 (U.S.A. and general type)	CL360
DIMENSION			
Overall length		2,040 mm (80.3 in.) **2,085 mm (82.1 in.)	2,040 mm (80.3 in.)
Overall width		775 mm (30.5 in.) * 800 mm (31.5 in.) ** 800 mm (31.5 in.)	820 mm (32.3 in.)
Overall height		1,125 mm (44.3 in.) *1,070 mm (42.1 in.) **1,070 mm (42.1 in.)	1,115 mm (43.9 in.)
Wheel base		1,345 mm (53.0 in.)	1,345 mm (53.0 in.)
Seat height		810 mm (31.9 in.)	810 mm (13.0 in.)
Ground clearance		160 mm (6.3 in.)	160 mm (6.3 in.)
Dry weight		162 kg (357 lbs) *165 kg (364 lbs) **165 kg (364 lbs)	162 kg (357 lbs)
FRAME			
Type		Semi-double cradle type	Semi-double cradle type
F. suspension, travel		Telescopic fork, 114.5 mm (4.5 in.)	Telescopic fork, 114.5 mm (4.5 in.)
R. suspension, travel		Swing arm, 77.6 mm (3.1 in.)	Swing arm, 77.6 mm (3.1 in.)
F. tire size, pressure		3.00-18-4 PR, 1.8 kg/sq. cm (26 psi)	3.00-18-4 PR, 1.8 kg/sq. cm (26 psi)
R. tire size, pressure		3.50-18-4 PR, 2.0 kg/sq. cm (28 psi)	3.50-18-4 PR, 2.0 kg/sq. cm (28 psi)
F. brake		Disc brake	Internal expanding shoes
R. brake		Internal expanding shoes	Internal expanding shoes
Fuel capacity		11.0 lit. (2.7 U.S. gal., 2.2 Imp. gal.)	9.0 lit. (2.4 U.S. gal., 2.0 Imp. gal.)
Fuel reserve capacity		2.5 lit (0.7 U.S. gal., 0.6 Imp. gal.)	1.8 lit. (0.5 U.S. gal., 0.4 Imp. gal.)
Caster angle		62.5°	62.5°
Trail length		92 mm (3.6 in.)	92 mm (3.6 in.)
ENGINE			
Type		Air cooled, 4-stroke, O.H.C. engine	
Cylinder arrangement		Vertical, twin parallel	
Bore and stroke		67.0 × 50.6 mm (2.638 × 1.992 in.)	
Displacement		356 cc (21.7 cu-in.)	
Compression ratio		9.3 : 1	
Valve train		Chain driven overhead camshaft	
Oil capacity		2.0 lit. (2.1 U.S. qt., 1.8 Imp. qt.)	
Lubrication system		Forced and wet sump	
Intake valve	Opens	At 5° (before top dead center)	
	Closes	At 40° (after bottom dead center)	
Exhaust valve	Opens	At 40° (before bottom dead center)	
	Closes	At 5° (after top dead center)	
Valve tappet clearance		IN : 0.05 mm (0.002 in.), EX : 0.08 mm (0.003 in.)	
Idle speed		1,200 rpm	
DRIVE TRAIN			
Clutch		Wet, multi-plate type	
Transmission		6-speed, constant mesh	
Primary reduction		3.714	
Gear ratio I		2.500	
Gear ratio II		1.750	
Gear ratio III		1.375	
Gear ratio IV		1.111	
Gear ratio V		0.965	
Gear ratio VI		0.866	
Final reduction		2.125	
Gear shift pattern		Left foot operated return system	
ELECTRICAL			
Ignition		Battery and ignition coil	
Starting system		Starting motor and kick starter	
Alternator		A.C. generator, 0.13 kW/5,000 rpm	
Battery capacity		12V–12AH	
Spark plug		NGK B 8ES, ND W 24ES	

* Indicates specifications of U.K. type.
** Indicates specifications of European type.

VII. SERVICE DATA

7. WIRING DIAGRAM

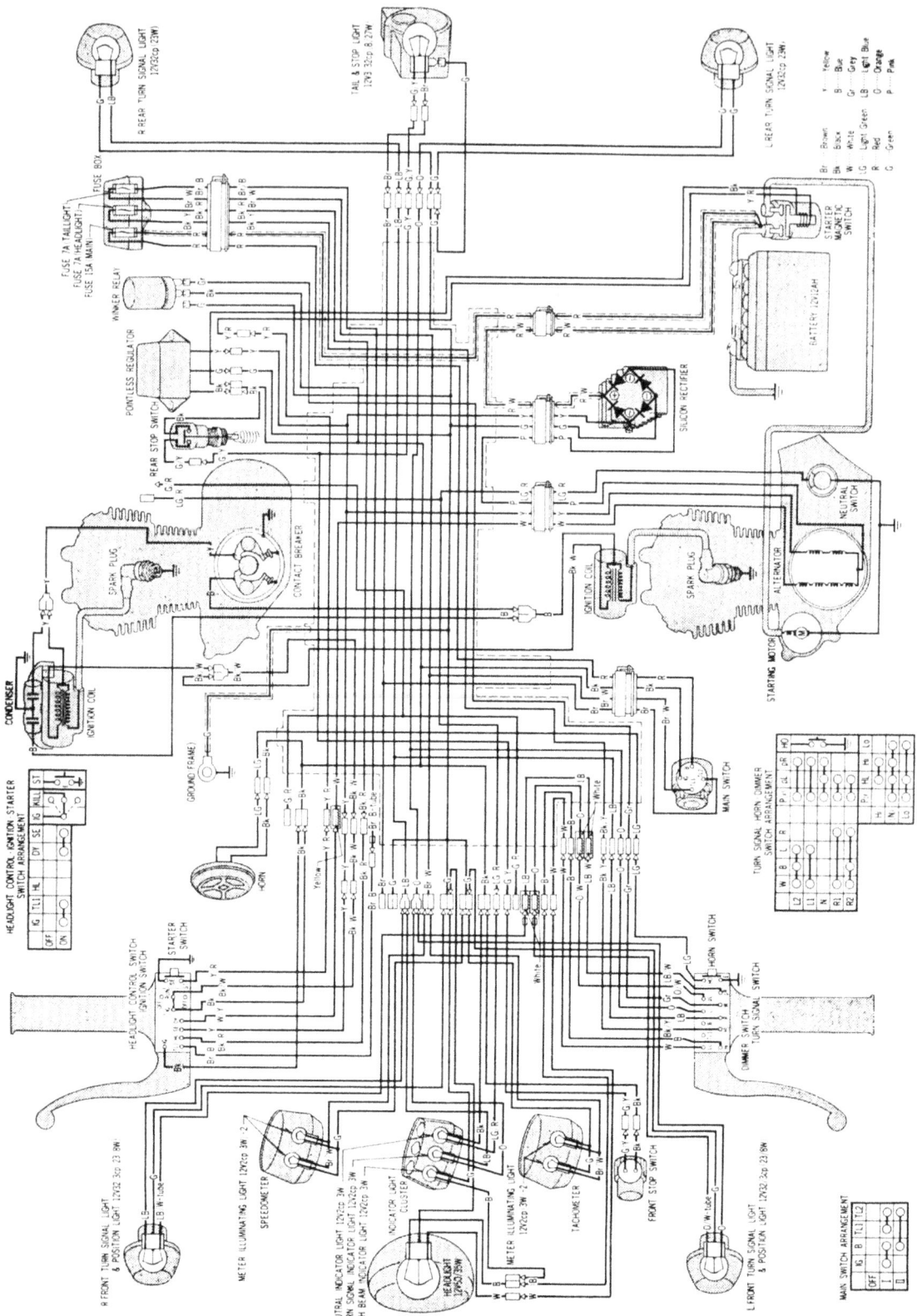

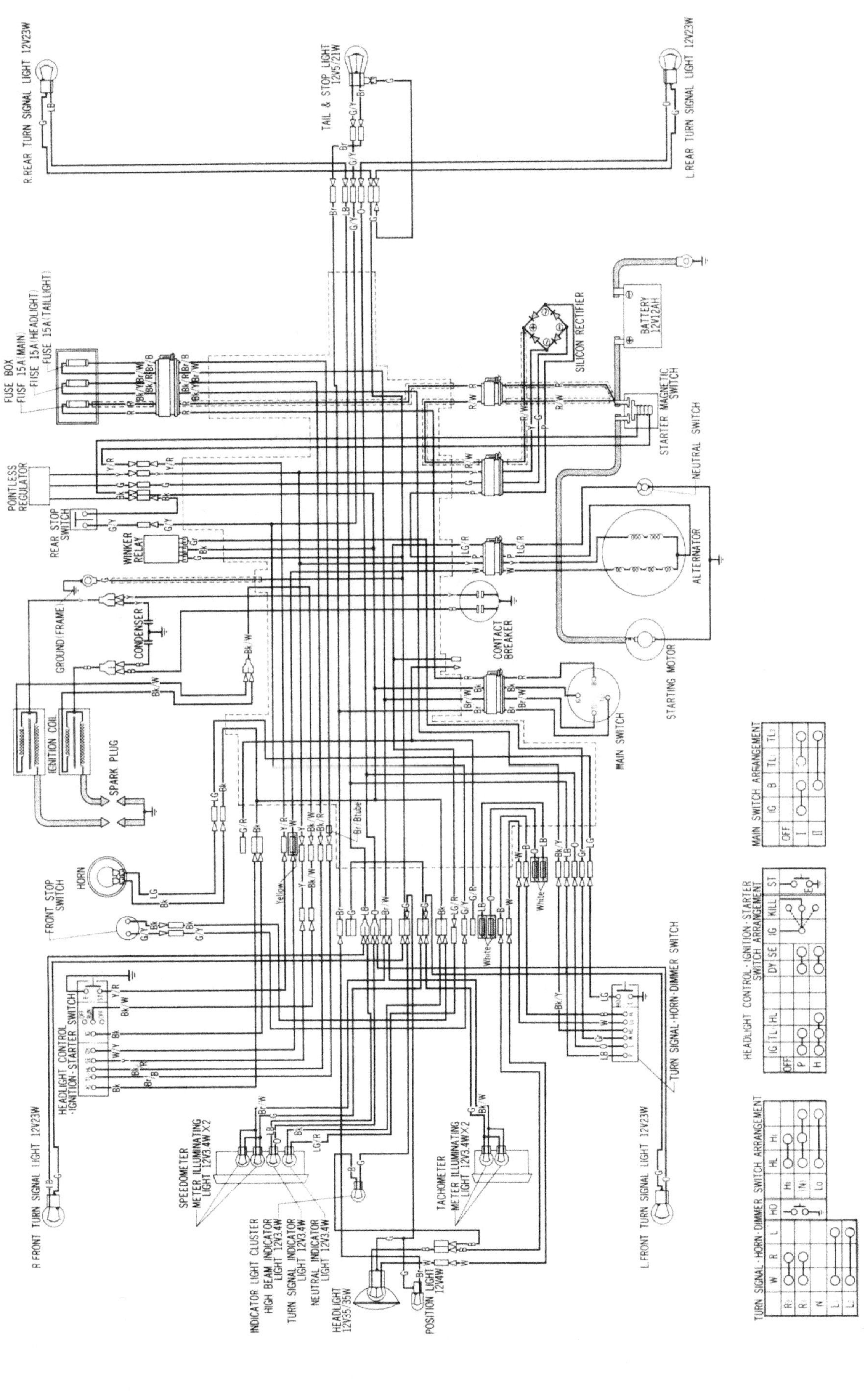

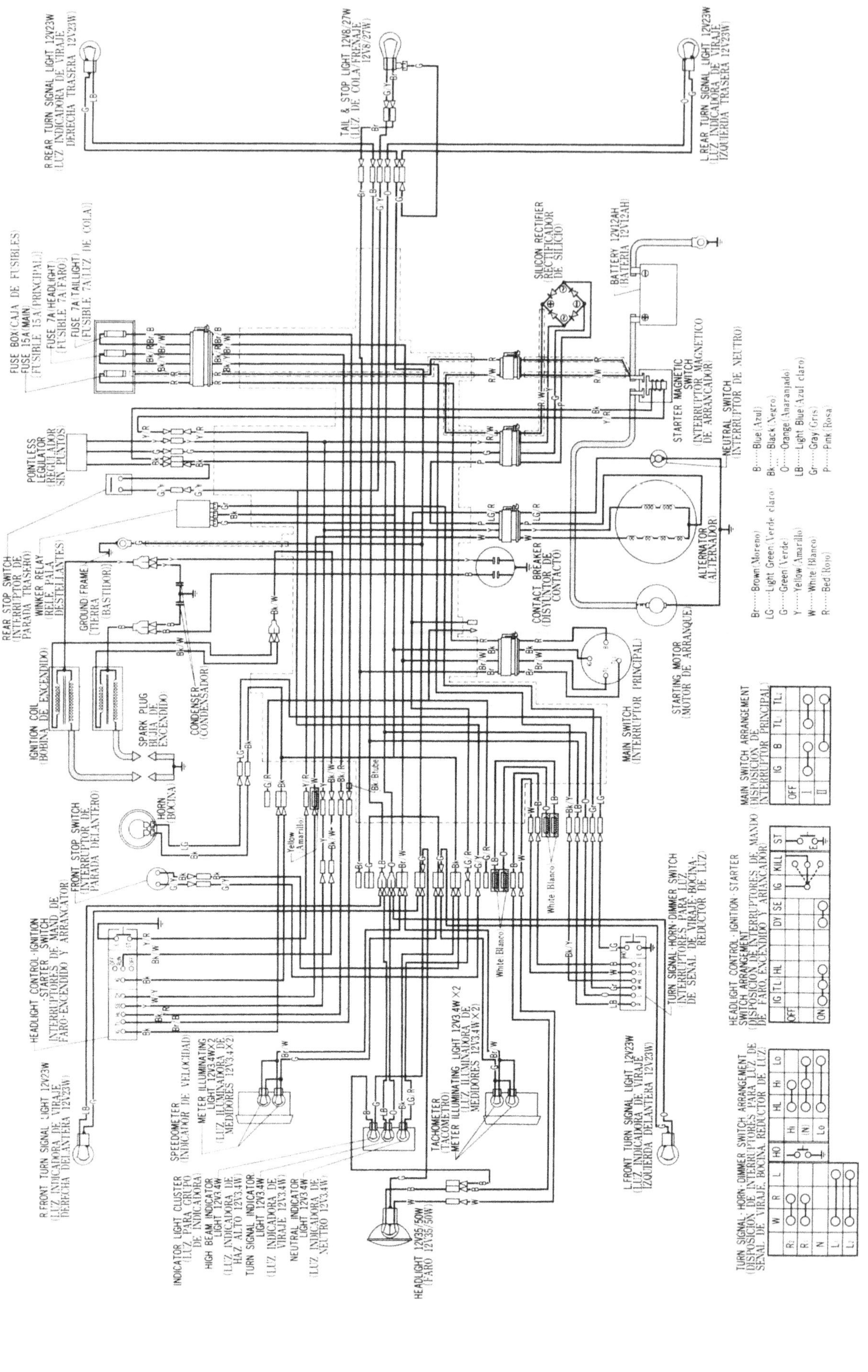

VII. SERVICE DATA

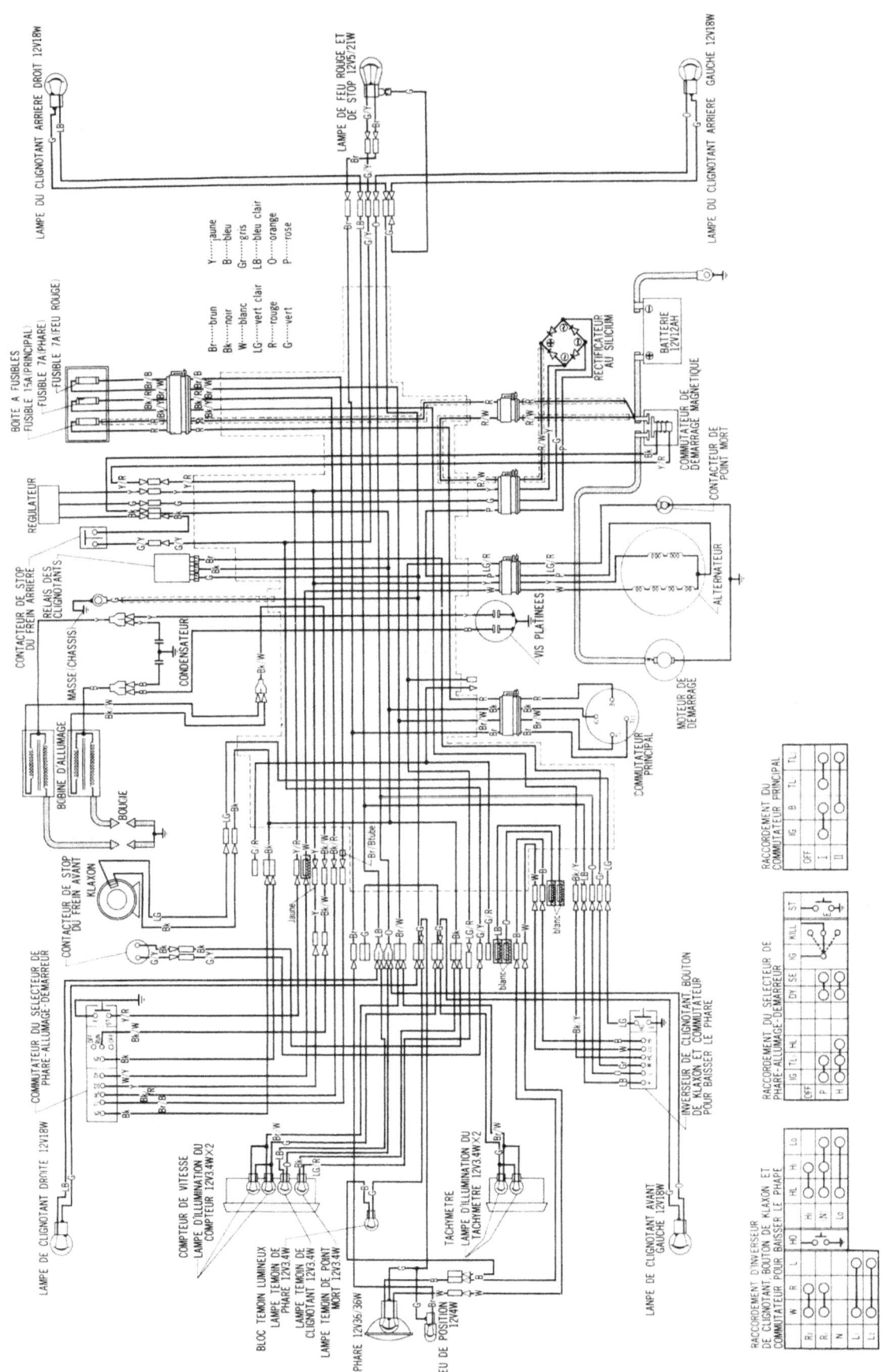

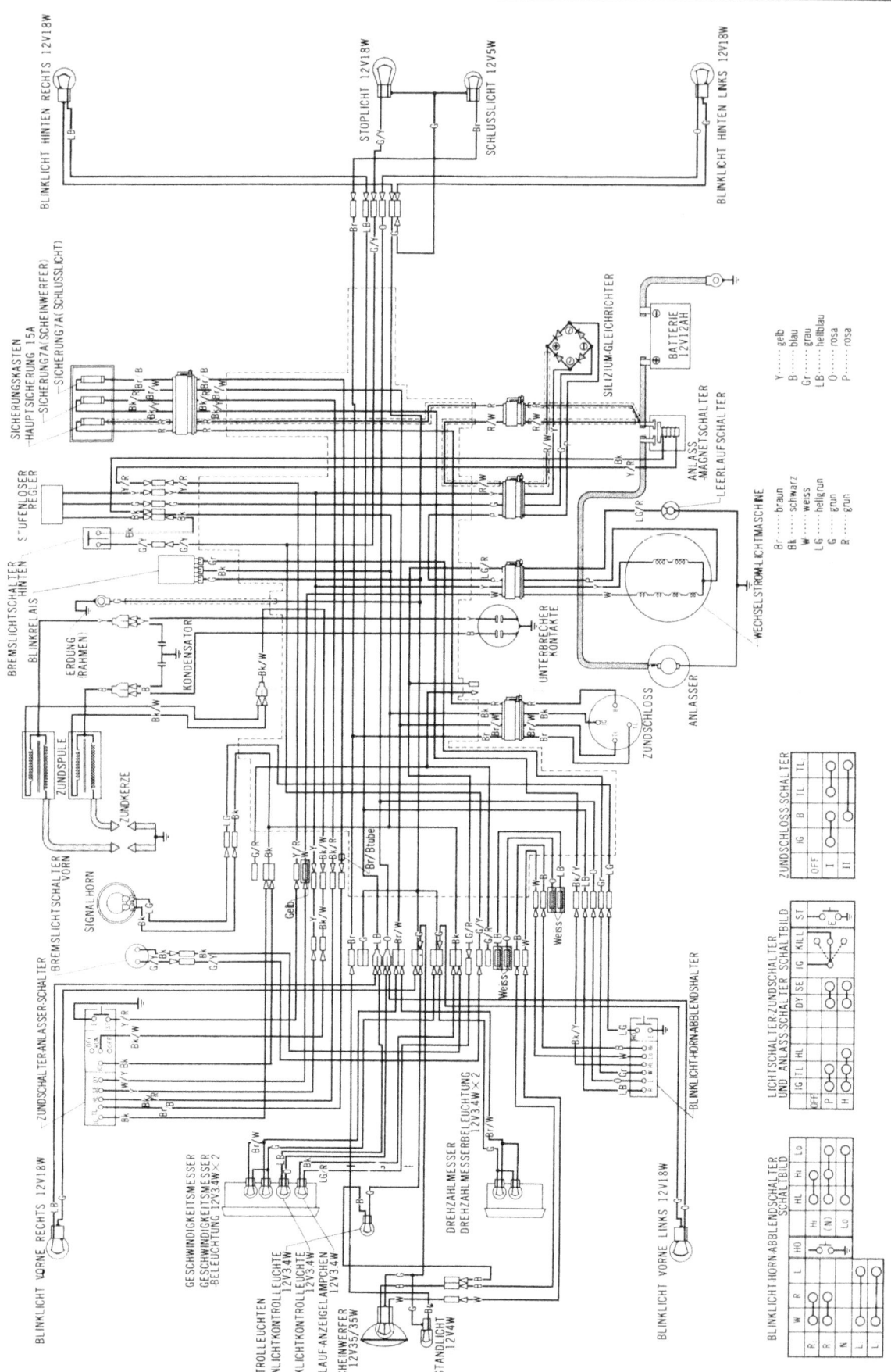

VII. SERVICE DATA

125

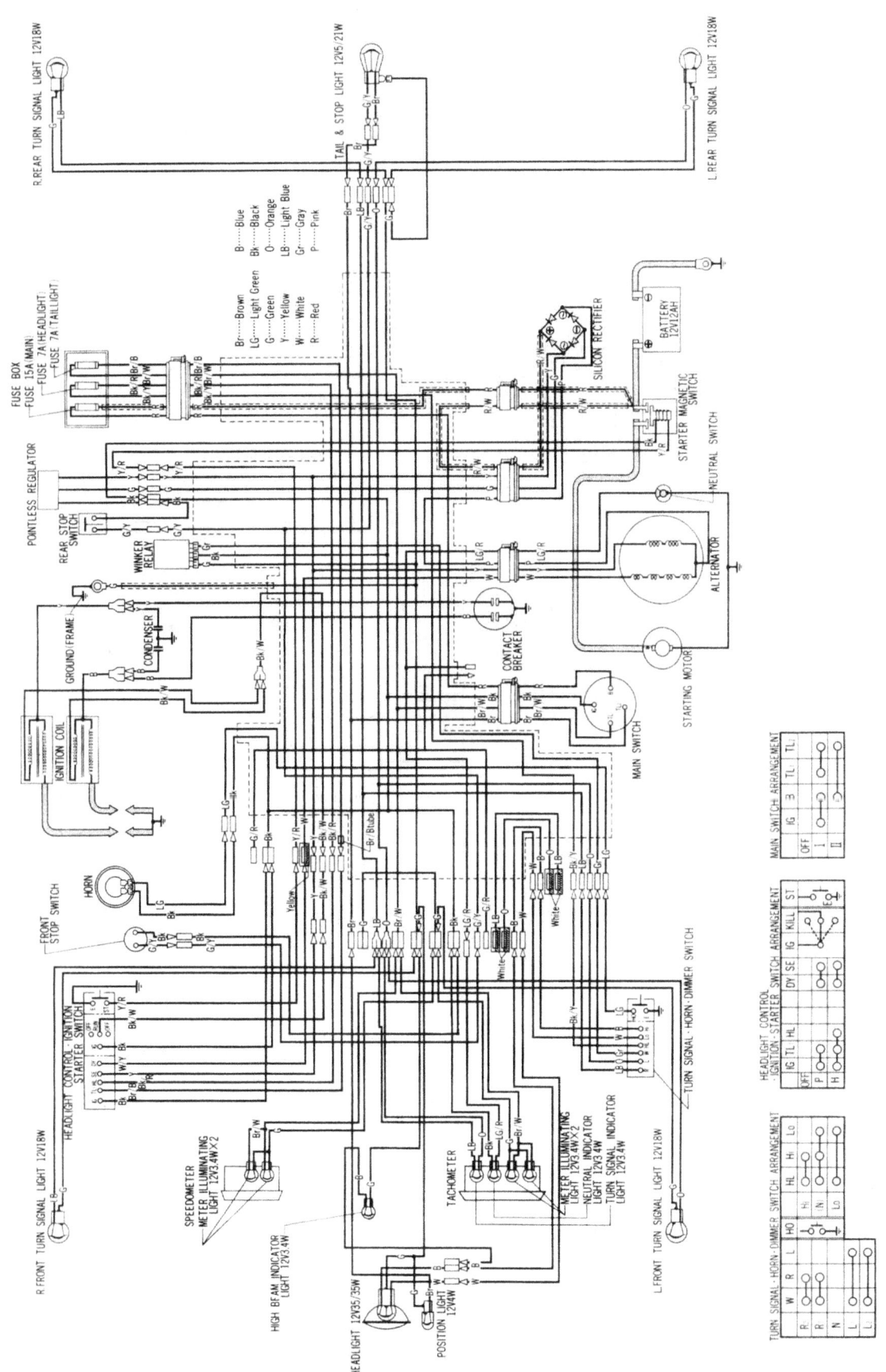

126　VII. SERVICE DATA

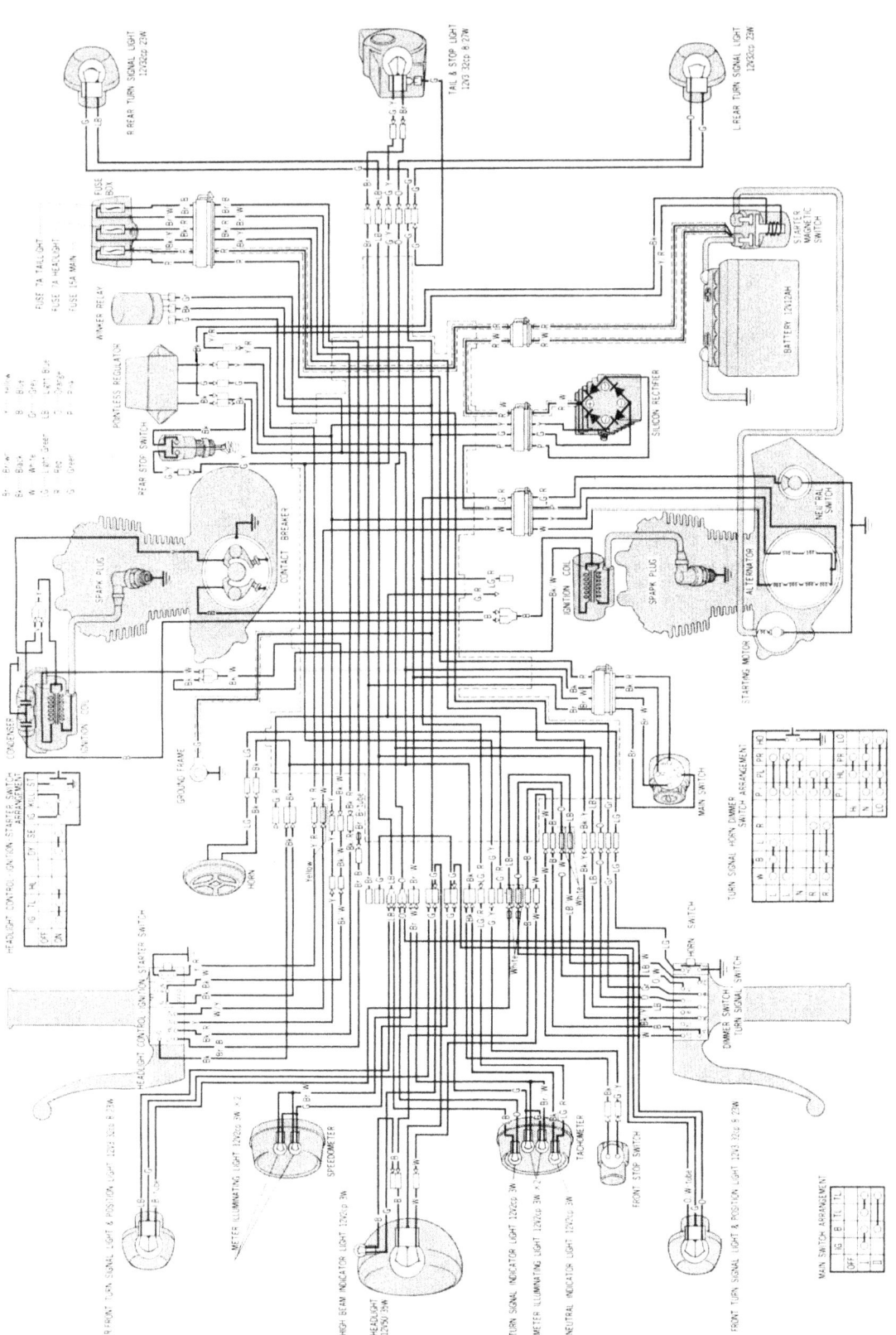

CL360 (U.S.A. TYPE)

VIII. SUPPLEMENT TO CB360T · CL360K1

1. FUEL COCK

The indication marks and their positions on the fuel cock was changed to a new type.

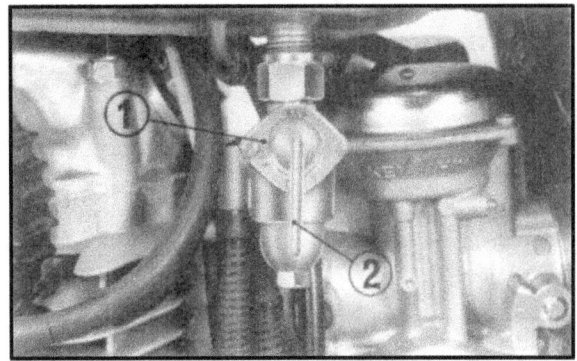

Fig. T-1 (1) Fuel cock
(2) Lever

2. SIDE STAND

The side stand was changed to a new type with a shock absorbing rubber pad.
The stand must be inspected periodically to determine that it is in good condition.

Inspection

1. Check the entire stand assembly (side stand bar, bracket and rubber pad) for installation, deformation or otherwise excessive damage.
2. Check the spring for freedom from damage or other defects.

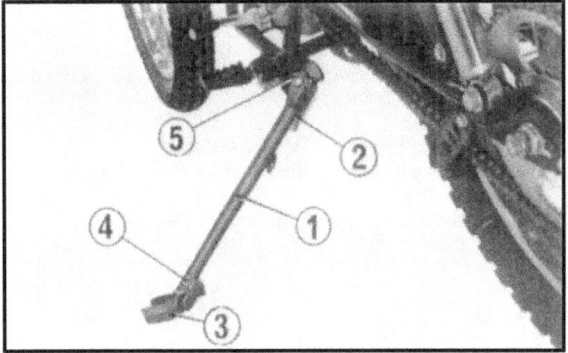

Fig. T-2 (1) Side stand bar   (4) 6 mm bolt
(2) Spring   (5) Side stand pivot bolt
(3) Rubber pad

3. Check the side stand for proper return operation:
   a. With the side stand applied, raise the side stand off the ground by using the main stand.
   b. Attach a spring scale to the lower end of the stand and measure the force with which the stand is returned to its original position.
   c. The stand condition is correct if the measurement falls within 2-3 kg (4.4-6.6 lbs.).
   If the stand requires force exceeding the above limit, this might be due to neglected lubrication, overtightened side stand pivot bolt, worn stand bar or bracket, or otherwise excessive tension. Repair as necessary.

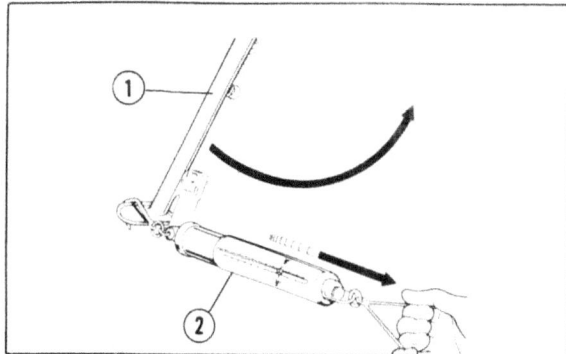

Fig. T-3 (1) Side stand bar
(2) Spring Scale

4. Check the rubber pad for deterioration or wear.
   When the rubber pad wear is excessive so that it is worn down to the wear line, replace it with a new one.

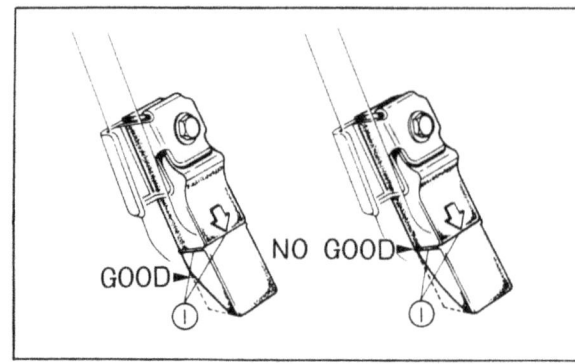

Fig. T-4 (1) Wear line

Rubber pad replacement

1. Remove the 6 mm bolt; separate the rubber pad from the bracket at the side stand.
2. After making sure the collar is installed, put a new rubber pad in place in the bracket with the arrow mark pointing toward out.
   NOTE:
   Use rubber pad having the mark "OVER 260 lbs ONLY".
3. Secure the rubber pad with the 6 mm bolt.

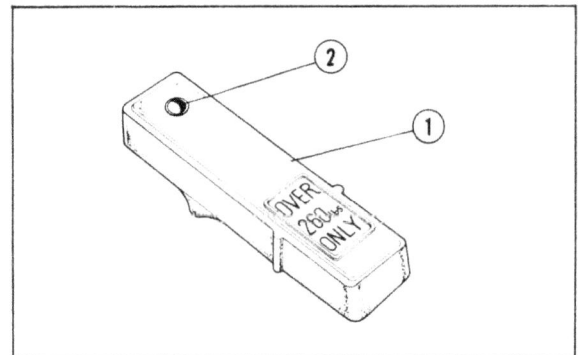

Fig. T-5 (1) Rubber pad
(2) Collar

3. MAINTENANCE SCHEDULE

Some additions occured in the MAINTENANCE SCHEDULE, of which details are as shown immediately below:

MAINTENANCE SCHEDULE This maintenance schedule is based upon average riding conditions. Machines subjected to severe use, or ridden in unusually dusty areas, require more frequent servicing.	INITIAL SERVICE PERIOD	REGULAR SERVICE PERIOD Perform at every indicated month or mileage interval, whichever occures first.			
	500 miles	1 month 500 miles	3 months 1,500 miles	6 months 3,000 miles	12 months 6,000 miles
* SIDE STAND—Check installation, operation, deformation, damage and wear.				O	

Items marked * should be serviced by an authorized Honda dealer, unless the owner has proper tools and is mechanically proficient. Other maintenance items are simple to perform and may be serviced by the owner.

VIII. SUPLEMENT TO CB360T · CL360K1

4. WIRING DIAGRAM
(CB360T)

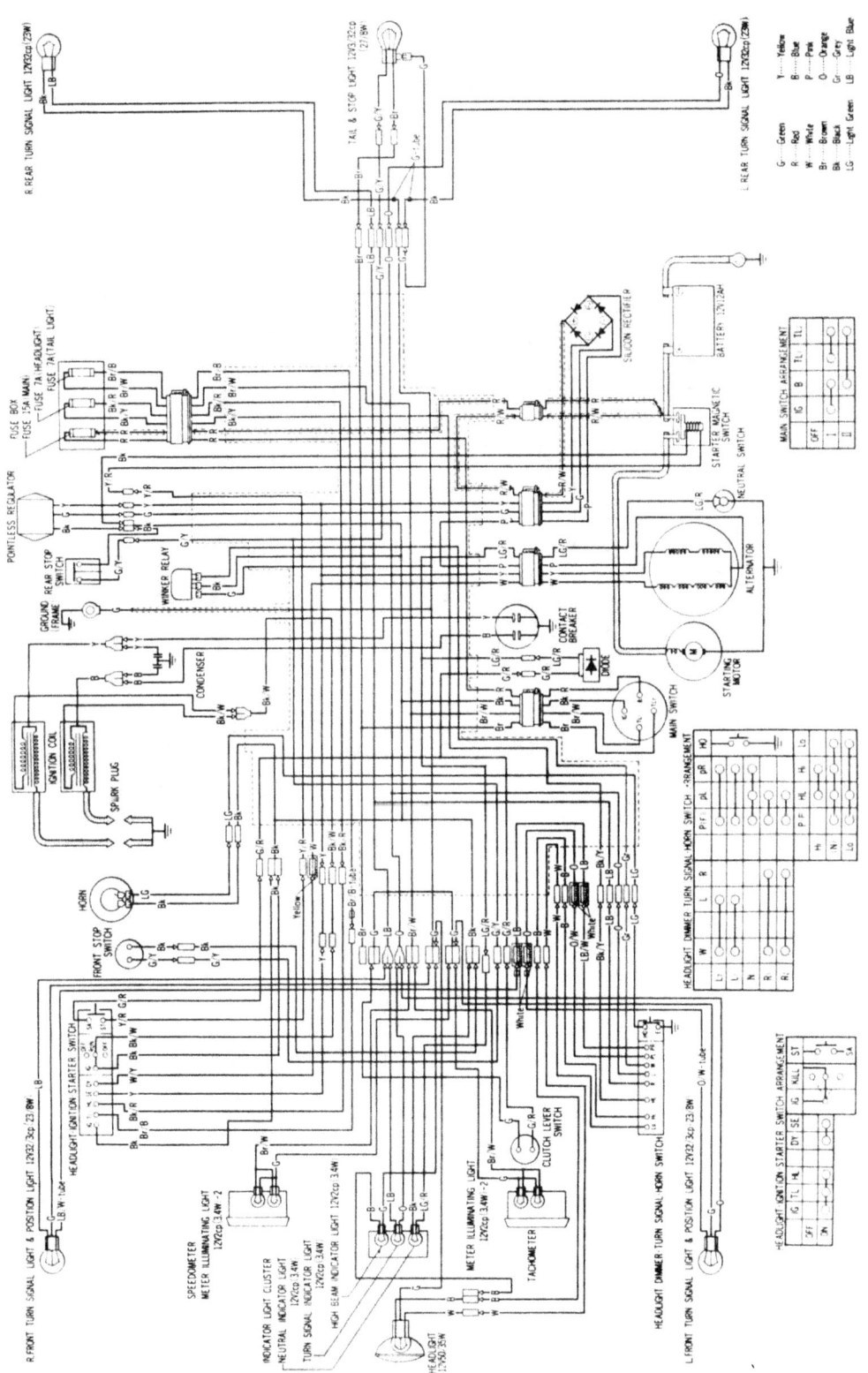

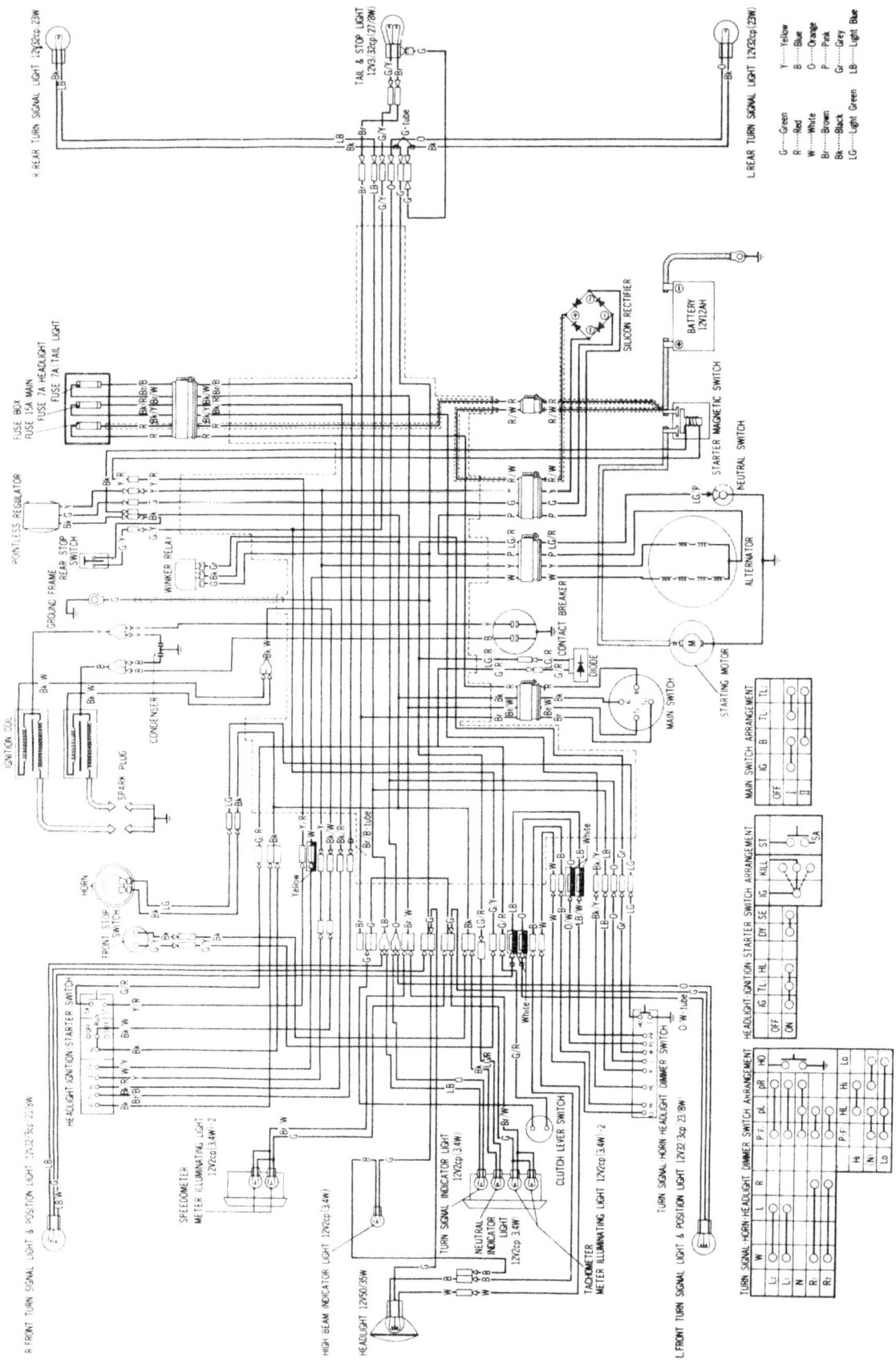

IX. SUPLEMENT TO CB360T (LATE MODEL)

1. AIR CLEANER

The following shows changes of the shape and disassembly procedure only.

Disassembly

1. Open the seat and remove the right and left side covers.
2. Remove the nuts (2), and remove the air cleaner case cover.
3. Remove the air cleaner bolt and loosen 5 mm screw and remove the air cleaner element.

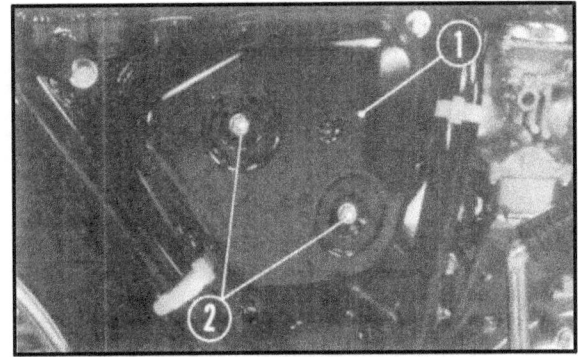

Fig. 1 (1) 6 mm nuts   (2) Air cleaner case cover

4. Separate each air cleaner element from the air cleaner case.
5. Loosen the inlet tube band and remove inlet tube.

Fig. 2 (1) Inlet tube band   (4) Air cleaner element
        (2) Inlet tube   (5) Air cleaner bolt
        (3) 5 mm screw

6. Loosen the inlet tube band and remove inlet tube.
7. Remove the 6 mm bolts and air cleaner case.

Fig. 3 (1) 6 mm bolts

8. Clean the air cleaner elements.
   Give a light tap to the air cleaner element to remove dirt and dust.
   If necessary, direct a blast of compressed air at the inner surface to blow off dirt and dust completely.
   CAUTION:
   If the air cleaner elements become oily or if they are broken, replace.

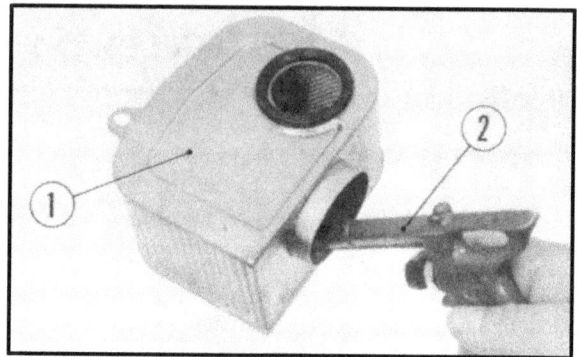

Fig. 4 (1) Air cleaner element (2) Air gun

Assembly

1. To install reverse the removal procedures.
   NOTE:
   For easier installation of inlet tube, remove screen and install band from inside by fingers.

Fig. 5 (1) Inlet tube
(2) Inlet tube band
(3) Screen

IX. SUPPLEMENT TO CB360T (LATE MODEL)

CHANGE TO THE CENTER CRANKSHAFT JOURNAL FIT MARKINGS

Applicable production Models and Engine Serial Nos.:

CB250G5 CB250E–6011678 and subsequent
  K5

CB360   CB350E–1055298 and subsequent
CB360G

CL360   CL360E–1012386 and subsequent

The fit markings of the center crankshaft journal have been changed as shown in the table below.
When replacing center crankshaft and center bearing assy, select the crankshaft and bearing with the same markings according to the right side table.

Select fit table of the center bearing
(radial clearance 12–20μ)

Center crankshaft marking	Center bearing assy. marking
イ or A	A
ロ or B	B
ハ or C	C
ニ or D	D
ホ or E	E

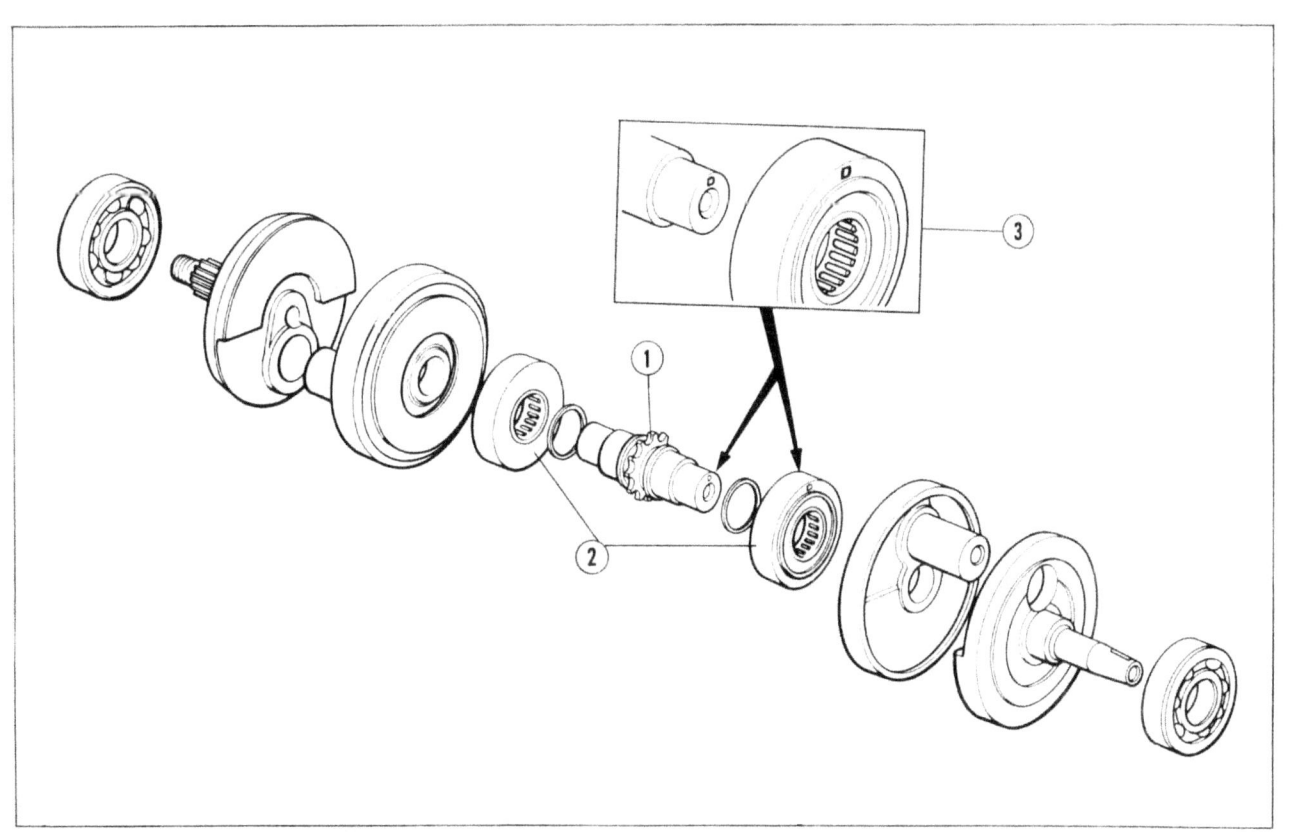

(1) Center crank
(2) Center bearing
(3) Marking position

ROCKER ARM SHAFT

The following shows rocker arm shaft disassembly and assembly procedures.

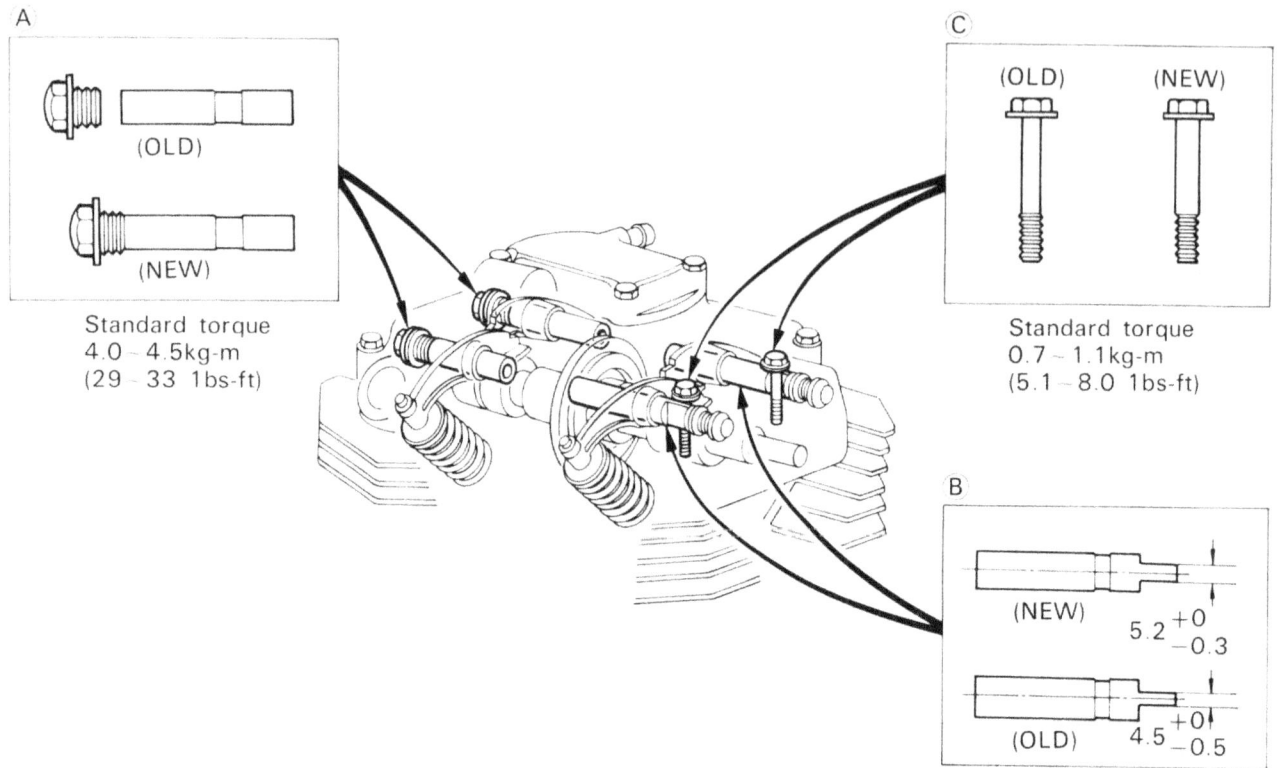

A — Standard torque 4.0 – 4.5 kg-m (29 – 33 1bs-ft)

C — Standard torque 0.7 – 1.1 kg-m (5.1 – 8.0 1bs-ft)

B — (NEW) $5.2^{+0}_{-0.3}$ (OLD) $4.5^{+0}_{-0.5}$

Application of Modifications

This changes have been applied on the production models starting with the following engine serial numbers.

TYPE	ENGINE No.
CB250 K5/G	6022201
CB360G	1088381
CL360K1	2008449
CB360T	2031164

Disassembly

Referring to disassembly procedures on page 38.
Except that Right rocker arm shaft is removed only loosening bolt.

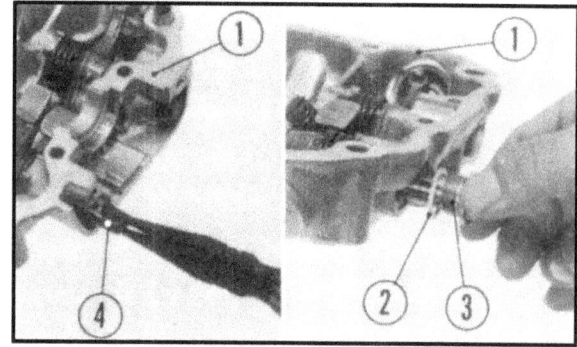

Fig. 1 (1) Cylinder head cover
(2) Sealing washer
(3) Right rocker arm shaft
(4) Left rocker arm shaft

IX. SUPPLEMENT TO CB360T (LATE MODEL)

Assembly

Referring to assembly procedure on page 44. Taking care of the following.

1. Install new rocker arm shafts into the bores with sealing washers.

   NOTE:
   The sealing washer cannot be re-used after once being tightened to the above specified torque, because of possible deforming or warpage.

2. Retighten the shaft/bolt to a torque of 4.0 to 4.5 kg-m (29 to 33 lbs-ft) using a **TORQUE WRENCH'**.

Cylinder head tightening torque is **0.7–1.1 kg-m (5.1–8.0 lbs-ft)** for 6 mm.

SPECIFICATIONS

Caster angle	63°
Trail	95 mm
Gear ratio I	2,438
Gear ratio II	1,667

Fig. 2 (1) Rubber plug   (2) Spark advancer

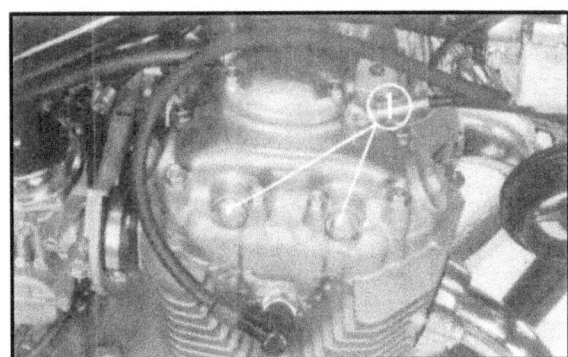

Fig. 3 (1) Right rocker arm shafts

Fig. 4 (1) Caster angle

IX. SUPPLEMENT TO CB360T (LATE MODEL)

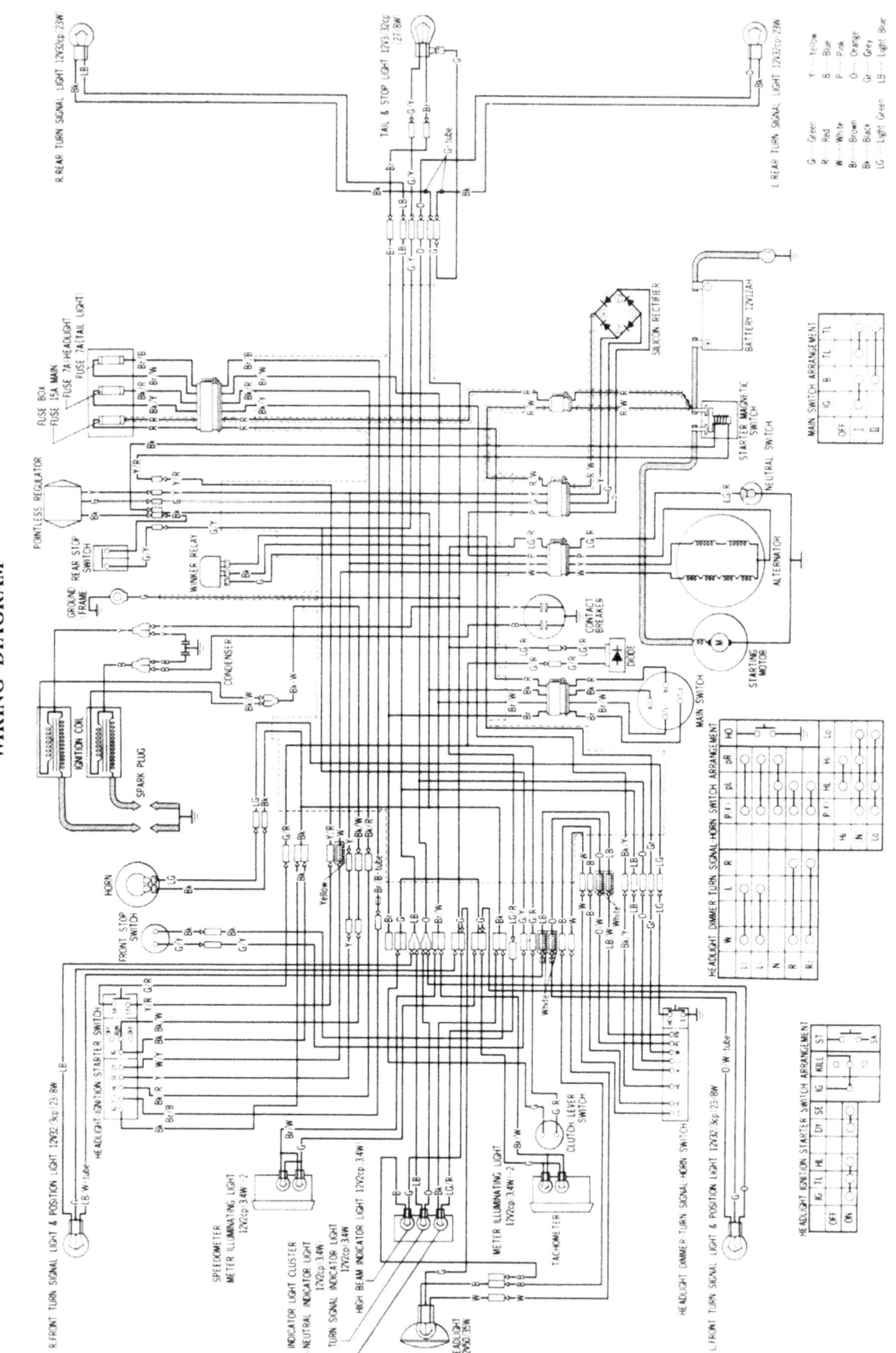

X. SUPPLEMENT TO CJ250T/CJ360T

SUPPLEMENT TO CJ250T/CJ360T

This addendum is a maintenance manual for the Honda CJ250T/CJ360T motorcycle. For information that is common to the CB250T, CB360T and CL360, refer to the preceeding pages.

1. CONSTRUCTION . . . . See page 2

1. Front Shock Absorber

The front shock absorbers are of a long-stroke, direct-acting type using a free valve. The bottom case is made of alminum alloy. The absorbers dampen out spring oscillation after siding over holes or bumps.
Stroke: Compression: 105 mm; Expansion: 34.5 mm
(Total: 139.5 mm)

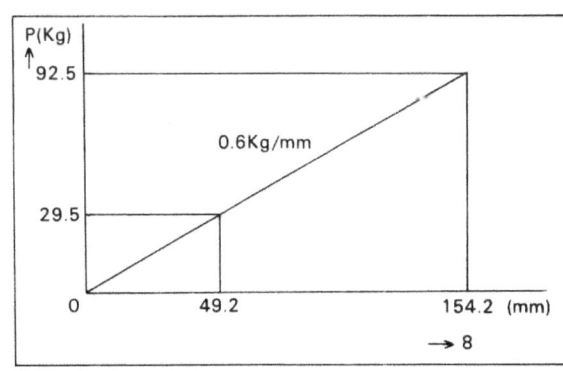

Fig. 1 Performance curves

2. Rear Shock Absorber

The two rear shock absorbers are direct-acting shock absorbers that are equipped with a bottom valve. An oil damper is utilized to prevent excessive wheel movement and dampen out spring oscillation.
Stroke: 77.3 mm

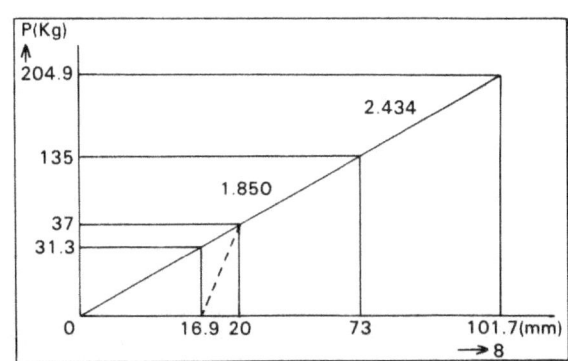

Fig. 2 Performance curves

3. Transmission

The transmission is a 5-speed constant-mesh type.

Gear ratios: Primary gear: 3.714; Secondary chain: 2.063
Gear ratios:
```
1st ............................. 2.438
2nd ............................. 1.667
3rd ............................. 1.375
4th ............................. 1.111
5th ............................. 0.965
```

4. Air Cleaner

The air cleaner uses a pleated paper element to prevent dust and grit in the air from entering the engine through the carburetor. It also muffles the noise resulting from the intake of air through the carburetor and valve ports. It is very important that the element be serviced carefully as grit and dust could, cause serious damage to the engine.

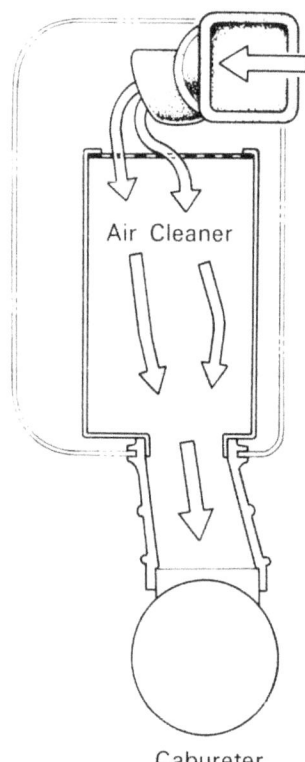
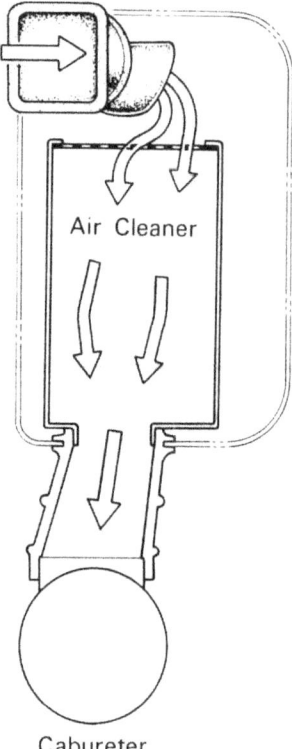

Fig. 3

11. INSPECTION AND ADJUSTMENT . . . . See page 17

1. FRONT FORK

Changing fork oil

1. Unscrew the front fork drain plug at the bottom of the fork leg. Drain the oil by pumping the fork while plug is out. Replace the plug securely after draining.
2. Set the motorcycle on the center stand.
3. Place a jack under the crankcase to control lowering of the front end.
4. Remove the handlebar by removing the four handlebar bolts.
5. Unscrew the fork filler plugs until free.
6. Lower the jack under the engine to extend the fork springs with the attached filler plugs.

Fig. 4 (1) Front fork drain plug

X. SUPPLEMENT TO CJ250T/CJ360T

7. Move the fork springs to one side and pour **120 cc** of premium quality ATF (automatic transmission fluid) into each fork leg.
8. Raise the jack under the engine to allow the fork springs and filler plugs to return into the fork legs.
9. Securely tighten the fork filler plugs.
10. Reinstall the handlebar, tightening the two front bolts first, then tightening the two rear bolts to the same torque.
11. Remove the jack from under the engine.
12. Pour **140–150 cc** of premium quality ATF into each fork leg if the fork has been disassembled.

Fig. 5 (1) Front fork filler plugs

2. Air Cleaner

1. Open the seat and loosen the screws (1).
2. Remove the three nuts (2) and remove the air cleaner case cover.

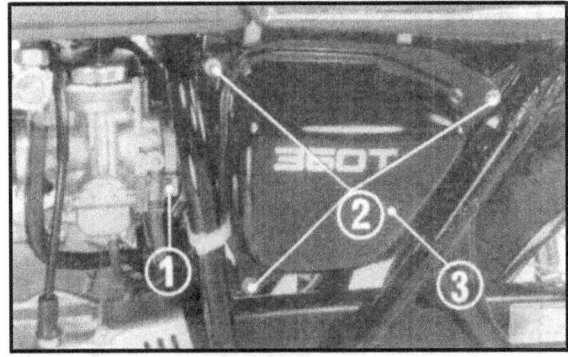

Fig. 6 (1) Screw
(2) Nut
(3) Air cleaner case cover

3. Unscrew the bolts (1) and remove the air cleaner case from the carburetor and frame body.
4. Remove the bolts (3) and screws (4) and take out the air cleaner element.

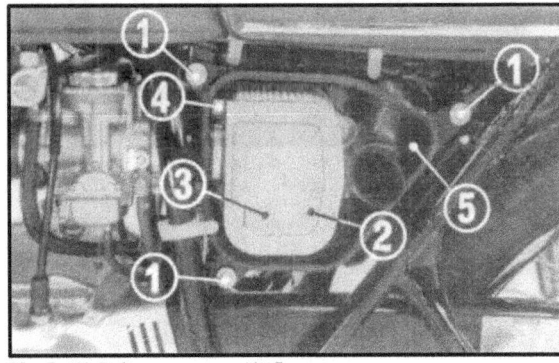

Fig. 7 (1) Bolts   (4) Screws
(2) Air cleaner case (5) Air cleaner element
(3) Bolts

5. Shake any dust off the cleaner element. Apply a blast of air from inside the element.
   CAUTION:
   Replace the element if it is found to be wet with oily or greasy substances.
6. To install, reverse the foregoing removal procedure.
7. Make sure that the inlet tube and connecting tube are secured in place and not leaking air.

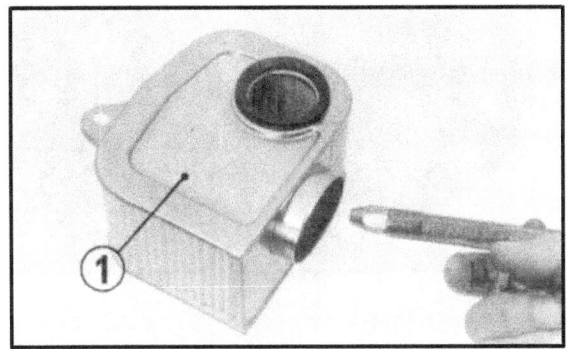

Fig. 8 (1) Air cleaner element

X. SUPPLEMENT TO CJ250T/CJ360T

III. ENGINE

1. ON-FRAME SERVICING (Engine Disassembly)

No.	Item	Ref. page
1	Cylinder head, cylinder and pistons	37
2	Left crankcase cover, A.C. generator	143
3	Right crankcase cover and clutch	47
4	Oil pump and oil filter	50
5	Gearshift spindle	57
6	Carburetor	63

2. ENGINE REMOVAL AND INSTALLATION

Removal

Remove, the engine for disassembly after the engine oil has been drained.

① Open the seat and remove the battery. To remove the battery, disconnect the negative terminal first.

(1) Battery
(2) Battery negative terminal
(3) Battery positive terminal

② Close the fuel cock and remove the fuel tube. Remove the fuel tank. Avoid damaging the fuel tube.

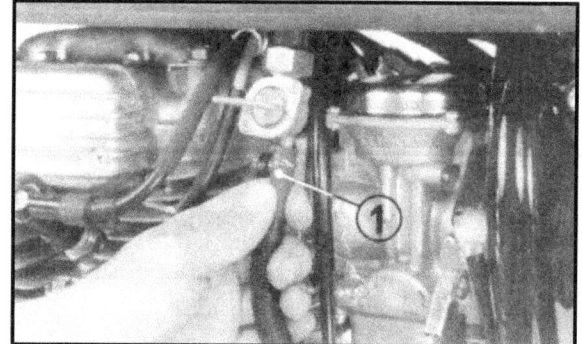

(1) Fuel tube

③ Remove the gear shift pedal and L-crankcase cover.

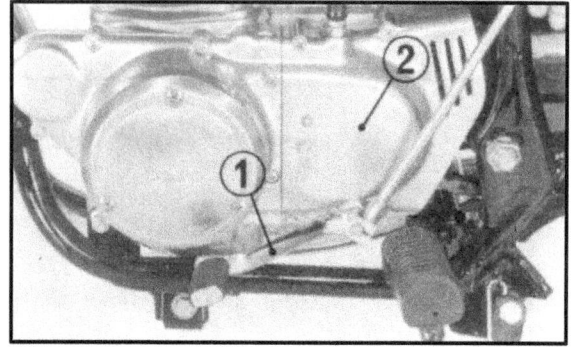

(1) Gear shift
(2) L-crankcase cover

④ Remove the drive chain together with the drive sprocket. Remove the drive sprocket fixing bolts.

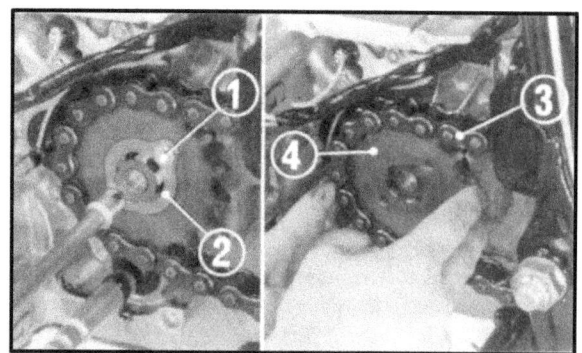

(1) Drive sprocket fixing bolts (3) Drive sprocket
(2) Lock plate   (4) Drive chain (endless)

X. SUPPLEMENT TO CJ250T/CJ360T

⑤ Remove the muffler by removing the nut (2) and bolt (3).

Remove the bolt (1).

(1) Muffler Assy

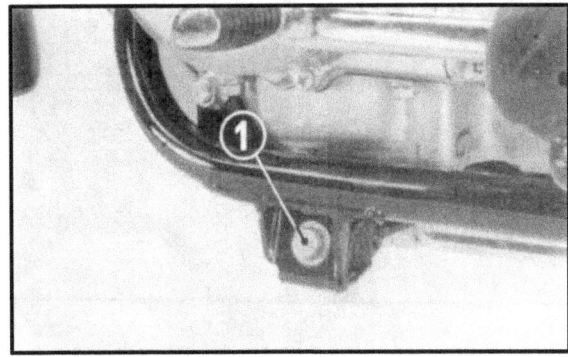

(1) Bolt

⑥ Disconnect the A.C. generator wires at the coupler as shown.

⑦ Drain the remaining fuel from the carburetor by loosening the drain screw. Loosen the clamp at the connecting tube. Use standard gasoline warning.

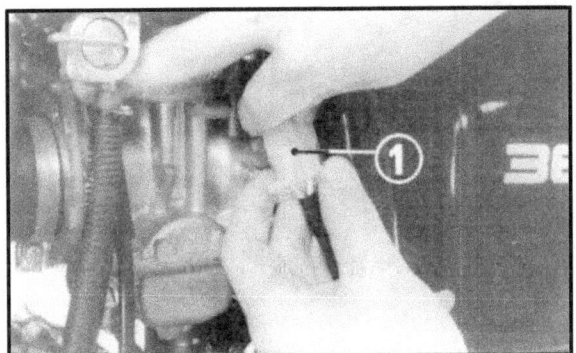

(1) A.C. generator coupler

(1) Drain screw
(2) Clamp
(3) Carburetor insulator band

⑧ Remove the carburetors toward the left while pushing them down toward the air cleaner.

⑨ Remove the tachometer cable, spark plug caps and breaker point wires.

(1) Carburetors

(1) Tachometer cable
(2) Spark plug cap
(3) Breaker point cord

X. SUPPLEMENT TO CJ250T/CJ360T

⑩ Remove the UBS nuts and nuts (3) and take out the engine upper hanger.

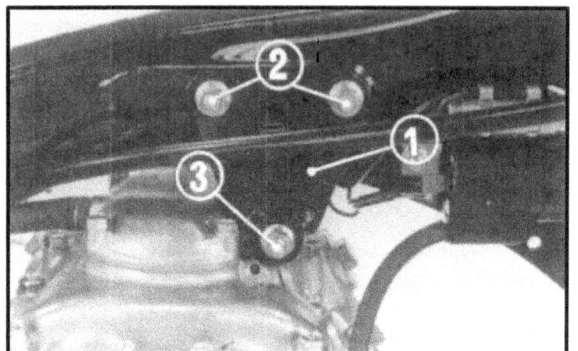

(1) Engine upper hanger

⑪ Remove the UBS nuts (2), (3) and (4). The left foot peg will be removed when the nut (3) is removed. Draw out the bolt by removing the nut (4).

(1) Left side step

⑫ Remove the bolt (3) and pull off the bolt (4). Take out the engine hanger plate. Remove the nut (5) and remove the plate complete with the right foot peg (with the bolt (6) and nut). Remove the kick starter pedal.

(1) Right foot peg
(2) Engine hanger plate
(3) Kick starter pedal

⑬ Remove the bolt (2) to take out the brake pedal.

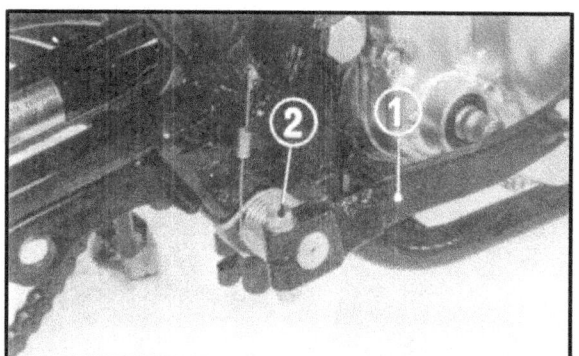

(1) Brake

⑭ Remove the bolts (2) and (3).

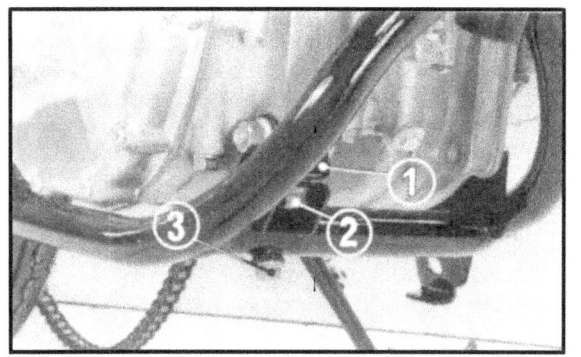

(1) Engine bottom hanger

⑮ With the aid of an assistant remove the engine from the right side. Before removing, install the kick starter pedal to facilitate the operation.

(1) Kick pedal

To install the engine, refer to page 34.

X. SUPPLEMENT TO CJ250T/CJ360T

3. CYLINDER HEAD, CAMSHAFT, CYLINDER AND PISTONS . . . . Refer to page 37

4. A.C. GENERATOR

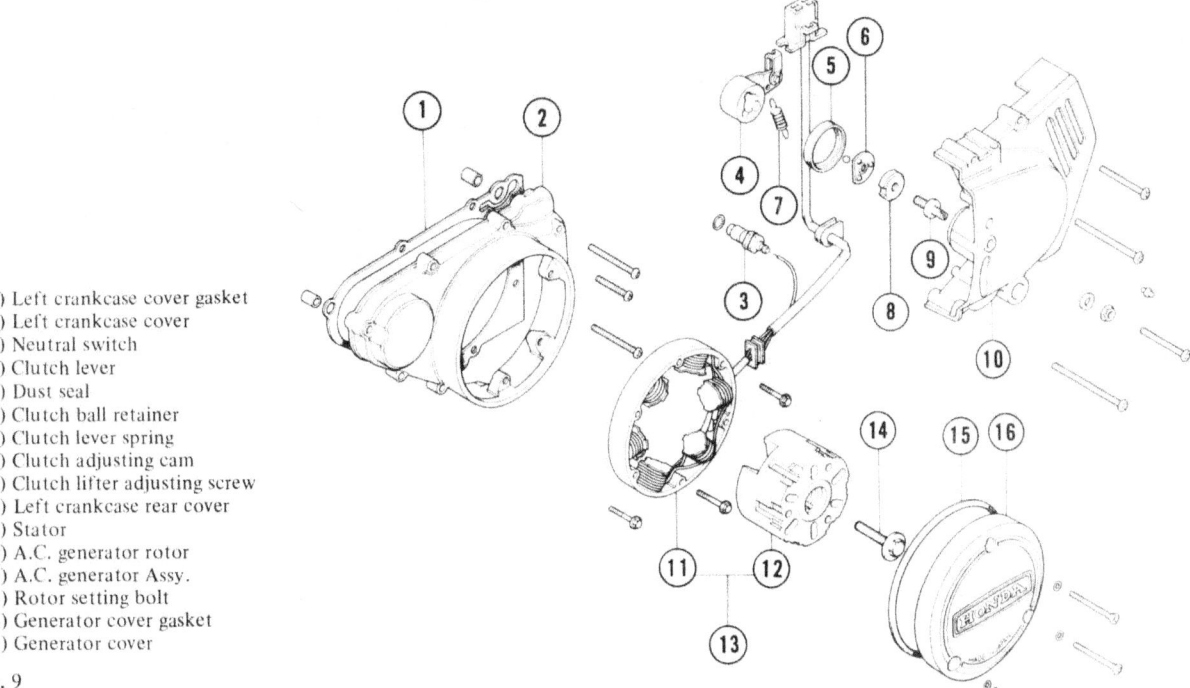

(1) Left crankcase cover gasket
(2) Left crankcase cover
(3) Neutral switch
(4) Clutch lever
(5) Dust seal
(6) Clutch ball retainer
(7) Clutch lever spring
(8) Clutch adjusting cam
(9) Clutch lifter adjusting screw
(10) Left crankcase rear cover
(11) Stator
(12) A.C. generator rotor
(13) A.C. generator Assy.
(14) Rotor setting bolt
(15) Generator cover gasket
(16) Generator cover

Fig. 9

The construction of the generator is as shown in Fig. 9 immediately above. The starting mechanism is eliminated.

Disassembly

1. Remove the change pedal.
2. Remove the L-crankcase rear cover.
3. Remove the clutch cable end off the clutch lever.

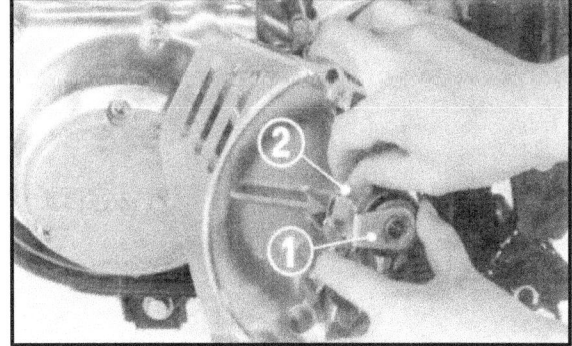

Fig. 10 (1) Clutch lever
(2) Clutch cable end

4. Disconnect the A.C. generator coupler and remove the cord from the neutral switch.
5. Remove the L-crankcase cover.
6. Remove the A.C. generator stator from the L-crankcase cover by backing off the bolts (5).

Fig. 11 (1) L-crankcase cover
(2) Stator
(3) Neutral switch cord
(4) Generator cord

X. SUPPLEMENT TO CJ250T/CJ360T

7. To remove the A.C. generator, remove the rotor set bolt and screw in the "Rotor Puller" (Tool No. 07933-2160000) as shown.

Assembly

Assembly is the reverse procedure of removal. However, observe the following assembly notes:
1. Before installing the generator rotor, make sure that the woodruff key is properly seated. Tighten to specified torque while holding the rotor by hand or with a suitable tool.

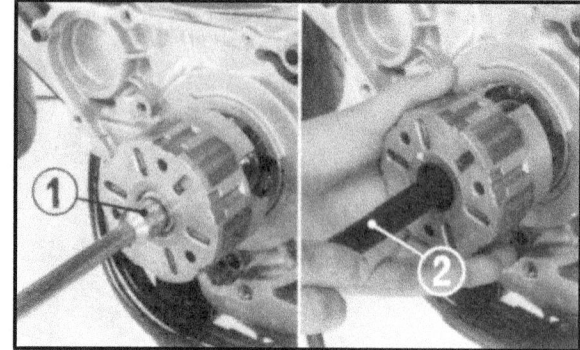

Fig. 12 (1) Rotor set bolt (2) Rotor Puller

5. RIGHT CRANKCASE COVER AND CLUTCH ...... Refer to page 47
6. OIL PUMP AND OIL FILTER ROTOR .... Refer to page 50
7. KICK STARTER AND LOWER CRANKCASE

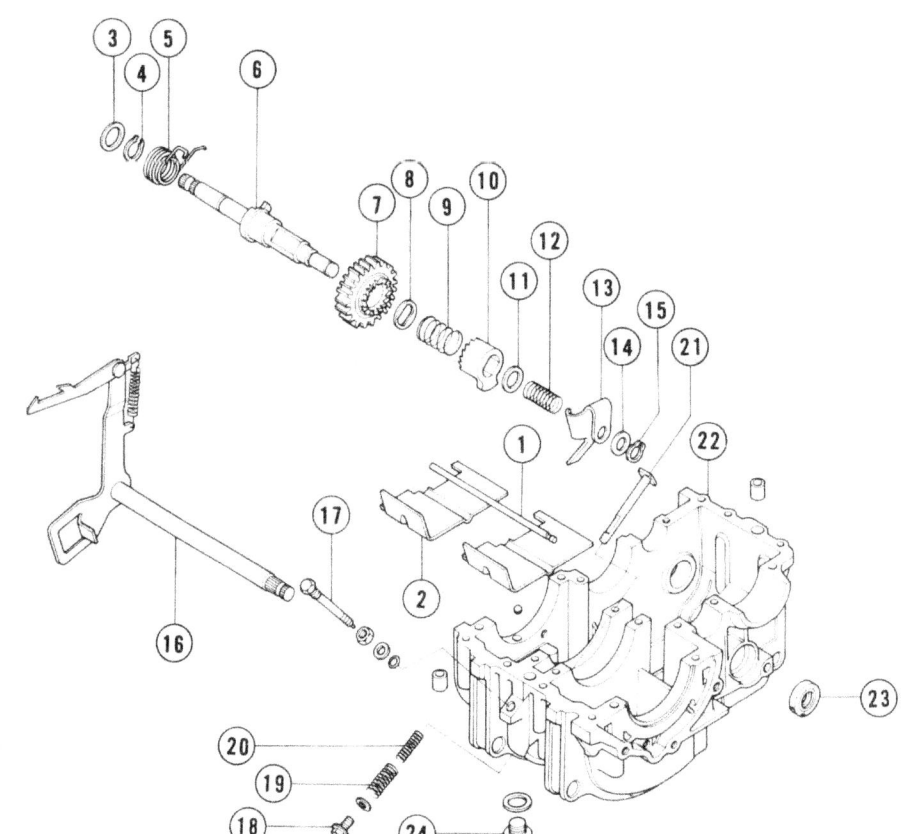

(1) Oil separator setting bar
(2) Oil separator
(3) 18 mm washer
(4) 18 mm snap ring
(5) Kick starter spring
(6) Kick starter spindle
(7) Kick starter pinion
(8) 20 mm thrust washer
(9) Setting spring
(10) Kick starter ratchet
(11) 15 mm thrust washer
(12) Ratchet spring
(13) Ratchet guide plate
(14) Thrust washer
(15) 12 mm snap ring
(16) Gear shift spindle
(17) Tensioner setting bolt
(18) Oil check bolt
(19) Tensioner outer spring
(20) Tensioner inner spring
(21) Tensioner puh bar
(22) Lower crankcase
(23) 14 x 28 x 7 oil seal
(24) Drain bolt

Fig. 13

Refer to page 53 for disassembly, inspection and assembly.
1. Assemble the parts in the order named.
2. Install the kick starter ratchet with the kick starter spindle placed in the position shown in Fig. 14.

Fig. 14 (1) Kick starter ratchet
(2) Kick starter spindle

X. SUPPLEMENT TO CJ250T/CJ360T

8. GEARSHIFT MECHANISM AND TRANSMISSION

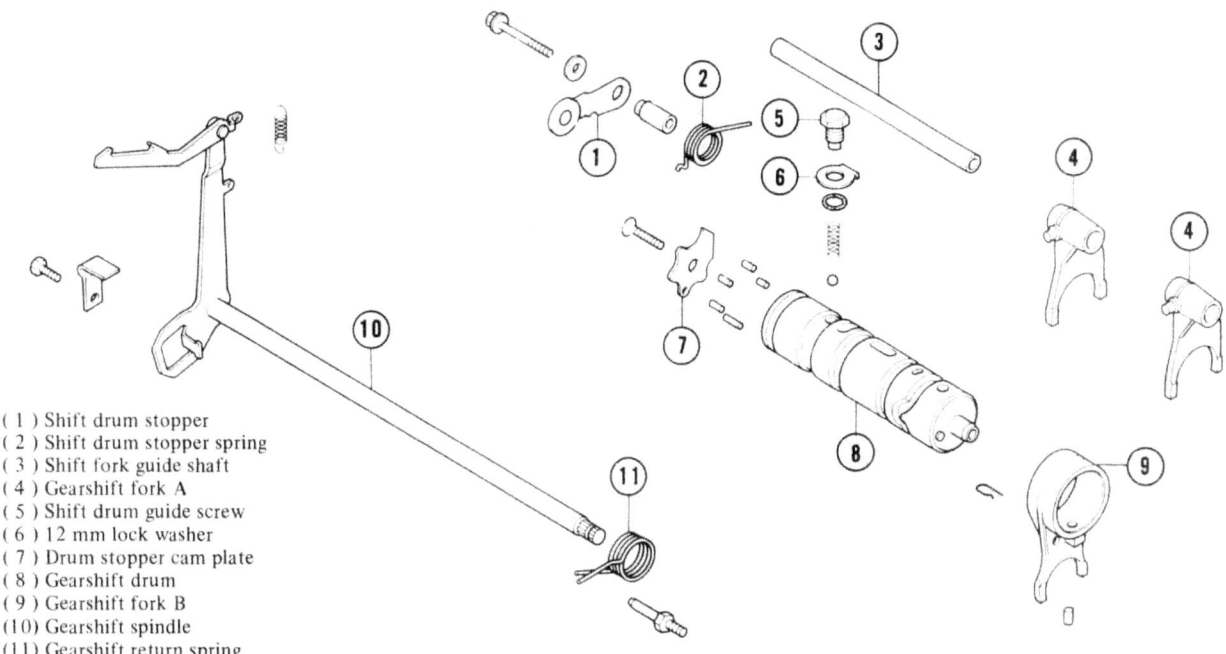

(1) Shift drum stopper
(2) Shift drum stopper spring
(3) Shift fork guide shaft
(4) Gearshift fork A
(5) Shift drum guide screw
(6) 12 mm lock washer
(7) Drum stopper cam plate
(8) Gearshift drum
(9) Gearshift fork B
(10) Gearshift spindle
(11) Gearshift return spring

Fig. 15

1. Refer to page 57 for disassembly, inspection and assembly. For assembling, refer also to the sketch immediately below.

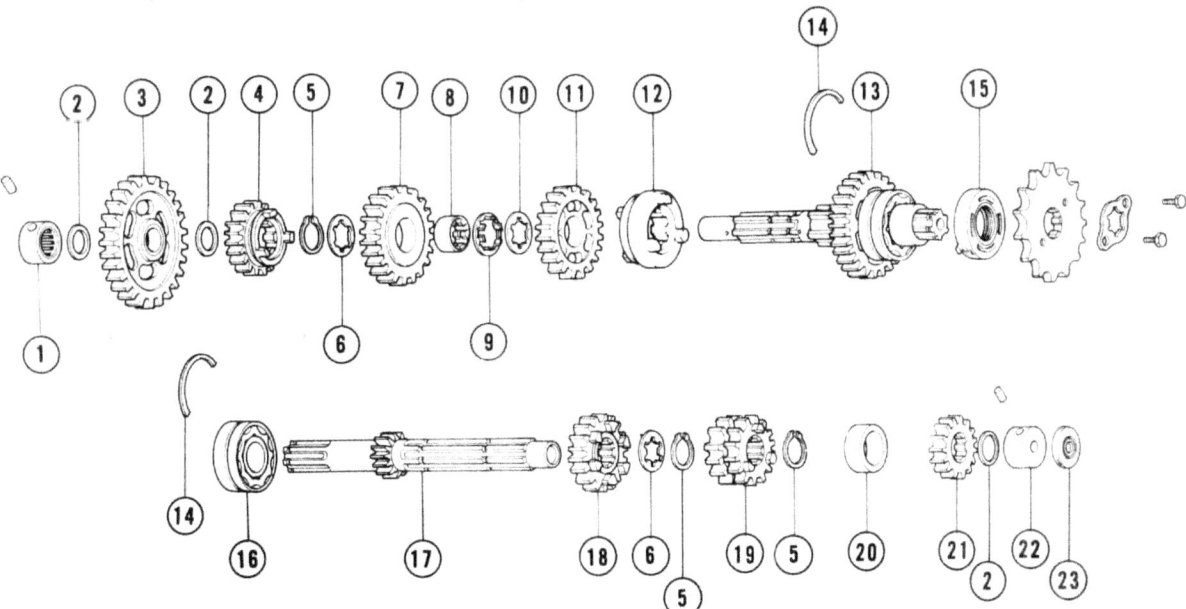

(1) 20 mm needle roller bearing
(2) 20 mm thrust washer
(3) C-1st gear
(4) C-5th gear
(5) 25 mm snap ring
(6) 25 mm thrust washer
(7) C-3rd gear
(8) 28 mm splined bushing
(9) 25 mm lock washer
(10) 25 mm thrust washer B
(11) C-4th gear
(12) Countershaft shifter
(13) Transmission countershaft
(14) 52 mm bearing set ring
(15) 34 x 52 x 13.5 x 15.5 oil seal
(16) 520S HS ball bearing
(17) Transmission main shaft
(18) M-5th gear
(19) M-3rd gear
(20) Collar
(21) M-2nd gear
(22) 20 mm needle roller bearing
(23) 8 x 34 x 8 oil seal

Fig. 16

X. SUPPLEMENT TO CJ250T/CJ360T

9. CRANKSHAFT AND UPPER CRANKCASE .... See page 55
10. CARBURETOR

Refer to page 63 for disassembly, inspection, adjustment and assembly. For carburetor adjustments, refer also to the instructions given in the table on the right.

Item	
Setting No.	759A
Main jet Primary	# 68
Secondary	#110
Slow jet	# 35
Jet needle setting	2nd
Pilot screw opening	2 (Standard)
Float level	18.5 mm

IV. FRAME

1. FRONT WHEEL AND FRONT BRAKE .... See page 68
2. REAR WHEEL AND REAR BRAKE .... See page 78

1. REAR BRAKE PEDAL

(1) Stop switch Assy
(2) Stop switch spring
(3) Brake pedal
(4) Brake pedal spring
(5) Rear brake pivot shaft
(6) Brake rod joint pin
(7) Cotter pin
(8) Rear brake rod
(9) Brake rod spring
(10) Rear brake arm joint
(11) Adjusting nut
(12) Change pedal
(13) Change pedal rubber

Fig. 17

Disassembly

1. Remove the stopper switch spring.
2. Remove the kick starter pedal.
3. Remove the right foot peg.

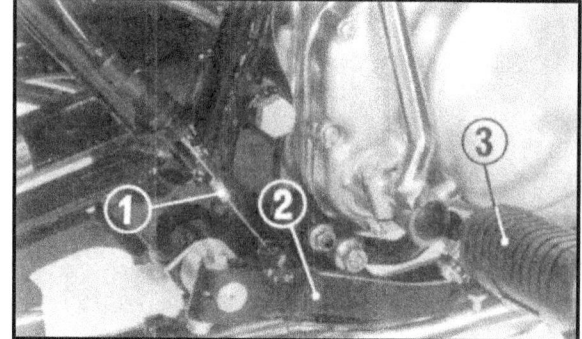

Fig. 18 (1) Stopper switch spring
(2) Kick starter pedal
(3) Right foot peg

X. SUPPLEMENT TO CJ250T/CJ360T

4. Remove the bolt (1) and remove the kick starter pedal.
5. Remove the brake pedal spring.

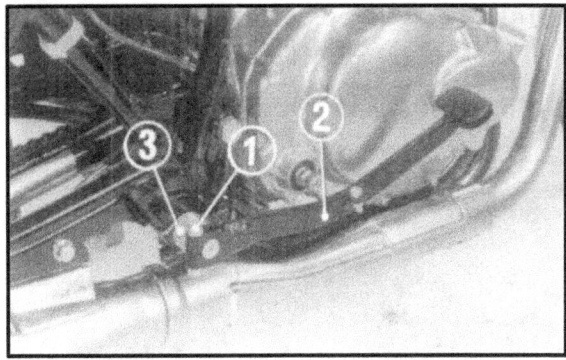

Fig. 19 (1) Bolt
(2) Kick starter pedal
(3) Brake pedal spring

6. Remove the brake adjusting nut, then remove the rear brake arm joint and brake rod spring.
7. Remove the rear brake pivot shaft from the frame.

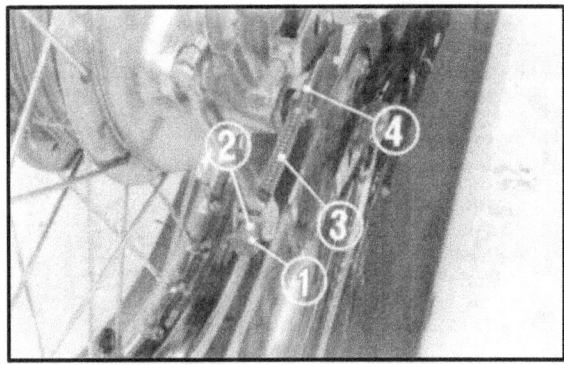

Fig. 20 (1) Brake adjusting nut
(2) Rear brake arm joint
(3) Brake rod spring
(4) Brake rod

Assembly

Assembly is the reverse of the removal. However, observe the following assembly notes:

1. Install the brake pedal spring with the end hooked on the pedal bracket as shown.

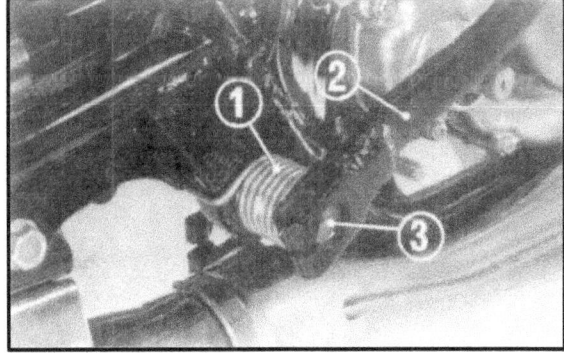

Fig. 21 (1) Brake pedal spring
(2) Brake pedal
(3) Pivot shaft

2. Align the punch mark on the pivot shaft with that on the brake pedal; then, tighten the pedal securely.
3. Adjust the rear brake pedal play and height.
4. To adjust, follow the instructions given on page 28.

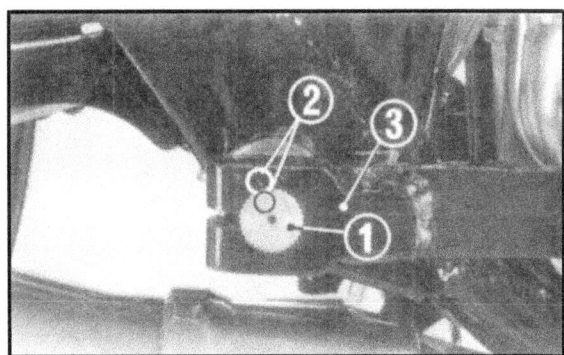

Fig. 22 (1) Pivot shaft
(2) Punch mark
(3) Rear brake pedal

X. SUPPLEMENT TO CJ250T/CJ360T

3. HANDLEBAR .... See page 81
4. FRONT SUSPENSION .... See page 85
5. STEERING STEM .... See page 87
6. REAR SHOCK ABSORBERS AND REAR SWING ARM ... See page 90

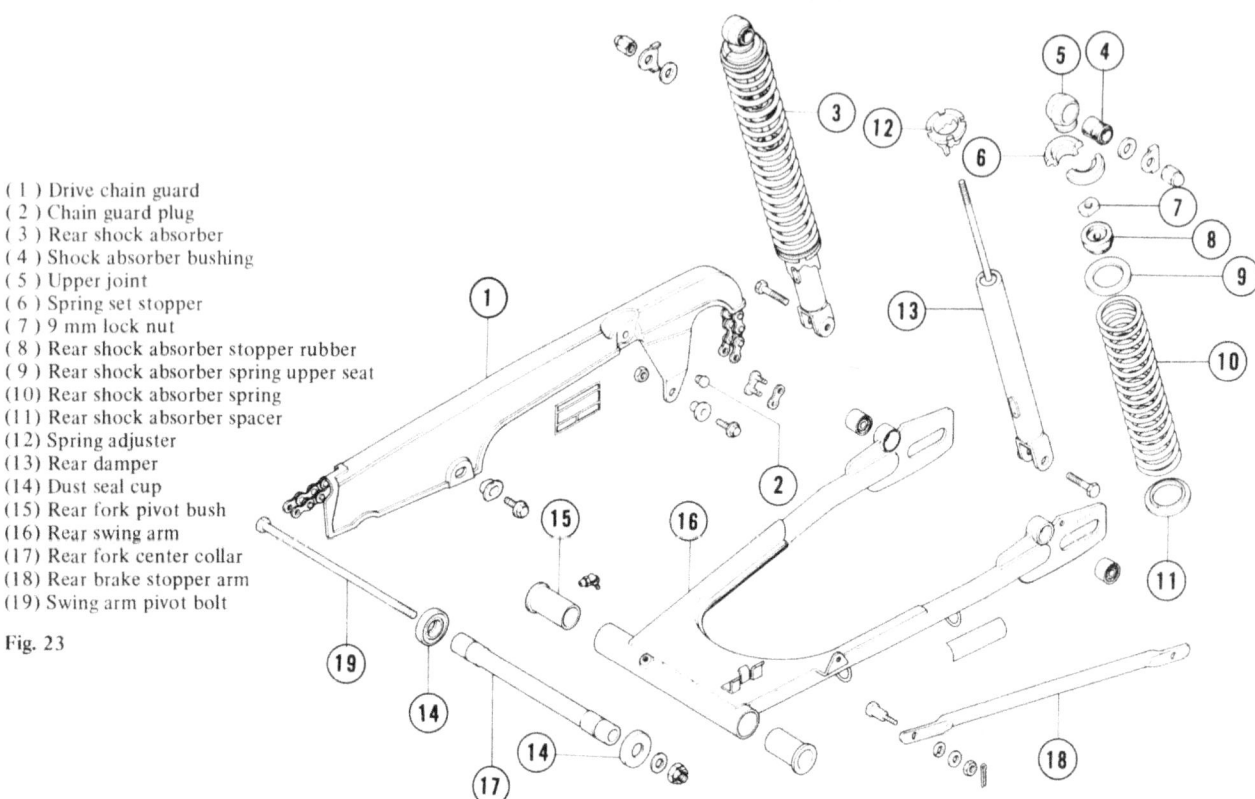

(1) Drive chain guard
(2) Chain guard plug
(3) Rear shock absorber
(4) Shock absorber bushing
(5) Upper joint
(6) Spring set stopper
(7) 9 mm lock nut
(8) Rear shock absorber stopper rubber
(9) Rear shock absorber spring upper seat
(10) Rear shock absorber spring
(11) Rear shock absorber spacer
(12) Spring adjuster
(13) Rear damper
(14) Dust seal cup
(15) Rear fork pivot bush
(16) Rear swing arm
(17) Rear fork center collar
(18) Rear brake stopper arm
(19) Swing arm pivot bolt

Fig. 23

Removal

1. Raise the rear of the motorcycle by placing a block under the engine.
2. Open the seat and remove the seat cowl by removing the three bolts (1).

Fig. 24 (1) Bolts
(2) Seat cowl

3. Remove the three bolts (1) and take out the rear fender stay.

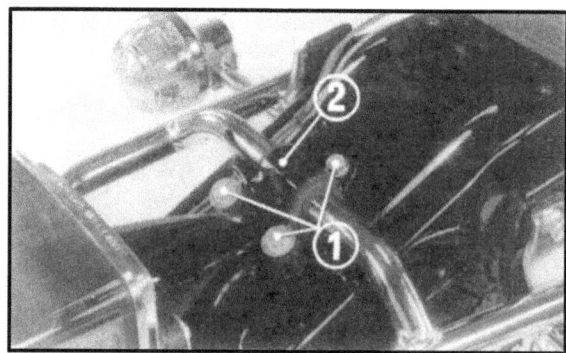

Fig. 25 (1) Bolt
(2) Rear fender stay

X. SUPPLEMENT TO CJ250T/CJ360T

4. Remove the nuts (3) and bolts (4) to remove the rear bumper and rear shock absorbers.

Fig. 26 (1) Rear bumper
(2) Rear shock absorber
(3) Nut
(4) Bolt

5. Remove the chain guard.
6. Pry off the cotter pin and remove the axle nut.
7. Loosen the right and left drive chain adjuster lock nuts and loosen the adjusting bolts.

Fig. 27 (1) Lock nut
(2) Adjusting bolt
(3) Axle nut
(4) Cotter pin

8. Remove the rear brake stopper arm from the brake panel.
9. Remove the rear brake adjusting nut and disconnect the brake rod from the brake arm.
10. While pushing the rear wheel forward, remove the drive chain from the driven sprocket.
11. Withdraw the rear wheel axle and remove the rear wheel.

Fig. 28 (1) Brake panel
(2) Rear brake stopper arm
(3) Rear brake adjusting nut
(4) Brake rod

12. Back off the 14 mm self-locking nut; and, remove the swing arm pivot bolt and rear fork in the swing arm.
13. Remove the rear brake stopper arm from the swing arm.
14. For inspection, refer to page 91.
15. To assemble, reverse the disassembly procedure.
16. Replace the rear axle cotter pin with a new one.

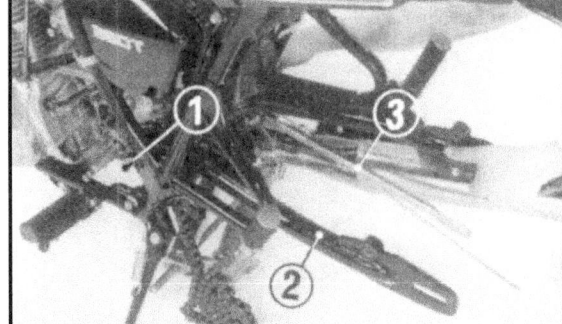

Fig. 29 (1) Swing arm pivot bolt
(2) Swing arm
(3) Rear brake stopper arm

7. FRAME BODY AND OTHER RELATED PARTS .... See page 93

1. Fuel Filter Cleaning

1. Turn the fuel cock lever to the OFF position, disconnect the fuel line, and remove the fuel tank.
2. Drain fuel from the fuel tank thoroughly.
3. Loosen the nut (2) and remove the fuel cock from the fuel tank.
4. Remove the fuel filter from the fuel tank.
5. Check the gasket and, replace if necessary.

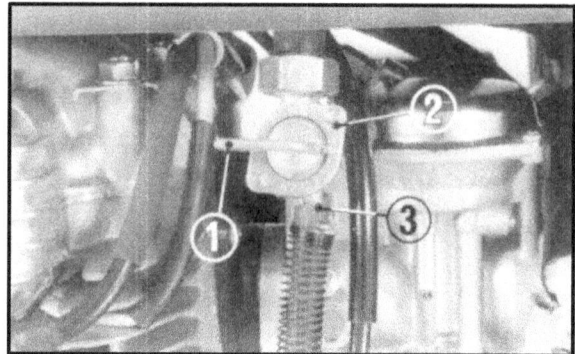

Fig. 30 (1) Fuel cock lever
(2) Fuel cock
(3) Fuel tube

6. Clean the fuel filter with solvent and blow dry with a compressed air. Discard the old filter element and install a new one if found to be clogged, broken or damaged.
7. Install the fuel filter in the fuel tank.
8. Install the fuel cock in the fuel tank.
9. Install the fuel tank. Connect the fuel line to the fuel cock.
10. Fill the tank with fuel. With the fuel cock lever in ON position, check for leaks past the mating surfaces of the fuel tube and fuel cock.

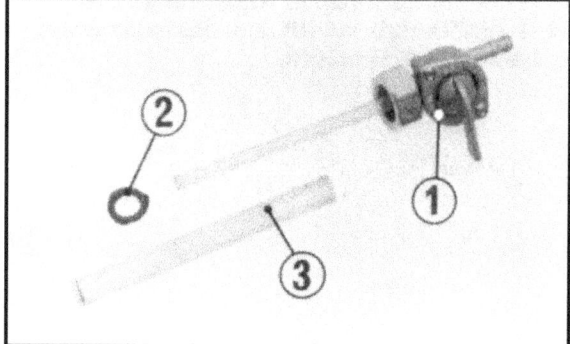

Fig. 31 (1) Fuel cock
(2) Gasket
(3) Fuel filter element

2. Battery Case

1. Open the seal and remove the fuel tank.
2. Remove the right and left air cleaners.
3. Remove the battery.
4. Disconnect the flasher relay and silicon rectifier wires at the battery case.
5. Remove the battery case by removing the three bolts (2).
7. To install the battery, reverse the foregoing removal procedure.
8. Apply grease to the battery terminals to prevent corrosion.
9. For inspection, refer to page 98.
10. Route the battery overflow tube as per the instructions given in the caution label, being sure that it is not bent or twisted.

Fig. 32 (1) Battery case

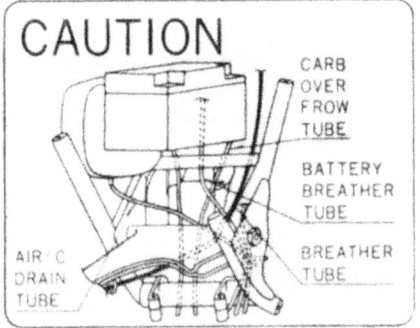

Fig. 33 (1) Battery caution label

X. SUPPLEMENT TO CJ250T/CJ360T

3. Muffler

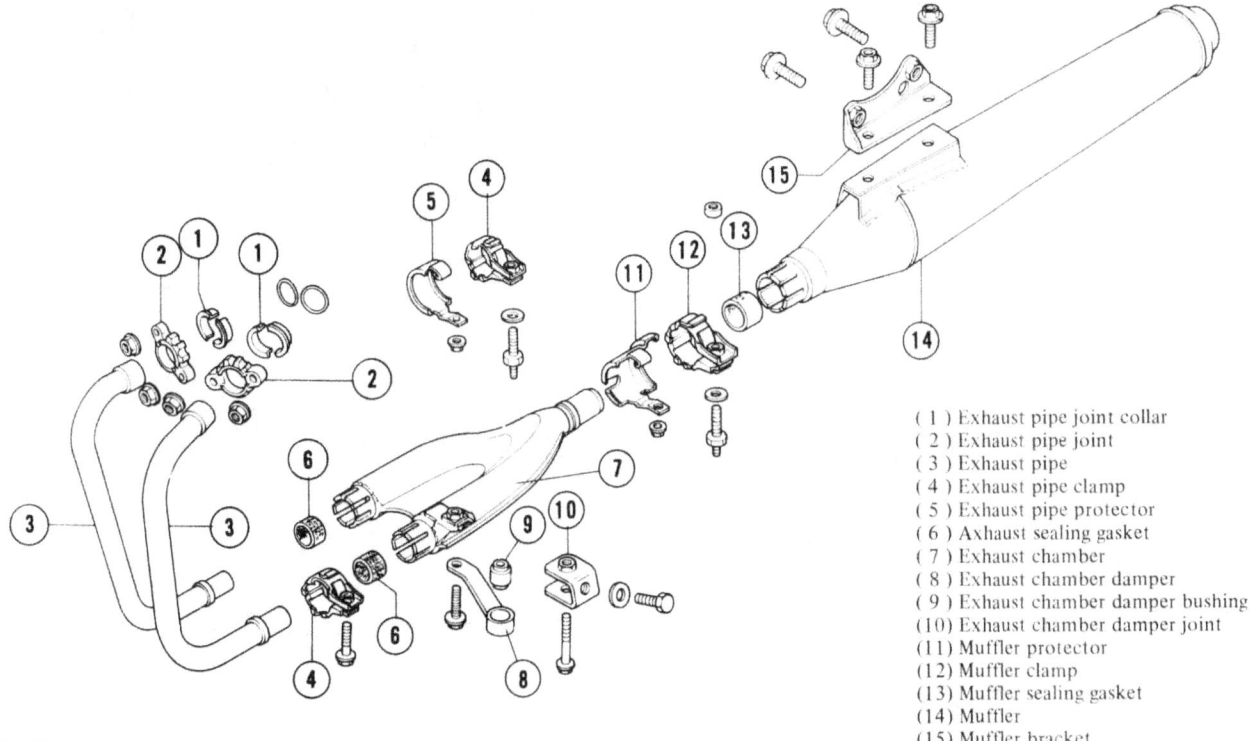

(1) Exhaust pipe joint collar
(2) Exhaust pipe joint
(3) Exhaust pipe
(4) Exhaust pipe clamp
(5) Exhaust pipe protector
(6) Axhaust sealing gasket
(7) Exhaust chamber
(8) Exhaust chamber damper
(9) Exhaust chamber damper bushing
(10) Exhaust chamber damper joint
(11) Muffler protector
(12) Muffler clamp
(13) Muffler sealing gasket
(14) Muffler
(15) Muffler bracket

Fig. 34

Disassembly

1. Remove the two bolts (1) and take out the muffler.

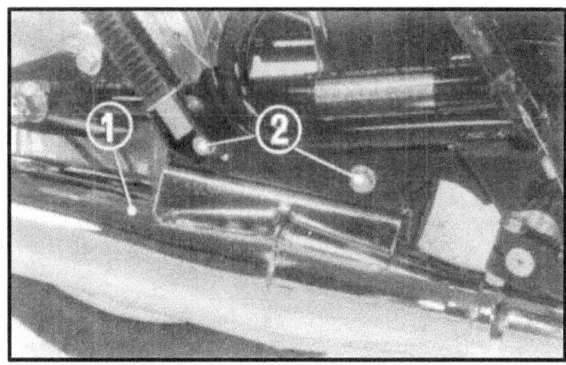

Fig. 35 (1) Muffler
(2) Bolt

2. Remove the exhaust chamber damper by removing the bolt (1).

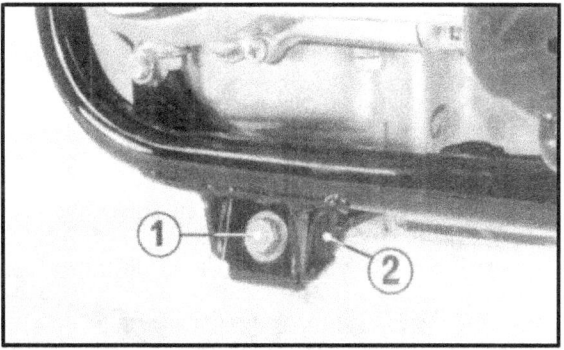

Fig. 36 (1) Bolt
(2) Exhaust chamber damper

3. Remove the exhaust pipe joints, collars and mufflers by removing the four joint nuts.

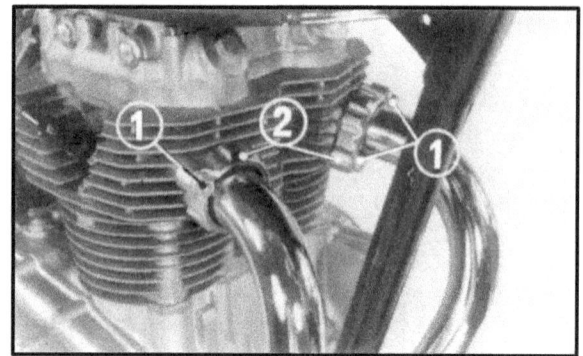

Fig. 37 (1) Joint nut
(2) Exhaust pipe joint

4. Remove the exhaust pipe and muffler protector.
5. Unscrew the two exhaust clamp bolts and remove the exhaust pipe and sealing gasket from the exhaust pipe chamber.
6. Remove the muffler clamp bolt; then, free the exhaust chamber from the muffler together with the sealing gasket.
7. Remove the muffler stay by backing off the two bolts.

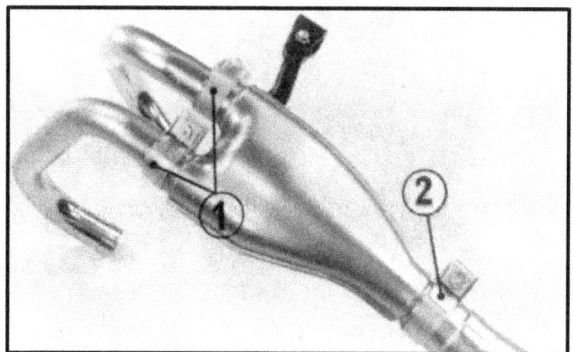

Fig. 38 (1) Exhaust pipe joint
(2) Muffler band

8. Free the damper joint and damper from the exhaust chamber by backing off the two bolts.

Inspection

1. Check the exhaust pipe gasket and, it necessary, replace.
2. Check the exhaust pipe and muffler sealing gasket for damage or other defects; if necessary, replace with a new one.
3. Check the damper rubber bushing and replace if damaged or deteriorated.

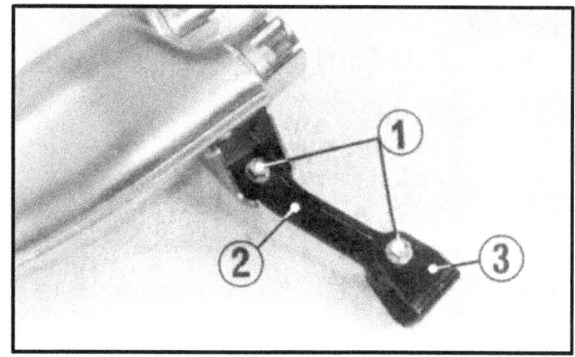

Fig. 39 (1) Bolt
(2) Damper joint
(3) Damper

Assembly

Assembly is the reverse order of the removal. However, observe the following assembly notes:
1. Put the sealing gaskets over the exhaust pipe and exhaust pipe chamber before assembling.
2. Tighten the muffler clamps in the location as per the instructions given in Fig. 40.
3. Place the protector over the muffler clamps protector stay, then tighten the protector and stay.
4. Install the exhaust pipe to the cylinder with the point, collar and nuts.
5. Install the damper to the muffler and frame.
6. If the cylinder gasket is renewed, retighten the band bolts after 500 km or riding.

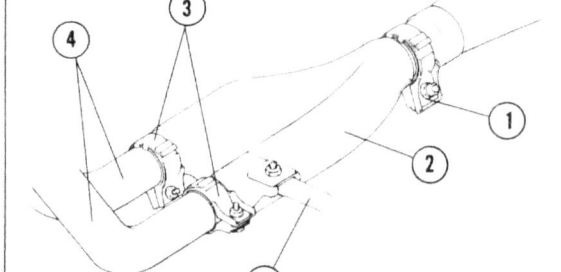

Fig. 40 (1) Muffler clamp   (4) Exhaust pipe
(2) Exhaust chamber   (5) Exhaust chamber damper
(3) Exhaust pipe clamp

X. SUPPLEMENT TO CJ250T/CJ360T

WIRING DIAGRAM

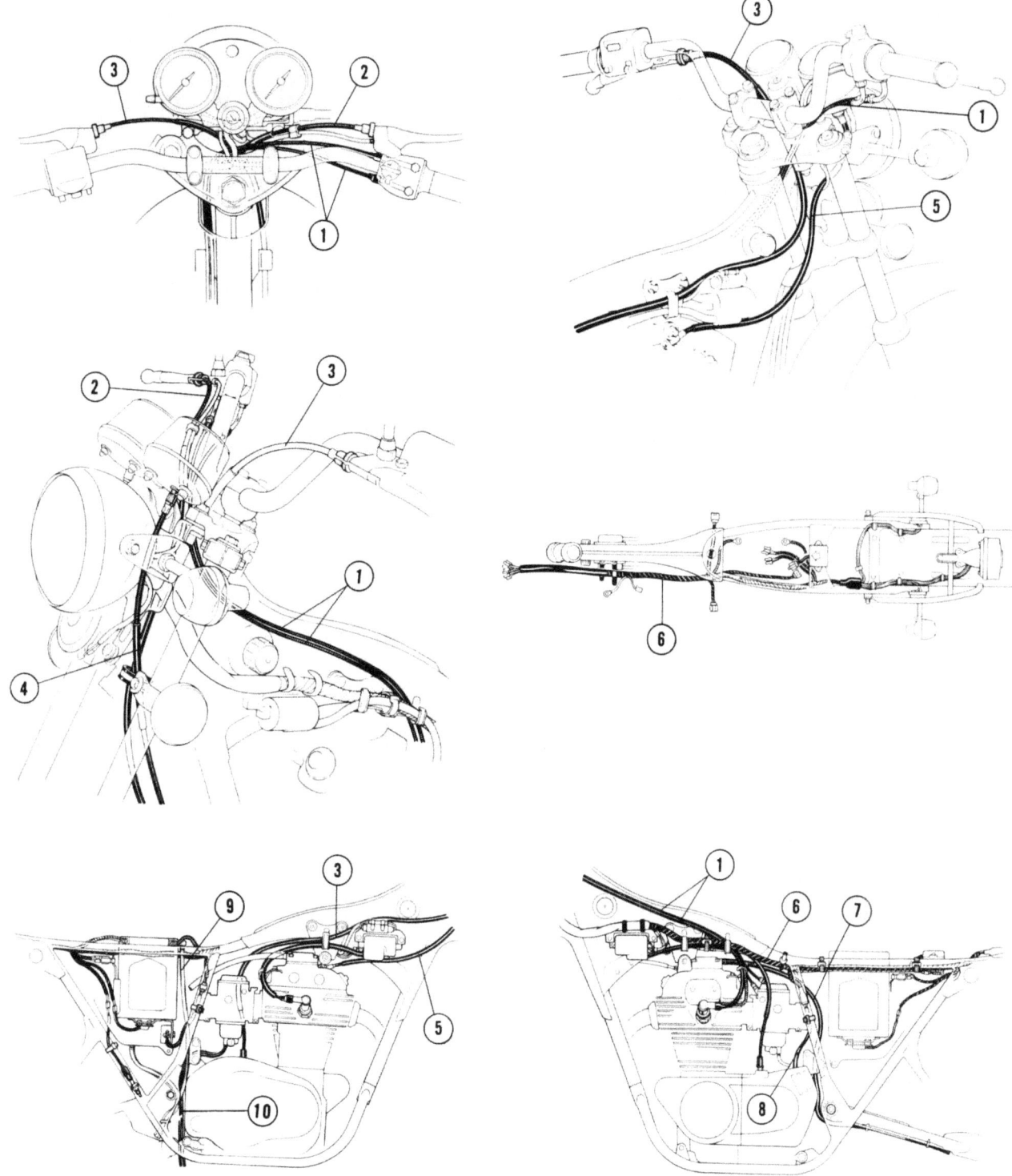

(1) Throttle cable
(2) Front brake cable
(3) Clutch cable
(4) Speedometer cable
(5) Tachometer cable
(6) Wire harness
(7) Breather tube
(8) Stop switch cord
(9) Battery breather tube
(10) Breather tube

X. SUPPLEMENT TO CJ250T/CJ360T

V. ELECTRICAL SYSTEM ....See page 97

1. INSPECTION

1. Main switch

Check for continuity between terminals. The switch is normal if continuity exists between terminals as shown (O–O). If there is no continuity, or if there is continuity in the circuits other than marked, discard the old switch and install new one.

	B	IG	TL1	TL2
OFF	○	○	○	○
1	○——○		○——○	
2	○			○
Cord color	Red	Black	Brown/white	Brown

Fig. 41 (1) Main switch

2. Front stop switch

Check for continuity between the black and green/yellow wires with an Ohm meter. The switch is normal if the stop lamp lights when the brake lever is pulled in 10–20 mm as measured at the lever tip.

Fig. 42 (1) Black wire (2) Green/yellow wire

3. Turn signal switch

Disconnect the switch wires in the headlight case and check for continuity between terminals. The switch is correct if there is continuity between the terminals as shown in the table below.

	W	L	R	PF	LP	RP
L2	○——○			○———		———○
L1	○——○			○———○		
(N)				○———○		
R1	○———		———○	○———○		
R2	○———		———○	○———		———○
Cord color	Gray	Orange	Blue	Black/yellow	Orange/white	Blue/white

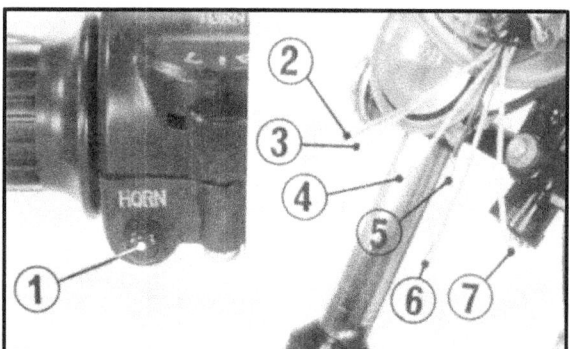

Fig. 43 (1) Turn signal switch (5) Black/yellow
(2) Gray (6) Orange/white
(3) Orange (7) Blue/white
(4) Blue

4. Dimmer switch

Disconnect the dimmer switch wires and check for continuity between terminals in each knob position.

	PF	HK	Hi	Lo
Hi	○——○	○———○		
(N)	○——○	○———○		○
Lo	○——○	○———○		○
Cord color	Black/yellow	Black/yellow	Blue	White

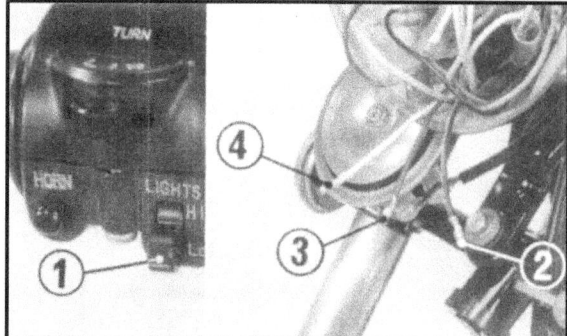

Fig. 44 (1) Dimmer switch (3) Blue
(2) Black/yellow (4) White

X. SUPPLEMENT TO CJ250T/CJ360T

5. Ignition switch

Disconnect the ignition switch wires and check for continuity between circuits. The switch is normal if continuity exists between the circuits as indicated by the mark "O–O" in the table shown immediately below:

	IG	KILL
OFF	O——————O	
RUN	O——————O	
OFF		
Cord color	Black	Black/white

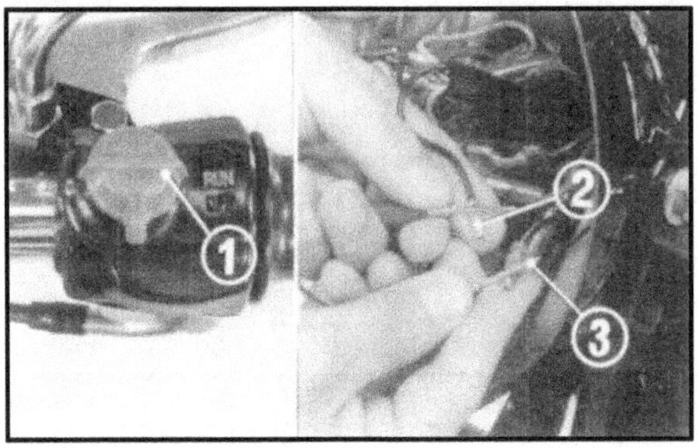

Fig. 45 (1) Kill switch
(2) Black/white

6. Horn switch

Disconnect the light green and green wires in the turn signal/dimmer switch and check for continuity between these two wires. The switch is correct if continuity exists when the switch button is depressed. Discard the old switch and install a new one if there is no continuity.

Fig. 46 (1) Horn switch

VI. SERVICE DATA

1. SPECIAL TOOLS

Ref. No.	Tool No.	Tool Name	Q'ty
1	07902–2400000	Spanner, pin 46 mm	1
2	07908–3230000	Wrench, tappet adjusting	1
3	07910–3290000	Wrench, R. retainer	1
4	07915–6390001	Wrench, lock nut 16 mm	1
5	07917–3230000	Wrench, hollow set 6 mm	1
6	07922–3000000	Holder driver sprocket	1
7	07933–2160000	Puller, rotor	1
8	07942–6110000	Driver, valve guide	1
9	07945–3330100	Driver, ATT bearing	1
10	07945–3330200	Driver, ATT bearing	1
11	07945–3330300	Driver, ball race	1
12	07947–3330000	Driver, fork seal	1
13	07949–6110000	Handle, driver	1
14	07953–3330000	Remover, ball race	1
15	07954–3690000	Compressor, piston ring	1
16	07957–3290001	Compressor, valve spring	1
17	07958–2500000	Base piston	1
18	07959–3290000	Compressor, shock absorber	1
19	07984–5900000	Reamer valve guide 7 mm	1
20	07797–2920300	Case tool set	1

OPTIONAL SPECIAL TOOL

Ref. No.	Tool No.	Tool Name	Q'ty
1	07504–3000100	Gauge set, vacuum	1
1-1	07504–3000200	Gauge vacuum	(1)
2	07510–3690100	Attachment A, gauge	2
3	07908–3690000	Wrench, carburetor adjusting	1
4	07975–3000001	Tool set, chain joint	1
4-1	07975–3000600	Bolt B, pressure	(1)
4-2	07975–3000700	Wedge set, joint	(1)

X. SUPPLEMENT TO CJ250T/CJ360T

2. MAINTENANCE STANDARDS

Engine

Unit: mm (in.)   [ ] : 360 cc only

Items to be inspected		Standard	Service Limit
Rocker arm-to-rocker arm shaft clearance		0.016–0.061 (0.0006–0.0024)	0.1 (0.0039
Cam lift	IN.	40.314 (1.5872)	40.1 (1.5787)
	EX.	40.339 (1.5882)	40.1 (1.5787)
Camshaft side clearance		0.07–0.3 (0.0028–0.0118)	Above and below standards
Valve seat width		1.0–1.3 (0.0394–0.0512)	2.0 (0.0787)
O.D. of valve stem	IN.	6.975–6.990 (0.2746–0.2752)	6.93 (0.2728)
	EX.	6.955–6.970 (0.2738–0.2744)	6.93 (0.2728)
Valve-to valve guide clearance	IN.	0.01–0.035 (0.0004–0.0014)	6.93 (0.2728)
	EX.	0.03–0.05 (0.0012–0.0020)	0.09 (0.0035)
Valve spring tension/ as compressed length	INNER	30.5–35.1 kg/31 (67.24–77.38 lbs/1.2205)	–
	OUTER	62.6–72.0 kg/31 (138.01–158.73 lbs/1.2205)	–
Free length of valve spring	INNER	39.8 (1.5669)	39.3 (1.5709)
	OUTER	49.0 (1.9291)	47.8 (1.8819)
Transverse warpage on cylinder head mating face		–	0.3 (0.0118)
I.D. of cylinder		56.01–56.02 (2.2051–2.2055) [67.01–67.02 (2.6382–2.6386)]	56.1 (2.2087) [67.1 (2.6417)]
O.D. of piston at skirt		55.97–55.99 (2.2036–2.2043) [66.97–66.99 (2.6366–2.6374)]	55.85 (2.1988) [66.85 (2.6319)]
Piston pin hole I.D.		15.002–15.008 (0.5906–0.5909) [16.002–16.008 (0.6300–0.6302)]	15.05 (0.5925) [16.05 (0.6319)]
O.D. of piston pin		14.994–15.00 (0.5903–0.5906) [15.994–16.00 (0.6297–0.6299)]	14.9 (0.5866) [15.9 (0.6260)]
Piston ring-to-ring groove clearance	TOP	0.02–0.06 (0.0008–0.0024)	0.15 (0.0059)
	SECOND	0.015–0.045 (0.0006–0.0018) [0.02–0.04 (0.0008–0.0016)]	0.15 (0.0059) [0.15 (0.0059)]
	OIL	0.010–0.045 (0.0004–0.0018)	0.15 (0.0059)
Piston ring end gap	TOP	0.15–0.35 (0.0059–0.0138) [0.2–0.4 (0.0079–0.0157)]	0.75 (0.0295) [0.8 (0.0315)]
	SECOND	0.15–0.35 (0.0059–0.0138)	0.75 (0.0295)
	OIL	0.2–0.4 (0.0079–0.0157)	0.8 (0.0315)
Oil pump outer rotor-to-pump body clearance		0.15–0.21 (0.0059–0.0083)	0.35 (0.0138)
Radial clearance of oil pump outer rotor		0.02–0.08 (0.0008–0.0032)	0.1 (0.0039)
Thickness of clutch friction disc		2.62–2.78 (0.1031–0.1095)	2.3 (0.9055)
Transverse warpage on clutch plate		0.1 (0.0039)	0.2 (0.0079)
Clutch spring tension		25/21.8–23.2 kg (0.984/48.06–51.15 lbs)	–
Free length of clutch spring		31.25 (1.2305)	29.7 (1.1693)
Gear shift fork width, A and B		5.93–6.00 (0.2335–0.2362)	5.5 (0.2165)
O.D. of gear shift guide shaft		12.957–12.984 (0.5101–0.5112)	12.9 (0.5079)

Items to be inspected	Standard	Service Limit
I.D. of gear shift fork A	13.000–13.018 (0.5118–0.5125)	12.95 (0.5098)
O.D. of gear shift drum	39.950–39.975 (1.5374–1.5384)	39.9 (1.5709)
I.D. of gear shift fork B	40.000–40.025 (1.5748–1.5758)	40.075 (1.5798)
Kick starter pinion-to-shaft clearance	0.04–0.082 (0.0016–0.0032)	0.1 (0.0039)
Gear shift fork-to-drum clearance (A and B)	0.05–0.22 (0.0020–0.0087)	0.3 (0.0118)
Thickness of cam chain tensioner slipper (at center)	4.0 (0.1575)	3.0 (0.1181)
Thickness of cam chain guide (at center)	6.1–6.3 (0.2402–0.2480)	5.9 (0.1969)
Crankshaft runout (See Fig. 4–101 on page 62)	–	Below 0.1 (0.0039)
I.D. of connecting rod small end	15.016–15.034 (0.5912–0.5919)	15.07 (0.5933)
Connecting rod big end side clearance on pin	0.07–0.33 (0.0028–0.0130)	0.60 (0.0236)
Connecting rod big end radial clearance on pin	0.004–0.012 (0.0002–0.0005)	0.05 (0.0020)

Frame

Items to be inspected	Standard	Service Limit
Wheel rim surface runout	0.5 (0.0197) max.	2.0 (0.787)
Wheel bearing axial play	0.07 (0.0276) max.	0.1 (0.0039)
Wheel bearing radial play	0.03 (0.0012) max.	0.05 (0.0020)
Front axle bend	0.01 (0.0004)	0.2 (0.0079)
Rear axle bend	0.01 (0.0004)	0.2 (0.0079)
Thickness of brake lining	4.9–5.0 (0.1929–0.1969)	2.5 (0.098)
I.D. of rear brake drum	160.0–160.3 (6.2992–6.3110)	161 (6.3386)
Free length of front suspension spring	478.6 (18.843)	468.0 (18.425)
I.D. of front fork bottom case	33.025–33.064 (1.3002–1.3017)	33.139 (1.3047)
O.D. of front fork pipe	32.97–32.985 (1.2980–1.2986)	32.25 (1.2697)
Free length of rear suspension spring	207.6 (8.1732)	
O.D. of rear fork center collar	21.427–21.460 (0.8436–0.8449)	21.46 (0.8449)
I.D. of rear fork bushing	21.5–21.552 (0.8465–0.8485)	21.70 (0.8543)

X. SUPPLEMENT TO CJ250T/CJ360T

3. TIGHTENING TORQUE STANDARD

Engine

Item	Size (mm)	Torque kg-m	Torque lbs-ft
R.L. crankcase cover bolt	6	0.7–1.1	5.1– 8.0
Cylinder head hold-down bolt	10	3.0–3.6	21.7–26.0
Cylinder head insulator bolt	6	0.7–1.1	5.1– 8.0
Camshaft sprocket fixing bolt	7	1.7–2.3	12.3–16.6
A.C. generator mounting bolt	8	3.5–4.5	25.3–32.5
Oil filter lock nut	16	4.5–5.5	32.6–39.7
Crankcase mounting bolt	6	0.9–1.4	6.5–10.1
	8	2.2–2.6	15.9–18.8

Frame

Item	Size (mm)	Torque kg-m	Torque lbs-ft
Steering stem nut	24	7.0–9.0	50.7–65.1
Fork bolt	27	2.5–3.0	18.1–21.7
Handlebar holder attaching bolt	8	1.8–2.5	13.1–18.1
Front fork bottom bridge	8	1.8–2.5	13.1–18.1
Spoke		0.15–0.20	1.1– 1.5
Rear fork pivot bolt	14	5.5–7.0	39.7–50.7
Front fork axle nut	12	5.5–6.5	39.7–47.0
Front fork under holder	8	2.7–3.3	19.5–23.8
Engine hanger bolt	8 UBS	2.7–3.3	19.5–23.8
Engine hanger bolt	10 UBS	4.5–6.0	32.5–43.4
Rear axle	16	8.0–10.0	57.9–72.3
Final driven sprocket	10 UBS	6.0–7.0	43.4–50.7
Brake arm	8	1.8–2.5	13.1–18.1
Rear brake stopper arm	8	1.8–2.5	13.1–18.1
Rear shock absorber	10	3.0–4.0	21.7–29.0
Foot rest	10 UBS	4.5–6.0	32.5–43.4
Change pedal	6	0.8–1.2	5.8– 8.7
Kick arm	8	2.5–3.0	18.1–21.7

X. SUPPLEMENT TO CJ250T/CJ360T

4. SPECIFICATIONS CJ360T (A TYPE)

Item		Metric	English
Overall length		2,075 mm	81.7 in.
Overall width		790 mm	31.1 in.
Overall height		1,110 mm	43.7 in.
Wheel base		1,375 mm	54.1 in.
Seat height		805 mm	31.7 in.
Foot peg height		345 mm	13.6 in.
Ground clearance		140 mm	5.5 in.
Dry weight		159 kg	351 lbs.
Type		Semi double crable	
F. suspension, travel		Telescopic fork, travel 139.5 mm 5.5 in.	
R. suspension, travel		Swing arm, travel 77.3 mm 3.0 in.	
F. tire size, pressure		3.00S 18 - 4PR Rib tire, tire air pressure 1.75/1.75 kg/cm², 25/25 psi	
R. tire size, pressure		3.50S 18 - 4PR Rib tire, tire air pressure 2.0/2.5 kg/cm², 28/36 psi.	
F. brake, lining area		Internal expanding shoe, lining swept area 104 cm², 16.1 sq.in.	
R. brake, lining area		Internal expanding shoe, lining swept area 70 cm², 10.9 sq.in.	
Fuel capacity		14 lit.	3.7 U.S. gal, 3.1 Imp. gal.
Fuel reserve capacity		2.5 lit.	0.7 U.S. gal, 0.6 Imp. gal.
Caster angle		63°30′	
Trail length		86 mm	3.4 in.
Front fork oil capacity		140 cc	
Type		Air cooled 4 stroke OHC engine	
Cylinder arrangement		2 cylinder in line	
Bore and stroke		67.0 x 50.6 mm	2.638 x 1.992 in.
Displacement		356 cc	21.7 cu. in.
Compression ratio		9.3 : 1	
Valve train		Chain driven over head camshaft	
Oil capacity		2.0 lit.	2.1 U.S. qt., 1.8 Imp. qt.
Lubrication system		Forced pressure and wet sump	
Cylinder head compression pressure		12 kg/cm² (170.7 psi.)	
Intake valve	Open	At 5° (before top dead center)	
	Close	At 40° (after bottom dead center)	
Exhaust valve	Open	At 5° (before bottom dead center)	
	Close	At 40° (after top dead center)	
Valve tappet clearance		IN: 0.05 EX: 0.08 mm	IN; 0.002 EX: 0.003 in.
Idle speed		1,200 rpm	
Type		CV Butterfly Tipe	
Setting mark		759A	
Main jet		Primary #68, Secondary #110	
Slow jet		#35	
Air screw opening		2	

X. SUPPLEMENT TO CJ250T/CJ360T

Item	Metric	English
Float height	18.5 mm	0.728 in.
Clutch	Wet multi plate type	
Transmission	5 speed constant mesh	
Primary reduction	3.714	
Gear ratio I	2.438	
Gear ratio II	1.667	
Gear ratio III	1.375	
Gear ratio IV	1.111	
Gear ratio V	0.965	
Final reduction	2.063, drive sprocket 16T, driven sprocket 33T	
Gear shift pattern	Left foot operated return system	
Ignition	Battery and Ignition coil	
Starting system	Kick pedal	
Alternator	A.C. generator 12V 0.11 kw 5,000 rpm	
Battery capacity	12V–9AH	
Spark plug	NGK D8ES ND W24EX	
Headlight	Low/High 12V 25/35 watt	
Tail/stoplight	Tail/stop 12V 8/27 watt 3/32 cp	
Turn signal-light	Front/rear 12V 23/23 watt 32/32 cp	
Speedometer light	12V 3.4 watt 2 cp	
Tachometer light	12V 3.4 watt 2 cp	
Neutral indicator light	12V 3.4 watt 2 cp	
Turn signal indicator light	12V 3.4 watt 2 cp	
High beam indicator	12V 3.4 watt 2 cp	

CJ250T/CJ360T (D.U. TYPE)

( ) : CJ250T

Item		Metric	English
Overall length		2,075 mm	81.7 in.
Overall width		790 mm	31.1 in.
Overall height		1,125 mm	44.3 in.
Wheel base		1,375 mm	54.1 in.
Seat height		805 mm	31.7 in.
Foot peg height		345 mm	13.6 in.
Ground clearance		140 mm	5.5 in.
Dry weight		162 kg	357 lbs.
Type		Semi double crable	
F. suspension, travel		Telescopic fork, travel 139.5 mm 5.5 in.	
R. suspension, travel		Swing arm, travel 77.3 mm 3.0 in.	
F. tire size, pressure		3.00S 18 - 4PR Rib tire, tire air pressure 1.75/1.75 kg/cm², 25/25 psi	
R. tire size, pressure		3.50S 18 - 4PR Block tire, tire air pressure 2.0/2.5 kg/cm², 28/36 psi.	
F. brake, lining area		Disk brake, disk pad swept area 38 cm², 5.9 sq.in.	
R. brake, lining area		Internal expanding shoe, lining swept area 150 cm², 23.2 sq.in.	
Fuel capacity		14 lit.	3.7 U.S. gal, 3.1 Imp. gal.
Fuel reserve capacity		2.5 lit.	0.7 U.S. gal, 0.6 Imp. gal.
Caster angle		63°30'	
Trail length		85 mm	3.4 in.
Front fork oil capacity		140 cc	
Type		Air cooled 4 stroke OHC engine	
Cylinder arrangement		2 cylinder in line	
Bore and stroke		67.0 x 50.6 mm (56 x 50.6 mm)	2.638 x 1.992 in. (2.205 x 1.992 in.)
Displacement		356 cc (249 cc)	21.7 cu. in. (15.2 cu. in.)
Compression ratio		9.3 : 1 (9.5 : 1)	
Valve train		Chain driven over head camshaft	
Oil capacity		2.0 lit.	2.1 U.S. qt., 1.8 Imp. qt.
Lubrication system		Forced pressure and wet sump	
Cylinder head compression pressure		12 kg/cm² (170.7 psi.)	
Intake valve	Open	At 5° (before top dead center)	
	Close	At 40° (after bottom dead center)	
Exhaust valve	Open	At 5° (before bottom dead center)	
	Close	At 40° (after top dead center)	
Valve tappet clearance		IN: 0.05 EX: 0.08 mm	IN; 0.002 EX: 0.003 in.
Idle speed		1,200 rpm	
Type		CV Butterfly Tipe	
Setting mark		759A	
Main jet		Primary #68, Secondary #110	
Slow jet		#35	
Air screw opening		2	

X. SUPPLEMENT TO CJ250T/CJ360T

Item	Metric	English
Float height	18.5 mm	0.728 in.
Clutch	Wet multi plate type	
Transmission	5 speed constant mesh	
Primary reduction	3.714	
Gear ratio I	2.438 (2.500)	
Gear ratio II	1.666 (1.170)	
Gear ratio III	1.375	
Gear ratio IV	1.111	
Gear ratio V	0.965	
Final reduction	2.062 (2.312), drive sprocket 16T, driven sprocket 33T (37T)	
Gear shift pattern	Left foot operated return system	
Ignition	Battery and Ignition coil	
Starting system	Kick pedal	
Alternator	A.C. generator 12V 0.13 kw 5,000 rpm	
Battery capacity	12V–9AH	
Spark plug	(NGK) B8ES (DENSO) W24ES	
Headlight	Low/High	12V 25/35 watt
Tail/stoplight	Tail/stop	12V 8/23 watt 3/32 cp
Turn signal-light	Front/rear	12V 23/23 watt 32/32 cp
Speedometer light		12V 3.4 watt 2 cp
Tachometer light		12V 3.4 watt 2 cp
Neutral indicator light		12V 3.4 watt 2 cp
Turn signal indicator light		12V 3.4 watt 2 cp
High beam indicator		12V 3.4 watt 2 cp

X. SUPPLEMENT TO CJ250T/CJ360T

CJ250T/CJ360T (G TYPE)

( ) : CJ250T

Item		Metric	English
Overall length		2,145 mm	84.5 in.
Overall width		710 mm	28.0 in.
Overall height		1,070 mm	42.1 in.
Wheel base		1,375 mm	54.1 in.
Seat height		805 mm	31.7 in.
Foot peg height		345 mm	13.6 in.
Ground clearance		140 mm	5.5 in.
Dry weight		162 kg	357 lbs.
Type		Semi double crable	
F. suspension, travel		Telescopic fork, travel 139.5 mm 5.5 in.	
R. suspension, travel		Swing arm, travel 77.3 mm 3.0 in.	
F. tire size, pressure		3.00S 18 - 4PR Rib tire, tire air pressure 1.75/1.75 kg/cm^2, 25/25 psi	
R. tire size, pressure		3.75S 18 - 4PR Block, tire air pressure 2.0/2.5 kg/cm^2, 28/36 psi.	
F. brake, lining area		Disk brake, disk pad swept area 38 cm^2, 5.9 sq.in.	
R. brake, lining area		Internal expanding shoe, lining swept area 150 cm^2, 23.2 sq.in.	
Fuel capacity		14 lit.	3.7 U.S. gal, 3.1 Imp. gal.
Fuel reserve capacity		2.5 lit.	0.7 U.S. gal, 0.6 Imp. gal.
Caster angle		63°30′	
Trail length		85 mm	3.4 in.
Front fork oil capacity		140 cc	
Type		Air cooled 4 stroke OHC engine	
Cylinder arrangement		2 cylinder in line	
Bore and stroke		67.0 x 50.6 mm (56 x 50.6 mm)	2.638 x 1.992 in. (2.205 x 1.992 in.)
Displacement		356 cc (249 cc)	21.7 cu. in. (15.2 cu. in.)
Compression ratio		9.3 : 1 (9.5 : 1)	
Valve train		Chain driven over head camshaft	
Oil capacity		2.0 lit.	2.1 U.S. qt., 1.8 Imp. qt.
Lubrication system		Forced pressure and wet sump	
Cylinder head compression pressure		12 kg/cm^2 (170.7 psi.)	
Intake valve	Open	At 5° (before top dead center)	
	Close	At 40° (after bottom dead center)	
Exhaust valve	Open	At 5° (before bottom dead center)	
	Close	At 40° (after top dead center)	
Valve tappet elearance		IN: 0.05 EX: 0.08 mm	IN; 0.002 EX: 0.003 in.
Idle speed		1,200 rpm	
Type		CV Butterfly Tipe	
Setting mark		759A	
Main jet		Primary #68, Secondary #110	
Slow jet		#35	
Air screw opening		2	

X. SUPPLEMENT TO CJ250T/CJ360T

Item	Metric	English
Float height	18.5 mm	0.728 in.
Clutch	Wet multi plate type	
Transmission	5 speed constant mesh	
Primary reduction	3.714	
Gear ratio I	2.437 (2.500)	
Gear ratio II	1.667 (1.750)	
Gear ratio III	1.375	
Gear ratio IV	1.111	
Gear ratio V	0.965	
Final reduction	2.062(2.312), drive sprocket 16T, driven sprocket 33T (37T)	
Gear shift pattern	Left foot operated return system	
Ignition	Battery and Ignition coil	
Starting system	Kick pedal	
Alternator	A.C. generator 12V 0.13 kw 5,000 rpm	
Battery capacity	12V–9AH	
Spark plug	(NGK) BR8ES (DENSO) W24ESR	
Headlight	Low/High 12V 40/45 watt	
Tail/stoplight	Tail/stop 12V 5/21 watt 3/32 cp	
Turn signal-light	Front/rear 12V 5/21 watt 32/32 cp	
Speedometer light	12V 3.4 watt 2 cp	
Tachometer light	12V 3.4 watt 2 cp	
Neutral indicator light	12V 3.4 watt 2 cp	
Turn signal indicator light	12V 3.4 watt 2 cp	
High beam indicator	12V 3.4 watt 2 cp	

X. SUPPLEMENT TO CJ250T/CJ360T

CJ250T/CJ360T (F.E.ED. TYPE)

( ) : CJ250T

Item		Metric	English
Overall length		2,145mm	84.5 in.
Overall width		710 mm	28.0 in.
Overall height		1,070 mm	42.1 in.
Wheel base		1,375 mm	54.1 in.
Seat height		805 mm	31.7 in.
Foot peg height		345 mm	13.6 in.
Ground clearance		140 mm	5.5 in.
Dry weight		162 kg	357 lbs.
Type		Semi double crable	
F. suspension, travel		Telescopic fork, travel 139.5 mm 5.5 in.	
R. suspension, travel		Swing arm, travel 77.3 mm 3.0 in.	
F. tire size, pressure		3.00S 18 - 4PR Rib tire, tire air pressure 1.75/1.75 kg/cm², 25/25 psi	
R. tire size, pressure		3.50S 18 - 4PR Block tire, tire air pressure 2.0/2.5 kg/cm², 28/36 psi.	
F. brake, lining area		Disk brake, disk pad swept area 38 cm², 28/25 psi. 16.1 sq.in.	
R. brake, lining area		Internal expanding shoe, lining swept area 150 cm², 23.2 sq.in.	
Fuel capacity		14 lit.	3.7 U.S. gal, 3.1 Imp. gal.
Fuel reserve capacity		2.5 lit.	0.7 U.S. gal, 0.6 Imp. gal.
Caster angle		63°30′	
Trail length		85 mm	3.4 in.
Front fork oil capacity		140 cc	
Type		Air cooled 4 stroke OHC engine	
Cylinder arrangement		2 cylinder in line	
Bore and stroke		67.0 x 50.6 mm (56 x 50.6 mm)	2.638 x 1.992 in. (2.205 x 1.992 in.)
Displacement		356 cc (249 cc)	21.7 cu. in. (15.2 cu. in.)
Compression ratio		9.3 : 1 (9.5 : 1)	
Valve train		Chain driven over head camshaft	
Oil capacity		2.0 lit.	2.1 U.S. qt., 1.8 Imp. qt.
Lubrication system		Forced pressure and wet sump	
Cylinder head compression pressure		12 kg/cm² (170.7 psi.)	
Intake valve	Open	At 5° (before top dead center)	
	Close	At 40° (after bottom dead center)	
Exhaust valve	Open	At 5° (before bottom dead center)	
	Close	At 40° (after top dead center)	
Valve tappet elearance		IN: 0.05 EX: 0.08 mm	IN; 0.002 EX: 0.003 in.
Idle speed		1,200 rpm	
Type		CV Butterfly Tipe	
Setting mark		759A	
Main jet		Primary #68, Secondary #110	
Slow jet		#35	
Air screw opening		2	

X. SUPPLEMENT TO CJ250T/CJ360T

Item	Metric	English
Float height	18.5 mm	0.728 in.
Clutch	Wet multi plate type	
Transmission	5 speed constant mesh	
Primary reduction	3.714	
Gear ratio I	2.438 (2.500)	
Gear ratio II	1.666 (1.750)	
Gear ratio III	1.375	
Gear ratio IV	1.111	
Gear ratio V	0.965	
Final reduction	2.062, drive sprocket 16T, driven sprocket 33T	
Gear shift pattern	Left foot operated return system	
Ignition	Battery and Ignition coil	
Starting system	Kick pedal	
Alternator	A.C. generator 12V 0.13 kw 5,000 rpm	
Battery capacity	12V–9AH	
Spark plug	(NGK) BR8ES (DENSO) W24ESR	
Headlight	Low/High 12V 40/45 watt	
Tail/stoplight	Tail/stop 12V 5/21 watt 3/32 cp	
Turn signal-light	Front/rear 12V 21/21 watt 32/32 cp	
Speedometer light	12V 3.4 watt 2 cp	
Tachometer light	12V 3.4 watt 2 cp	
Neutral indicator light	12V 3.4 watt 2 cp	
Turn signal indicator light	12V 3.4 watt 2 cp	
High beam indicator	12V 3.4 watt 2 cp	

5. WIRING DIAGRAM CJ360T (A TYPE)

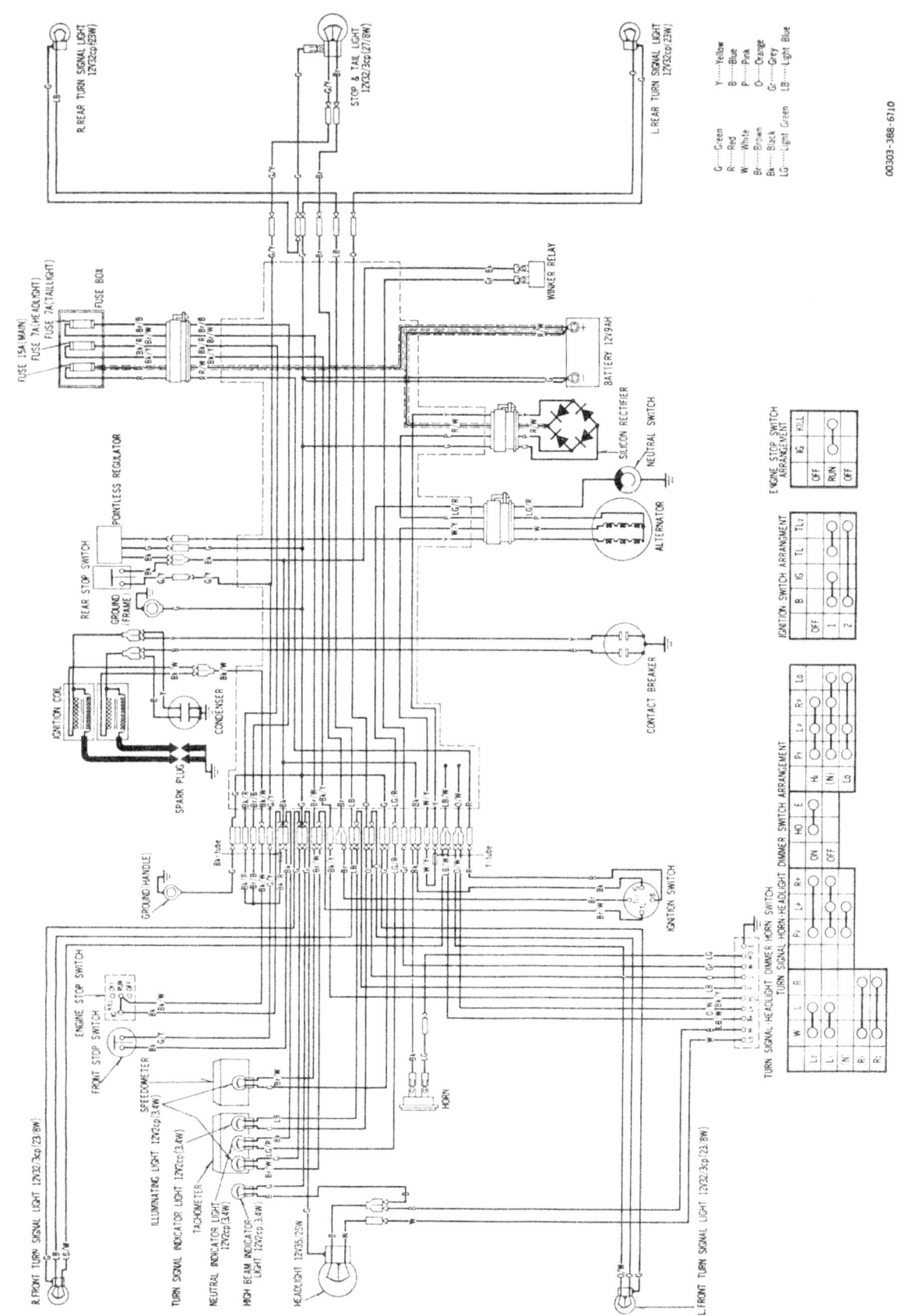

X. SUPPLEMENT TO CJ250T/CJ360T

CJ250T/CJ360T (GENERAL AND AUSTRALIAN TYPES)

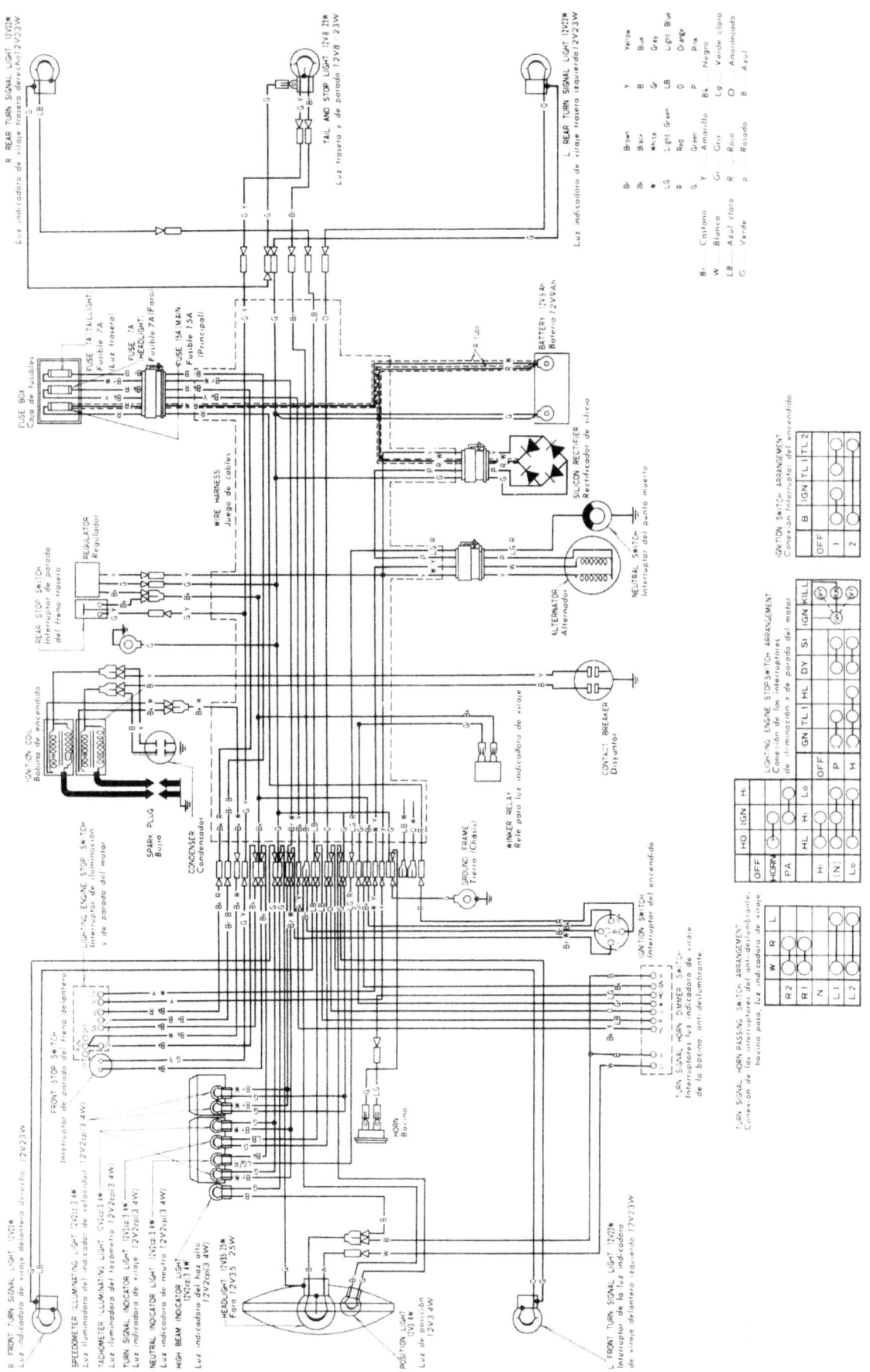

X. SUPPLEMENT TO CJ250T/CJ360T

CJ250T/CJ360T (U.K. · FRENCH · GERMANY · EUROPEAN TYPES)

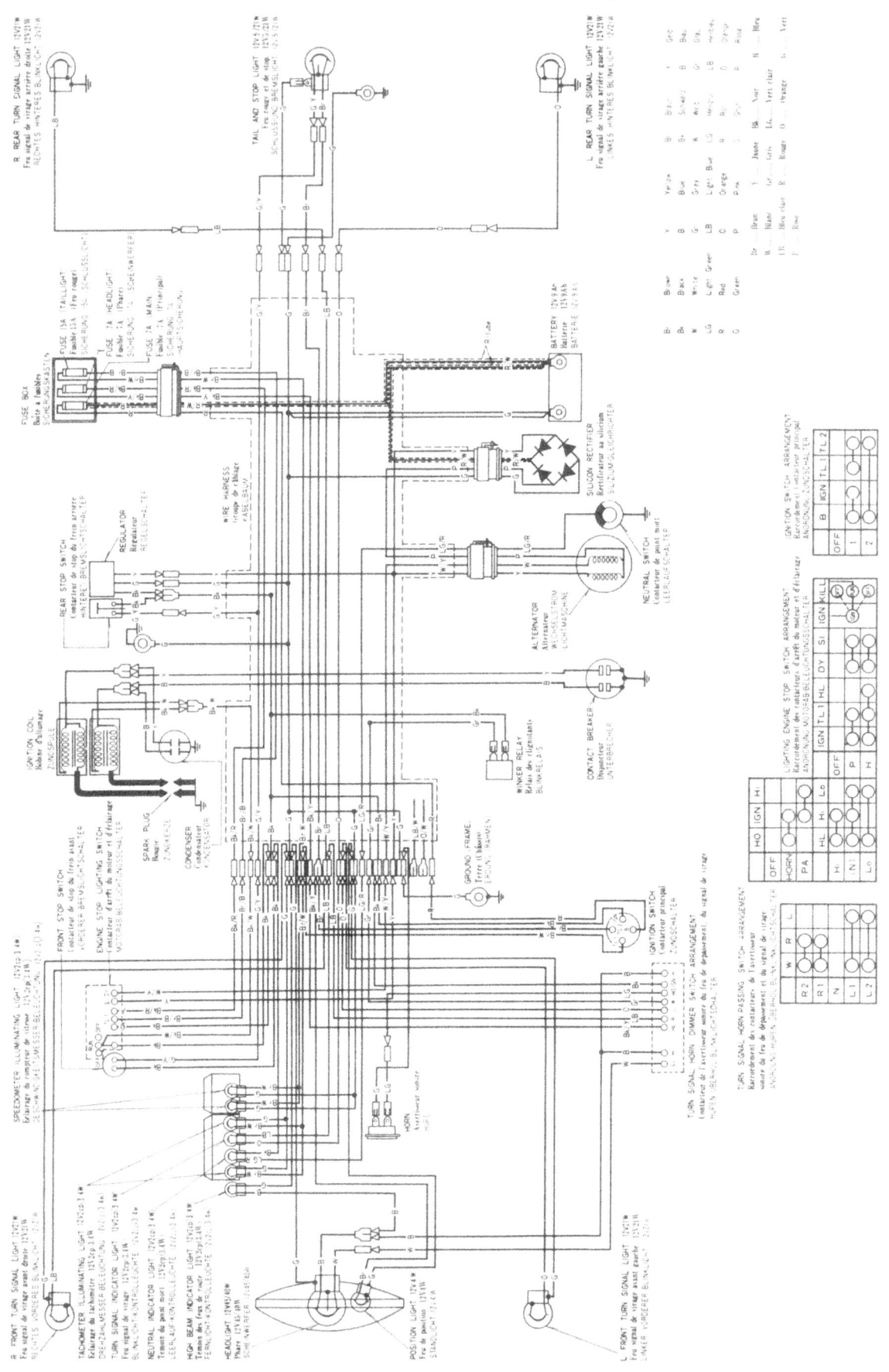

VELOCEPRESS MANUALS – MOTORCYCLE BY MAKE

AJS 1932-1948 SINGLES & TWINS 250cc THRU 1000cc (BOOK OF)
AJS 1945-1960 SINGLES 350cc & 500cc MODELS 16 & 18 (BOOK OF)
AJS 1955-1965 SINGLES 350cc & 500cc (BOOK OF)
AJS 1957-1966 FACTORY WSM - ALL SINGLES & TWINS
ARIEL UP TO 1932 (BOOK OF)
ARIEL 1932-1939 PREWAR MODELS (BOOK OF)
ARIEL 1933-1951 (WORKSHOP MANUAL)
ARIEL 1939-1960 4 STROKE SINGLES (BOOK OF)
ARIEL 1958-1964 LEADER & ARROW FACTORY WSM & PARTS LIST
ARIEL 1958-1964 LEADER & ARROW (BOOK OF)
BMW R26 R27 (1956-1967) FACTORY WORKSHOP MANUAL
BMW R50 R50S R60 R69S (1955-1969) FACTORY WORKSHOP MANUAL
BRIDGESTONE 90 SERIES FACTORY WSM & PARTS CATALOGUE
BRIDGESTONE 175 SERIES FACTORY WSM & PARTS CATALOGUE
BRIDGESTONE 350 SERIES FACTORY WSM & PARTS CATALOGUES
BSA SERVICE SHEETS MASTER CATALOGUE ALL MODELS 1945-1967
BSA BANTAM D1 TO D7 1948-1966 FACTORY SERVICE SHEETS MANUAL
BSA BANTAM ALL MODELS FROM 1948 ONWARDS (BOOK OF)
BSA DANDY FACTORY WORKSHOP MANUAL (COMPILATION)
BSA SINGLES & V-TWINS UP TO 1927 (BOOK OF)
BSA SINGLES & V-TWINS UP TO 1930 (BOOK OF)
BSA SINGLES & V-TWINS UP TO 1935 (BOOK OF)
BSA SINGLES & V-TWINS 1936-1939 (BOOK OF)
BSA C10, C11 & C12 1945-1958 FACTORY SERVICE SHEETS MANUAL
BSA OHV & SV SINGLES 250-600cc 1945-1959 (BOOK OF)
BSA C15 & B40 1958-1967 FACTORY SERVICE SHEETS MANUAL
BSA OHV & SV SINGLES 250cc (ONLY) 1954-1970 (BOOK OF)
BSA B31, B32, B33 & B34 1945-60 FACTORY SERVICE SHEETS MANUAL
BSA OHV SINGLES 350 & 500cc 1955-1967 (BOOK OF)
BSA M20, M21 & M33 1945-1963 FACTORY SERVICE SHEETS MANUAL
BSA TWINS A7 & A10 1948-1962 FACTORY SERVICE SHEETS MANUAL
BSA TWINS A7 & A10 1948-1962 (BOOK OF)
BSA TWINS A50 & A65 1962-1965 FACTORY WORKSHOP MANUAL
BSA TWINS A50 & A65 1962-1969 (SECOND BOOK OF)
DOUGLAS 1929-1939 PREWAR ALL MODELS (BOOK OF)
DOUGLAS 1948-1957 POSTWAR ALL MODELS FACTORY SHOP MANUAL
DUCATI 160cc, 250cc & 350cc OHC MODELS FACTORY SHOP MANUAL
HONDA 50cc ALL MODELS UP TO 1970 INC MONKEY & TRAIL (BOOK OF)
HONDA 90cc ALL MODELS UP TO 1966 (BOOK OF)
HONDA 50-65-70-90cc OHC SINGLES 1959-1983 FACTORY WSM
HONDA 100-125cc SINGLES CB/CD/CL/SL/TL 1970-1984 FACTORY WSM
HONDA 125-150cc TWINS C/CS/CB/CA FACTORY WORKSHOP MANUAL
HONDA 125-160-175-200cc TWINS 1965-1978 WORKSHOP MANUAL
HONDA 250-305cc TWINS C/CS/CB 1959-1967 FACTORY WSM
HOHDA 250-350cc TWINS CB/CL/SL 1968-1973 FACTORY WSM
HONDA 250-360cc TWINS CB/CL/CJ 1974-1977 FACTORY WSM
HONDA 450cc TWINS CB/CL 1965-1974 K0 TO K7 WORKSHOP MANUAL
HONDA 500cc & 550cc 4CYL 1971-1978 FACTORY WORKSHOP MANUAL
HONDA 750cc SHOC 4 CYL 1969-1978 K0~K8 WORKSHOP MANUAL
HONDA C100 SUPER CUB FACTORY WORKSHOP MANUAL
HONDA C110 SPORT CUB 1962-1969 FACTORY WORKSHOP MANUAL
HONDA TWINS & SINGLES 50cc THRU 305cc 1960-1966 (BOOK OF)
HONDA TWINS ALL MODELS 125cc THRU 450cc UP TO 1968 (BOOK OF)
INDIAN PONYBIKE, BOY RACER & PAPOOSE ILL PARTS LIST & SALES LIT
J.A.P. ENGINES 1927-1952 & MOTORCYCLES 1934-1952 (BOOK OF)
MATCHLESS 1931-1939 ALL MODELS 250cc THRU 990cc (BOOK OF)
MATCHLESS 1945-1956 350 & 500cc SINGLES (BOOK OF)
MATCHLESS 1955-1966 350 & 500cc SINGLES (BOOK OF)
MATCHLESS 1957-1966 FACTORY WSM - ALL SINGLES & TWINS
NEW IMPERIAL ALL SV & OHV FROM 1935 ONWARDS (BOOK OF)
NORTON 1932-1939 PREWAR MODELS (BOOK OF)
NORTON 1932-1947 (BOOK OF)
NORTON 1938-1956 (BOOK OF)
NORTON 1945-1963 MODELS 16H, Big4, ES2, 19 & 50 WSM'S & PARTS
NORTON 1955-1963 MODELS 19, 50 & ES2 (BOOK OF)
NORTON 1948-1970 DOMINATOR TWINS FACTORY WSM'S & PARTS
NORTON 1955-1965 DOMINATOR TWINS (BOOK OF)
NORTON 1960-1970 TWIN CYLINDER FACTORY WORKSHOP MANUAL
NORTON 1970-1975 COMMANDO 850 & 750cc FACTORY WSM
NORTON 1975-1978 MK 3 COMMANDO 850 cc FACTORY WSM
PANTHER 1932-1958 LIGHTWEIGHT MODELS 250 & 350cc (BOOK OF)
PANTHER 1938-1966 HEAVYWEIGHT MODELS 600 & 650cc (BOOK OF)
RALEIGH MOTORCYCLES 1919-1933 (BOOK OF)
ROYAL ENFIELD 1934-1946 SINGLES & V TWINS (BOOK OF)
ROYAL ENFIELD 1937-1953 SINGLES & V TWINS (BOOK OF)
ROYAL ENFIELD 1946-1962 SINGLES (BOOK OF)
ROYAL ENFIELD 1958-1966 250cc & 350cc SINGLES (SECOND BOOK OF)
ROYAL ENFIELD 1962-1970 INTERCEPTOR WSM'S & PARTS (Compilation)
RUDGE 1933-1939 (BOOK OF)
SUNBEAM 1928-1939 (BOOK OF)
SUNBEAM 1946-1957 S7 & S8 (BOOK OF)
SUZUKI 50cc & 80cc UP TO 1966 (BOOK OF)
SUZUKI T10 1963-1967 FACTORY WORKSHOP MANUAL
SUZUKI T20 & T200 1965-1969 FACTORY WORKSHOP MANUAL
SUZUKI TWINS 1962 ONWARDS 125-500cc WORKSHOP MANUAL
TRIUMPH 1935-1949 SINGLES & TWINS (BOOK OF)
TRIUMPH 1937-1951 (WORKSHOP MANUAL)
TRIUMPH 1945-1955 FACTORY WORKSHOP MANUAL
TRIUMPH 1945-1959 TWINS (BOOK OF)
TRIUMPH 1956-1969 TWINS (BOOK OF)
TRIUMPH 1963-1970 UNIT CONSTRUCTION 650cc FACTORY WSM
TRIUMPH 1963-1974 UNIT CONSTRUCTION 350-500cc FACTORY WSM
TRIUMPH 1968-1974 TRIDENT T150 & T150V FACTORY WSM
VELOCETTE 1925-1970 ALL SINGLES & TWINS (BOOK OF)
VELOCETTE 1933-1952 MOV-MAC-MSS RIGID FRAME FACTORY WSM
VELOCETTE 1954-1971 MSS-VENOM-THRUXTON-VIPER FACTORY WSM
VILLIERS ENGINE UP TO 1959 INC. 3 WHEELERS (BOOK OF)
VILLIERS ENGINE UP TO 1969 (BOOK OF)
VINCENT 1935-1955 (WORKSHOP MANUAL)
YAMAHA 1961-1967 YA5 & YA6 (WORKSHOP MANUAL & ILL PARTS LIST)
YAMAHA 1971-1972 JT1& JT2 (WORKSHOP MANUAL & ILL PARTS LIST)

VELOCEPRESS TECHNICAL BOOKS – MOTORCYCLE

1930'S BRITISH MOTORCYCLE CARBS & ELEC COMPONENTS (BOOK OF)
1930'S BRITISH MOTORCYCLE ENGINES (OVERHAUL & MAINTENANCE)
1930'S BRITISH MOTORCYCLE GEARBOXES & CLUTCHES (BOOK OF)
CATALOG OF BRITISH MOTORCYCLES (1951 MODELS)
LUCAS ELECTRONICS BRITISH M/CYCLES REPAIR & PARTS (1950-1977)
MOTORCYCLE ENGINEERING (P.E. Irving)
MOTORCYCLE ROAD TESTS 1949-1953 (Motor Cycle Magazine UK)
SPEED AND HOW TO OBTAIN IT (Motor Cycle Magazine UK)
TUNING FOR SPEED (P.E. Irving)
WIPAC (COMBO) MANUAL NUMBER 3 + M/CYCLE & SCOOTER MANUAL

VELOCEPRESS MANUALS – SCOOTERS BY MAKE

BSA SUNBEAM SCOOTER WORKSHOP MANUAL 1959-1965
BSA SUNBEAM SCOOTER 1959-1965 (BOOK OF)
LAMBRETTA 1947-1957 ALL 125 & 150cc MODELS (BOOK OF)
LAMBRETTA 1957-1970 LI & TV MODELS (SECOND BOOK OF)
NSU PRIMA 1956-1964 ALL MODELS (BOOK OF)
TRIUMPH TIGRESS SCOOTER WORKSHOP MANUAL 1959-1965
TRIUMPH TIGRESS SCOOTER (BOOK OF)
VESPA 1951-1961 (BOOK OF)
VESPA 1955-1963 125 & 150cc & GS MODELS (SECOND BOOK OF)
VESPA 1955-1968 GS & SS (BOOK OF)
VESPA 1963-1972 90, 125 & 150cc (THIRD BOOK OF)

VELOCEPRESS MANUALS – MOPEDS & MOTORIZED BICYCLES

CYCLEMOTOR (BOOK OF)
NSU QUICKLY 1953-1963 ALL MODELS (BOOK OF)
PUCH MAXI N & S MAINTENANCE & REPAIR (3 MANUAL COMPILATION)
RALEIGH MOPEDS 1960-1969 (BOOK OF)

VELOCEPRESS MANUALS - THREE WHEELER'S

BOND MINICAR THREE WHEELER 1948-1967 (BOOK OF)
BMW ISETTA FACTORY WORKSHOP MANUAL
BSA THREE WHEELER (BOOK OF)
RELIANT REGAL THREE WHEELER 1952-1973 (BOOK OF)
VINTAGE MORGAN THREE WHEELER (BOOK OF)

VELOCEPRESS MANUALS – AUTOMOBILE BY MAKE

ALFA ROMEO GIULIA WORKSHOP MANUAL 1300 TO 2000cc 1962-1975
ALFA ROMEO GIULIA TECH MANUAL CARBURETED CARS FROM 1962
ALFA ROMEO GIULIA TECH MANUAL FUEL INJECTED CARS FROM 1969
ALFA ROMEO GIULIETTA & GIULIA 750 & 101 SERIES 1955-1965 WSM
AUSTIN-HEALEY SPRITE & MG MIDGET WORKSHOP MANUAL 1958-1971
BMW 600 LIMOUSINE FACTORY WORKSHOP MANUAL
BMW 600 LIMOUSINE OWNERS HAND BOOK & SERVICE MANUAL
BMW 2000 & 2002 1966-1976 WORKSHOP MANUAL
CORVAIR 1960-1969 WORKSHOP MANUAL
CORVETTE V8 1955-1962 WORKSHOP MANUAL
FERRARI HANDBOOK ROAD & RACE CARS (SERVICE/SPECS) 1948-1958
FERRARI 250/GT SERVICE & MAINTENANCE MANUAL 1956-1965
FIAT 500 FACTORY WORKSHOP MANUAL 1957-1973
FIAT 600, 600D & MULTIPLA FACTORY WORKSHOP MANUAL 1955-1969
JAGUAR E-TYPE 3.8 & 4.2 SERIES 1 & 2 WORKSHOP MANUAL
JAGUAR MK 7, 8, 9 & XK120, 140, 150 WORKSHOP MANUAL 1948-1961
METROPOLITAN FACTORY WORKSHOP MANUAL
MGA & MGB OWNERS HANDBOOK & WORKSHOP MANUAL
MG MIDGET TC, TD, TF & TF1500 WORKSHOP MANUAL
PORSCHE 356 1948-1965 WORKSHOP MANUAL
PORSCHE 911 2.0, 2.2, 2.4 LITRE 1964-1973 WORKSHOP MANUAL
PORSCHE 911 2.7, 3.0, 3.2 LITRE 1973-1989 WORKSHOP MANUAL
PORSCHE 912 WORKSHOP MANUAL
PORSCHE 914/4 & 914/6 1.7, 1.8, 2.0 LITRE 1970-1976 WSM
TRIUMPH TR2, TR3, TR4 1953-1965 WORKSHOP MANUAL
VOLKSWAGEN TRANSPORTER, TRUCKS & WAGONS 1950-1979 WSM
VOLVO 1944-1968 ALL MODELS WORKSHOP MANUAL

VELOCEPRESS TECHNICAL BOOKS - AUTOMOBILE

HOW TO BUILD A FIBERGLASS CAR
HOW TO BUILD A RACING CAR
HOW TO RESTORE THE MODEL 'A' FORD
MASERATI OWNER'S HANDBOOK
PERFORMANCE TUNING THE SUNBEAM TIGER
SOUPING THE VOLKSWAGEN
SOLEX CARBURETORS (EMPHASIS ON UK & EU AUTOMOBILES)
SU CARBURETORS (EMPHASIS ON UK AUTOMOBILES)
WEBER CARBURETORS (EMPHASIS ON ALFA & FIAT)

VELOCEPRESS BOOKS & GUIDES - AUTOMOBILE

COMPLETE CATALOG OF JAPANESE MOTOR VEHICLES
FERRARI 308 SERIES BUYER'S AND OWNER'S GUIDE
FERRARI BROCHURES AND SALES LITERATURE 1968-1989
FERRARI SERIAL NUMBERS PART I - ODD NUMBERS TO 21399
FERRARI SERIAL NUMBERS PART II - EVEN NUMBERS TO 1050
HENRY'S FABULOUS MODEL "A" FORD
MASERATI BROCHURES AND SALES LITERATURE

VELOCEPRESS BOOKS – RACING

CARRERA PANAMERICANA - MEXICAN ROAD RACE (BOOK OF)
DIALED IN - THE JAN OPPERMAN STORY
VEDA ORR'S NEW REVISED HOT ROD PICTORIAL

Please check our website:

www.VelocePress.com

for a complete
up-to-date list of
available titles

www.ingramcontent.com/pod-product-compliance
Lightning Source LLC
Chambersburg PA
CBHW080738300426
44114CB00019B/2620